It's a wonderful life!

CLIFF JONES

It's a wonderful life!

MY STORY

WITH IVAN PONTING

VSP

Published by Vision Sports Publishing in 2016

Vision Sports Publishing
19-23 High Street
Kingston upon Thames
Surrey
KT1 1LL

www.visionsp.co.uk

ISBN: 978-1909534-64-3

© Cliff Jones and Ivan Ponting, 2016

Authors: Cliff Jones with Ivan Ponting
Editor: Paul Baillie-Lane
Design: Doug Cheeseman

A CIP record for this book is available from the British library

Printed and bound in the UK by TJ International, Padstow, Cornwall

MIX
Paper from
responsible sources
FSC
www.fsc.org   FSC® C013056

CONTENTS

Foreword
by Ryan Giggs

It's an honour and a privilege for me to write a few words about Cliff Jones, one of the greatest Welsh footballers of all time, a star many years before I was born and a man for whom I have the warmest regard and admiration.

Having mentioned that he played long ago, I should say that he has looked after himself so well down the years, and is such a lively character, that I find it very difficult to take on board that he's entered his eighties. I think there must be some mistake on his birth certificate!

Although I was brought up on stories of the heroes who took Wales to the quarter-finals of the World Cup in Sweden in 1958, I had never met Cliff until one evening at White Hart Lane after Manchester United had played Spurs. As I was waiting on the coach before going back up north, he put his head round the door and introduced himself, saying that we might have a bit in common.

And certainly we do. In a football sense, he grew up at The Vetch Field in Swansea, which I visited for the first time to play in a schoolboy international when I was only 14. Mind you, that day I captained England to victory over Wales, but Cliff didn't hold that against me, and I enjoyed giving him my impressions of the old ground, which has now been demolished. I remember having to slip through a small gap between houses to reach the pitch – it felt like strolling through somebody's garden.

Throughout my life I have heard so much about Cliff Jones. People I trust tell me that, despite the fact that he wasn't very big, he was absolutely brilliant in the air and so incredibly brave. Then there's the way he used to run with the ball at speed, which is also something I can identify with.

I wasn't aware he was watching at the time, but Cliff now tells me how he saw me playing for Salford Boys against Islington Boys in the quarter-finals of the English Schools Trophy and how he picked me out as having a bit of potential, which was nice of him. We knew we were in for a hard game that day because Islington were an excellent side, but we gave one of our best performances and managed to win.

I'm delighted to say that there are even more footballing connections between the two of us. Cliff was a key member of the wonderful Spurs team which became the first in the twentieth century to lift the League and FA Cup double, and winning that pair of trophies was an uplifting experience which I was fortunate enough to share in my own career, although I wasn't a pioneer like he was.

Also he was in the first British side to win European silverware, when Tottenham brought home the Cup Winners' Cup in 1963, and once again I've had the luck to be involved in success on the continent, following the trail that he blazed so gloriously so many years before me.

On the international front, of course, I could never equal what he did in becoming a World Cup quarter-finalist. Looking back, it's such a shame that the incomparable John Charles was injured and forced to miss the last-eight clash with a Brazil team that included the young Pele. Still, the fact that Wales got so far in the competition, and held their own against such top opposition, is a colossal achievement of which Cliff and his teammates could be so, so proud. The scale of what they did is only emphasised by the fact that it has taken our country more than half a century to reach the finals of another major competition.

All this underlines the status of Cliff Jones in the history of Welsh football. Truly he is, and will always remain, one of our game's principal figures. This was illustrated vividly to me at a function organised by the National Football Museum in Manchester at which he got up to speak at the inauguration of his old friend the late Ivor Allchurch, another all-time great.

Cliff held the floor for about 15 minutes and he had the place spellbound with his stories and his insights. People were hanging on his every word. The venue was full of famous football folk that night, some of the biggest names you can imagine, but there was never any doubt who everyone wanted to have their picture taken with afterwards. I'm not just talking about fans, either, but top players from all eras – they all sought out Cliff and wanted to share a bit of his time.

And it's easy to understand why. Not only is Cliff a true legend of Welsh football, but he's a lovely man, full of fun and wisdom, so humble and accessible and down-to-earth. I hope his book sells a million.

Ryan Giggs, September 2016

Foreword
by Gareth Bale

I first met Mr Jones, as I used to call him at the time, when I signed for Tottenham in 2007, although I already knew of his legendary success as a footballer for Spurs and Wales.

He was often around the training ground and the stadium before games and he spoke regularly with me, giving me advice and encouragement. It meant so much when he said to me that his words were coming from the old Welsh Wizard to the new Welsh Wizard!

It's an honour in itself to be compared to the first Welsh Wizard and I hope that I can emulate Cliff in representing our country as he did in the past, especially as I seem to have followed in his footsteps, with the current Wales team qualifying for a major tournament.

Cliff has told me he waited a long time for this to happen and I hope he feels we did the nation proud in France by reaching the semi-finals of Euro 2016.

I am so looking forward to reading this book. I am sure that it will give me a great insight into the experiences that he has encountered during his magnificent career and will also inspire the next generation of young Welsh footballers. I would like to wish Cliff every success with *It's A Wonderful Life*.

Gareth Bale, September 2016

Prelude

I look on myself as one of the luckiest men in the world. Both personally and professionally, this little Swansea Jack – as male natives of my lovely hometown are known – has tasted the best life has to offer. Now, as I embark on my ninth decade, I'm still amazingly busy and, as I write these words, I'm as fit as a flea.

My time on this planet has been bound up inextricably with football in general, more particularly with Swansea Town (now City) and Wales and, most vividly of all, with my beloved Tottenham Hotspur.

I was privileged to be a part of the marvellous team which, under the inspirational guidance of the great Bill Nicholson in 1960/61, became the first team in the twentieth century to lift the long-coveted League and FA Cup double. Others went on to emulate our achievement but, as with Edmund Hillary climbing Mount Everest and Roger Bannister breaking the four-minute mile barrier, it's being first that matters most, that carves your name most indelibly into the history of your time.

Along the way I was fortunate enough to play alongside and against some of the finest footballers who ever drew breath. To wear the White Hart Lane cockerel on my chest in comradeship with the likes of Dave Mackay and Danny Blanchflower, John White and Bobby Smith, Jimmy Greaves and Pat Jennings and so many more, was an unbelievable honour.

So was pulling on the blood-red shirt of Wales in the company of some of the game's immortals, such as my dear old Swansea mates Ivor Allchurch and Mel Charles, the magnificent goalkeeper Jack Kelsey of Arsenal –

nobody's perfect! – and, best of all, the incomparable John Charles, Mel's brother and a player without a single weakness.

With the irrepressible Jimmy Murphy driving us on we reached the quarter-finals of the 1958 World Cup in Sweden and, despite being deprived of our top man, Big John, by injury, we bowed out only to a 1–0 defeat by Brazil, then emerging as one of the mightiest sides of all time.

That day in Gothenburg we were beaten by a goal from a 17-year-old rookie named Pele, who is joined on my list of most illustrious opponents by Sir Stanley Matthews, Tom Finney, Bobby Charlton, Duncan Edwards, Johnny Haynes, Eusebio, Bobby Moore, George Best... I could go on and on.

It still takes my breath away to ponder how incredibly fortunate I have been to share my days with such people, sensational crowd-pleasers every one of them.

Playing as a winger as I did, I like to think that, on my day, I could entertain a bit, too. My game was all about running with the ball – I very rarely passed it, as Danny Blanchflower never tired of telling me, often in the most colourful language imaginable! – and it would send an electric shock through my system when I took possession, and could hear the fans murmuring in anticipation.

It didn't always come off, of course, but I had my moments, and I must have done something right because in the early 1960s Juventus attempted to make me the most expensive footballer in the world. Had the lucrative deal gone through, I would have been following in the record-breaking footsteps of my uncle, Bryn, when he moved from Wolves to Arsenal shortly before the war. But Bill Nick was unmoved by the Italians' colossal bid and in the end, despite the untold riches that were beckoning, I was more than happy to stay at White Hart Lane, knowing full well that some things are far more important than money.

Crucially for my sanity and wellbeing down the years, I have benefited from a large and loving family, and I enjoyed a deeply fulfilling second career, spending some 30 years as a physical education teacher at Highbury Grove School. But no life as long as mine can run unremittingly smoothly, and I have not been immune from tragedy or struggle.

Joan – my wonderful and supportive wife of more than 60 years – and I were blessed with four children, but we lost our beautiful daughter, Deborah, to cancer in 2006. My best friend in football, the brilliant Scottish international inside-forward John White, was killed by a bolt of lightning in 1964. Later in life I fell prey to one of the scourges of mankind, alcoholism, but it's now more than 30 years since I last took a drink, and these days I'm still striving to balance the books, as it were, by trying to help people currently facing a similar problem.

Meanwhile, I keep out of mischief by working for Spurs as a matchday host and glorying in the progress being made at White Hart Lane by Mauricio Pochettino and his exciting young team; by indulging my insatiable appetite for sporting competition on the greens and fairways of West Essex Golf Club; and by keeping in close touch with (and counting) my many great grandchildren. A lucky man? I invite you to consider the evidence in these pages and to judge for yourself.

CHAPTER ONE

A Swansea Jack with brains in his feet

The origin of the term 'Swansea Jack' to describe any lad born in our dear old town is open to lively debate. Some say it was a nineteenth-century nickname coined to describe locally-born sailors, or Jack Tars, who always enjoyed a glowing reputation for their exceptional seamanship. Others get a bit more technical, reckoning Swansea-based miners, the hard men who dug coal and copper from the earth, used something called a jack tin to carry their lunch.

Then there is a third theory, perhaps the most romantic, that the name derives from an extremely brave dog who rejoiced in that title, a muscular black Newfoundland with a long coat, who made a habit of rescuing people from drowning in Swansea Docks in the 1930s. Local legend declares that the courageous hound saved 27 lives over the span of around half a decade before he fell victim to rat poison.

That particular Swansea Jack became a national hero, winning an award as the Bravest Dog of the Year from a London newspaper and being named Dog of the Century by a rescue organisation as recently as 2000. There is a monument to the canine hero on the dock promenade, close to St Helen's rugby and cricket grounds.

Finally, though rather less acceptably, there is the notion that Swansea Jack was an alias used by a fellow from the town accused of murdering a Cardiff man in 1847, and that it was adopted to describe any man or boy hailing from the thriving community at the mouth of the River Tawe.

Whatever the truth of the matter, and I have to say I like the idea of the fearless dog who was in his intrepid prime around the time of my birth, the fact remains that I am, and always will be, a Swansea Jack through and through, from topknot to toes. True, I have lived in London or the surrounding area for more than half a century now, and have been immensely happy there, but I remain fiercely proud of my birthplace and my heritage, and I get back to Swansea, where I have countless friends and family members, as often as ever I can.

It's not my intention to paint my childhood in a rose-tinted light that might have seeped from some cosy Sunday-evening television drama set in the good old days, but the fact remains that my growing-up years were happy and contented ones, broadly speaking.

I was born into a remarkable family of professional footballers, and such were my own talents and inclinations that I was always going to follow in their sporting footsteps, but much more of that later. Let me first attempt to paint a picture of the earliest daily life I can remember.

I first saw the light of day on 7 February 1935 and was brought up at 8 Beach Street, Sandfields, which was very much a working-class area of Swansea situated, as the name implies, very close to the waterside.

Our house was very ordinary, terraced, three-up-and-three-down with not a lot of spare space, no front garden and only a small vegetable patch at the back, but it was home to seven of us – my dad, Ivor; May, my mother; and five children. In descending order of age there was Bob, Valerie, Bryn, myself and Freda.

The world we inhabited was very close-knit, with friends and relatives nearby in all directions, all living in very similar houses. It seems almost like a cliché to mention it now, but it really was true that most families didn't lock their doors, and folk wandered in and out of each other's homes pretty much at will, often without even knocking. Nearly all communication was by word of mouth. Hardly anyone had telephones, although there were red boxes on many corners. Nobody had cars, so the streets were safe and the kids could play in them. There were little pubs everywhere, which were key focal points of the community. Socially and work-wise you lived your lives in a very small area.

They were different days, very rough and ready, but people were more grounded in reality, mindful of the things that really matter in life. Although there was plenty of hardship around, folk were grateful and relieved to have come through the war. They were more easily satisfied, more ready to make do and mend, weren't consumed by the absurd and unrealistic aspirations that appear to obsess so many people today.

Close by us was a cobbler's run by Bryn Wilkie; Dolly Furseland had a greengrocer's shop; there was Thomas's, the Welsh shop, and Puddicombs, the butcher, where we would go every Thursday without fail to get our faggots and peas. Also nearby was Joe's ice-cream parlour and I shall always remember his sales pitch: 'There's ice-cream, and then there's Joe's.' Finally there was Cambden the barber with the red-and-white pole outside – short back and sides for one shilling and sixpence (seven and a half pence in modern money).

Best of all, my maternal grandfather, Bob Messer, lived next to me and he ran a fish-and-chip shop which had a deserved reputation as the best in Swansea. It even had a bus stop named after it. When I popped home from school at lunchtimes – it was only a stone's throw away and school dinners were rare in those times – he always let me help myself to the freshly-cooked chips, which I loved. They never made me put on weight, no matter how many I ate, because I was always so active.

Granddad Bob was a central figure in my young life and I spent a lot of time with him, especially relishing our joint excursions to the fish market. He was a former rugby league player who had moved down from the north, and in later years when I developed into a pretty nippy winger, people used to say I had inherited my pace from him.

That said, I was never going to be anything less than as fit as a whippet because, I am reliably informed, all through my childhood I never stayed still for a moment. I was always on the go with my mates, either playing football or cricket or any one of the usual games like cops-and-robbers and hide-and-seek.

I was probably a bit of a scamp, roaming round with the other kids and getting into scrapes – always wholesome scrapes, mind, just ordinary naughtiness, nothing malicious. I always threw myself wholeheartedly into every activity, some might say recklessly, and there were times when I paid for my overwhelming determination. Too often for coincidence, I would end up in the casualty department of Swansea hospital, more likely than not having to hold still while stitches were inserted into my latest wound.

At least that stood me in good stead for my football career, during which I suffered no shortage of injuries. At Tottenham they used to tell me I had more scars around my eyes than legendary boxer Henry Cooper, most of them caused by heading the ball and sometimes making contact with my marker's nut. In some ways, I suppose, I was a victim of my own enthusiasm, but I can honestly say that whenever the ball came near me it didn't even cross my mind that I might get hurt, I just threw everything I had at putting it into the net. Fools rush in, you might say!

Back in my time as a schoolboy adventurer, there were other discomforts, too, notably a food shortage on one ridiculously disorganised occasion. Together with a group of friends I went camping in woods not all that far out of town. We had planned to make our expedition last for a couple of days – it was meant to be a real Swiss Family Robinson affair – so we had taken plentiful supplies with us. But, being typical lads with healthy appetites, by lunchtime on the first day we had gobbled the lot. Soon I was pining for my grandfather's fish and-chip shop and we made an emergency return to base for extra supplies, shrugging off the severe ribbing we received in the interest of re-lining our stomachs.

Given all the energy we burned, we used to get tired so on one trip we planned to go to sleep early in the evening, as soon as it started to get dark. One of my pals suggested we stuff something in our ears to keep out the bugs, and I thought I was being clever by rolling up pieces of newspaper, then forcing them in as far as they would go. Of course, they went a bit too far, right into my inner ear, and pretty soon I was on one of my hospital visits to have them extracted. I felt pretty daft, and everybody had a good laugh at my expense, but at least the doctor didn't need a needle and thread on this occasion.

Many of the most vivid recollections from my boyhood involve the Blitz. Swansea was targeted repeatedly by the Luftwaffe because it was a very industrial area, with the steelworks and the docks, and all the kids were given Mickey Mouse gas masks to protect them during the frequent air raids.

Though I was only six at the time, I can recall with absolute clarity three or four consecutive nights of bombing in 1941 when I had to race to the bomb shelter and dive into it with lots of other people. Looking back, I suppose it was quite eerie because you'd hear the bombs coming down but you wouldn't know where they were going to land. We called them whistlers, which was a pretty cheerful name for something so deadly, but it was very important for everybody to keep their spirits up.

There were Anderson shelters in many of the gardens in our terrace, some of them shared by three or four families. They were made of corrugated iron with sacks stuffed in to block up holes. Of course, all this would have been utterly useless against a direct hit but it was needed to deflect the flying shrapnel, of which there was plenty. During the daytime we youngsters would comb the area, collecting shards of the shrapnel that had been blasted seemingly into every corner, then we would swap pieces with each other.

To us it was all a bit of a lark, a dash of adventure which broke up the routine of daily life, but to the grown-ups, who truly understood what was at stake every time they heard the drone of an approaching bomber, it must have been terrifying.

At one point I was evacuated, along with my brothers and sisters, to the comparative safety of Merthyr Tydfil, where my father's folk were based, and other members of the clan turned up from all over the place, including Birmingham and the London area. Because there were five of us we all slept in different houses but we saw each other every day, being part of a close-knit and extended family. Even to a child, the sense of community was obvious, and it was extremely reassuring. There was a feeling that everyone would look after everyone else, which is an ideal way to live. Sadly, that ethos seems to have seeped away from many areas of modern life, and that's a shame.

Another positive memory from the war was the fun we had when the Americans arrived in Swansea. Generally speaking, we children got on well with them. They were lively and ready for a laugh, and suddenly there seemed to be a lot of chewing gum around. With so many of our local lads away on active service, all the girls seemed to fancy these glamorous newcomers and, in an era of sharp cultural change, it's hardly surprising that there were plenty of GI brides.

For me, though, everything always came back to football and, for all the closeness of my relationship with Granddad Bob, there was never any way that I was going to follow him into the oval-ball code. Football was part of my DNA, hardly surprising when you consider that my father was a Welsh international inside-forward who collected ten caps between 1920 and 1926 and his four brothers – that's Will John, Emlyn, the famous Bryn and Bert – also played the game to a high level, three of them professionally.

Dad's family hailed from Merthyr Tydfil, some 30 miles along the Rhondda Valley, and their collective aptitude for football was truly astonishing. Among such a keen bunch you might expect one or two to excel, but for the whole lot to be blessed with rich talent with a ball at their feet defies belief.

The eldest of the quintet, Will John, was the only one to remain in the amateur ranks, turning out for Merthyr, Ton Pentre and Porth, but opting to make his living in business.

Next came my dad, Ivor, to whom I'll return shortly. Then there was Emlyn, a clever inside-forward like most of my clan, and he played for Everton and Southend United. The fourth brother was Bryn, who served Wolverhampton Wanderers, Arsenal and Norwich City at club level while winning 17 caps for Wales, and finally there was young Bert, apparently the most gifted of all, who gave exciting notice of his potential with Southend and Wolves before being killed in the war in Burma, cut down tragically before what should have been his prime.

As for my father, he left school while playing his football to a commendably high level as a centre-half with Merthyr, then headed down a local pit shaft to start work as a coalminer, as was the inevitable custom for young men in those parts.

But then his way of life was turned upside down as, in 1917 while he was still only 18, he was called up to serve in the Army in the First World War. When peace was declared he came home and shifted his football activity to Caerphilly, for whom he shone brightly in a game with Swansea reserves, mightily impressing new Vetch boss Joe Bradshaw. Accordingly in 1919 he was recruited by the Town for a transfer fee of just £50 – how incredible to reflect that such a sum wouldn't pay for more than a few minutes of a Premier League player's time today.

By all accounts my dad was a lovely ball player, very smooth in possession and a natural schemer who could pick a pass and then place it on a sixpence. Strong and stockily built, he didn't score too many goals but he created plenty for others and soon enough the news of his talent spread well beyond South Wales, so much so that by the spring of 1920 the club had received 25 enquiries about signing him, nearly all from Football League clubs.

At that time the Swans were members of the Southern League, but for the 1920/21 season they became founder members of the Football League's new Third Division. It was at that point that my father, who had just become the first Swansea man to enter the international arena – making his Wales debut in a 2–2 draw against Ireland in Belfast – became very much in demand.

The approaches continued to pour into The Vetch until April 1922, when finally he was transferred, to West Bromwich Albion of the top division at a cost of £2,500.

Reporters of the day were mostly very complimentary about Ivor's clever play, though I read one account where he was criticised for attempting more than he could hope to achieve single-handedly. That might be translated as hanging on to the ball too long, and my only comment on that would be: Like father, like son! I was never over-keen on passing either, a tendency which used to have Spurs captain Danny Blanchflower tearing out his hair at times. As he put it to me once, lacing his customary eloquence with heartfelt profanity: "The ball is f****** round, and it rolls, so why not f****** pass it occasionally?" Of course, that wasn't my style, but I'll make my excuses for that later in my story.

My dad seemed to fit in well at The Hawthorns, filling both inside-forward positions at various times and linking beautifully with excellent wingers such as Howard Gregory, Jack Byers and Tommy Glidden. He stayed there until 1926, the year he received the last of his caps and when injury problems began to hamper him seriously.

Probably his proudest achievement in the game was being part of the squad which lifted the Triple Crown in 1923/24. He operated at inside-right in the 2–0 victory over Scotland at Ninian Park, but was replaced by Newport County's Jack Nicholls for the subsequent wins over England and Ireland.

After leaving the Throstles – that was Albion's nickname in the old days, before everyone started calling them the Baggies in modern times – he returned to Swansea, as a player-coach, then had further footballing billets with Aberystwyth Town, Aldershot, Thames, Eastside and Aberavon Harlequins, but eventually left the game to make a living for his growing brood.

Meanwhile Bryn, who was a dozen years younger, was working his way towards what would become an illustrious career, and which took off when he moved to Wolverhampton Wanderers from Aberaman Athletic in 1933.

Up to that point, though clearly endowed with enormous talent, he had wandered from club to club, completing a trial here and a brief stint there before starting to dazzle at Molineux. Over the next five years his displays in the famous gold shirt, usually with a number ten on his back, made him one of the hottest properties around.

Come 1937/38, in his mid-twenties and probably at his peak, he hit the form of his life, scoring 15 goals in 36 games and proving inspirational as Major Frank Buckley's Wolves finished as runners-up in the title race, only a point behind the champions, Arsenal.

My Uncle Bryn's burgeoning influence was duly noted at Highbury, and that August he broke the world transfer record when he moved to Arsenal for £14,000, a deal which made him an instant celebrity.

To anyone who knew him, that was a strange state of affairs because Bryn was a quiet, modest, delightfully unassuming character who would never seek the limelight. Certainly he was never concerned about being feted as the most expensive player there had ever been. Rather it was just something he took in his stride. After all, it wasn't something he was going to make a fortune from – things have changed a bit now, you might say!

Unfortunately, although he remained at Arsenal for 11 years, his time at the club was not the glorious sojourn which had been anticipated. Soon after he arrived in north London – he had completed only one season, in which he had struggled to settle into producing the best of himself for George Allison's star-studded side – along came the Second World War and he joined the Army, thus finding himself involved in an altogether deadlier type of action than what he had had in mind.

Happily he survived, but the conflict had cost him and his generation what should have been the finest years of their careers. Six years on, it must have been monstrously difficult to pick up the threads and he never really

Back where it all began, at Oxford Street Secondary School in Swansea. I don't recall the name of the lad in the blazer on the left of the back row, but I do remember the rest. Standing, left to right after the mystery man, are John Williams, Buller Champion, Freddie Spridgeon and Alan Blewitt. In the middle row are our maths and games teacher Mr Ebo Evans, Billy Peters, Alan Davies (who became a top comedian at the local dockers' club), Gerald Griffiths, Brian Parker, Terry Tracey and headmaster Mr Logan. That's me cross-legged at the front on the left with Aubrey Argent on the right and some hard-earned silverware in between us.

managed it, making precious little impact over the next three campaigns before enlisting with Norwich City, then in the old Third Division South, as player-coach in the summer of 1949.

In such poignant circumstances, a lot of people might have fallen prey to bitterness, blaming others for their own misfortunes, but Bryn was never going to be like that. When his playing days were done, Arsenal helped him to get a little newspaper shop in Islington, north London, in which he worked successfully for a long time, and he always retained enormous respect for the club. He spoke as he found, declaring that they looked after their former players fantastically well, and I feel that attitude reflected immense credit on Bryn, who died in 1985 at the age of 73.

Normally I'm not one for looking back and eating my heart out for what might have been, but I have to say that one of the most intense regrets of my life is that I never saw my father – who didn't fight in the war because he was working below ground in a Merthyr coalmine during the hostilities – or any of my uncles in action on the pitch. Dad's career was over before I was born and even though I was ten when the war ended, with Bryn still playing for Arsenal, those were very different days, with practically no live football on television – and anyway, for many years we didn't have a set!

Meanwhile, I must admit to not being the most avid of readers, but even if I had been there would have been nothing but the occasional match report in the London newspapers from which I might have gleaned some precious information. Remember, this was a time before magazines such as *Charles Buchan's Football Monthly* and *Soccer Star* – both long disappeared and much lamented – so there was precious little for a young lad in South Wales to consult.

Still, I do have some treasured memories of my father with a ball at his feet. Sometimes when I was a little boy he would take a few of us on to the beach, or to a local pitch, for a bit of a kickabout and you could see even then, though he was in his forties and cutting a distinctly portly figure, that he could do a bit. Oh yes, I have no doubt that Ivor Jones was some player in his day.

So, with so much emphasis on football in my family and in my everyday life, it always seemed completely natural, totally inevitable, even a matter-of-fact circumstance, that I would grow up to play the game professionally. To most boys of my age, back then and even more so now, becoming a footballer was little more than a dream. To me it was reality.

My earliest memory of playing anything close to a structured football match is on the beautiful expanse of open space that is the beach at Sand-fields. Every Sunday morning there would be a communal game, perhaps 20-a-side, mostly made up of older boys but also including tiddlers like me who were keen to have a go. For loads of football-crazy youngsters, it was the big occasion of their week.

And it wasn't just the Sandfield boys in action. You could gaze around Swansea Bay, a glorious sweep of about seven miles of hard-packed sand when the tide was out, and there were pockets of football all the way along. There'd be the Brynmill Boys and the Port Tenant Boys and many more, an amazing sight, an inspirational one really, the mere thought of which transports me back to my childhood. They talk about the beach football of Brazil, but I can vouch for the fact that the Swansea version wasn't bad, either!

I suppose it was our local equivalent of Hackney Marshes, where there are nearly a hundred full-sized pitches which have been the subject of some fantastic photographs – I only wish I had a picture of Sandfields in its footballing prime. Of course, it was much more informal than Hackney, with no marked lines, but it lifted the heart to see it. Once again, we come back to the notion of community, and this was a truly powerful illustration of that, with so many folk immersed in their sport together.

Mind, I wasn't having such profound thoughts at the time. I was just having fun while soaking up experience that would stand me in good stead even when I was running up and down the wing for Swansea, Spurs and Wales.

What I learned most surely was that, with so many people in the same team, when you passed the ball you might not see it again for another 20 minutes. My solution to that was simple – I would hang on to the ball as long as I could. That's where I honed my dribbling technique, it's as basic as that. Obviously I had a certain fundamental ability and the athleticism to avoid some of the, shall we say, rather vigorous challenges that came my way, but in the final analysis, I owed my progress to my time on the sand.

Even before those tumultuous Sunday morning sessions, I used to nip out of our back door and over to the beach to kick a ball around at every opportunity. Every time I stepped outside to join my friends, out would come a ball. Any lad who owned anything like a proper one was a top man. I never possessed one myself, but there was always someone who did.

We had one favourite location, a bombsite on the corner of Beach Street, a sandy piece of ground where we would play for hours on end. There wasn't much space, it was probably no more than half the size of a penalty area, but there was one sound wall from which we would get reliable rebounds. We would improvise goalposts with anything that came to hand, often a coat or a stray piece of wood, and employ our vivid imaginations, transforming our humble venue into whatever famous stadium took our fancy – Wembley, Ninian Park, Hampden, Old Trafford, White Hart Lane... you name it and we played there! There was even a handily placed street lamp which served as our floodlight. What more could a bunch of football-mad kids ask?

Often, too, I'd be playing street games with a tennis ball in the time-honoured tradition followed all over the world. With the smaller ball bouncing at any old awkward angle off kerbstones and boot-scrapers and door-handles, it was brilliant for perfecting your skills.

That's me sitting on the left, looking a fair bit younger than most of my mates in the Swansea Schoolboys team in the mid-1940s. On the other end of the bench is Lenny Allchurch, whom I went on to play alongside for Swansea Town and Wales, while the fellow with the ball at his feet is Jim Pressdee, who found fame as a Glamorgan county cricketer.

Tellingly, back in the 1940s there were no distractions such as television or computers and, even more crucially, it was absolutely safe to stage a football game on the street because there was virtually no traffic around. Also – and it makes me feel very sad to say this – the community was far, far safer than it is today. Parents had no qualms about sending their children outside to play for hours on end, confident that no harm would come to them, and if they did take a tumble then there would always be somebody sympathetic on hand to pick them up.

Our local copper was old Dai Salmon, who would go through the motions of chasing the young footballers off the streets, but we weren't bothered by him and, anyway, he knew we weren't doing any harm. The cry 'Old Dai's coming!' would go up and we'd all scarper somewhere else to re-start our game. Honour was satisfied all round.

The important thing was that in all the years I was growing up, I never felt threatened or in any sort of danger. Of course, in any neighbourhood at any time there is the odd dodgy character, but we knew everybody in Sandfields, especially the ones who might be described as villains, and we knew the ones to stay away from.

My first school was St Helen's Infants, where there was no organised team. That step up came when I made it to the Oxford Street Secondary Modern at the age of 11, by which time, without being big-headed because genuinely I hate to blow my own trumpet, I knew I was pretty good at football. It became clear that I had something a little bit extra to most of the lads because they couldn't get the ball off me, even boys who were much bigger and older.

When I was 12 I was picked for the first time for Swansea Schoolboys, which had become quite a breeding ground for professional footballers over the years. At the time I was an inside-forward, like my dad and all my uncles before me, and I was captain in 1950, my last year at school when we won the English Schools Trophy, beating Manchester Boys in the final.

We drew 1–1 at The Vetch in front of 20,000 fans, then we travelled north to Maine Road – then the home of Manchester City – and we won 1–0, with Bryn Evans from Gorseinon getting the goal.

Before the game we had the thrill of our lives when Dai Beynon, a marvellous

Slurping my soup (centre of picture) after Swansea Schoolboys had beaten Manchester Boys 1–0 on their own turf to win the English Schools Shield in 1950. To my left are teammates Bryn Evans, who scored the goal, Gerald Griffiths, a cherubic Mel Charles and Dai Davies.

man who organised our football and looked after us magnificently, introduced us to the great Billy Meredith, the original Welsh Wizard.

Billy, who has been called football's first superstar and not without reason, shone for both Manchester clubs, emerging as a City hero in the late nineteenth century, then winning everything in sight with United before returning to City to finish his career in the early 1920s.

Along the way he accumulated 48 Welsh caps, a vast total in those days of fewer internationals per season, and still found time to be one of the main moving forces behind the players' union, which was needed desperately at a period in history when footballers tended to be exploited mercilessly by club owners. Billy was a genuine pioneer, a true trailblazer.

Dai got him to talk to us, which was really uplifting. The wisdom was

The spoils of victory. As the Swansea captain, it fell to me to receive the English Schools Shield in 1950.

practically dripping out of him and he was superb at motivation, telling us to go and win it for Wales. As for that famous toothpick with which he was always pictured by cartoonists, I can confirm that it was no myth, he really did have it in his mouth all the time.

It was a privilege for me to play in that schoolboy side, which lifted a prestigious double that season as we also won the Welsh Shield, though it did surprise me when I was the only one who went on to become a professional. It was thought at the time that the centre-forward, Dai Davies, had a good chance. He was quick and strong, an outstanding prospect, but he never developed. I guess it's fair to say that size is a massive advantage for any reasonably talented lad at that age, but often the young giants just don't go on. Another pair, the wing-half Gerald Griffiths and defender Kenny Chard, did join the Swansea Town groundstaff at the same time as me but they never progressed, and there were a few more who had trials at The Vetch without making the grade.

I suppose if any confirmation were ever needed that I was destined to make my living in the game, it came when I didn't pass my 11-plus examination. I have to admit that the result came as a disappointment because I believed I was bright enough to succeed. The truth is that, although I always had a certain intelligence, being capable of expressing myself, I was never genuinely academic. I was never too bad at English and I had decent handwriting, but I was never much good at maths, history, geography or science. My heart just wasn't in those subjects. My development was all geared around sport in general and football in particular.

One of my teachers, an enormously encouraging individual called Gabe Williams, had helped me a lot and now he attempted to let me down lightly, telling me that there was more to life than exams. "Anyway," he added, "your brains are in your feet!" No argument from me about that. I recounted that story in July 2014 when I was elected an Honorary Fellow of The University of Wales, Trinity Saint David, at an awards ceremony held in The Grand, Swansea.

Still, for all my lack of significant classroom achievement, I do have plenty of worthwhile recollections of my schooldays, even some which had nothing to do with football. For example, there was the time when I was late and was sent to the headmaster, who caned me. Then he gave me an extra whack because I had blamed my mum for my lack of punctuality, telling me: "Jones, you shouldn't blame your mother. She's the best friend any boy ever has!" And he wasn't wrong, was he?

CHAPTER TWO

Taking flight at The Vetch

By the time I was growing up in the late 1940s, my father's football days were well and truly over. He was working in the local steelworks at Cwm-felin, not a particularly enjoyable job, quite a rotten one from what I remember him saying, but it involved hard manual labour which kept him in shape. He had no other skill so he had little choice if he was going to put food on the family table, but he didn't want me ever to find myself in the same predicament.

When I joined the Swansea Town groundstaff straight from school at the age of 15 in 1950, I had every confidence that I was embarking on a long and fulfilling career in the game – and that's how it turned out, thank goodness – but there were no guarantees. At the time, lots of fathers were saying the same thing because they'd been through some hard, chastening experiences.

He made me understand the many pitfalls, reminding me that a lot of talented footballing hopefuls fell by the wayside. Sometimes, no matter how gifted a lad might be, no matter how hard he's prepared to work, things just don't pan out, often through no fault of his own. It might just be a matter of bad luck, perhaps getting injured or not hitting form at the crucial time when a breakthrough might have been possible.

Also, there is the possibility that a boy who looks a world-beater at 15 might fail to develop as expected, and by the time he is 18 or 19 he finds himself surplus to requirements, effectively on the scrapheap. Most managers will tell you that the most painful aspect of their job is breaking the news to a bright-eyed teenager, who has devoted his life to becoming a footballer, that he is not going to make the grade after all. It amounts to trampling on their dreams, and it is exceedingly distressing for all concerned.

Having taken this on board, and despite the natural boldness of youth, I heeded Dad's eminently sound advice and, as soon as I was able to do so at the age of 16, started a five-year apprenticeship as a sheet-metal worker at the Prince of Wales dry dock, not far from where we lived.

It was hard graft involving a lot of lifting and everybody was kept very busy, there was never any chance of slacking on the job. I clocked on at 7.30am and knocked off at 5pm, as well as fitting in a rigorous training session every Tuesday and Thursday evening. In addition, I had to spend all day Monday on a course at Swansea Technical School, and go to classes on Wednesday and Friday evenings. Certainly it wasn't easy, but it rammed home to me one of the most valuable lessons of my life. It made me understand that, no matter how much effort you put into the game, football is not work. It's not the same as labouring on a building site or beavering away all day at a factory bench. The truth is that most players don't know they're born, especially in the modern era when they're so well paid. Their lives simply don't bear any resemblance to those of ordinary working people.

As it turned out, I was one of the lucky ones. With all due modesty, I have to say that there were plenty of talent scouts from big clubs buzzing around during my time with Swansea Schoolboys. Bolton Wanderers were very keen, and they were a major power in the land at that point, and there was interest from at least two leading clubs from the Midlands, Wolverhampton Wanderers and Aston Villa.

I thought very hard about what prospects I might have with them, especially as they were all in the First Division while the Swans were in the Second, and I did come very close to signing for Bolton, who had liked what they had seen from me in a schoolboy international against England at Hillsborough.

What made it seem for a while that I was destined for Burnden Park was that a Bolton scout, Bob Thomas, worked with my father at the steelworks and had impressed him with the Lancashire club's credentials. They had even agreed to set me up with an engineering apprenticeship and it was arranged for me to travel north by train to seal the deal.

Is it a bird? Is it a plane? No, it's a young Swansea Jack taking to the air against England Schoolboys. I was the Welsh skipper and that's my opposite number, Johnny Haynes, in the background on the left. I can't quite recall the venue or the year.

But I was very much a Swansea Jack at heart, I loved my life in the town where I was born and moving away was not an attractive proposition at that point. So only two days before I was due to set off into the unknown, I opted to stay on home territory. My parents hadn't attempted to influence me one way or the other, telling me I had to make up my own mind, but I think they were secretly relieved at my decision.

And so I started on The Vetch ground staff, on the princely sum of two pounds and ten shillings a week (£2.50p in modern money) and my first immediate boss was a wonderful man named Joe Sykes, who coached the youngsters at the club and also did a lot of the scouting. He knew me well already, having watched me play countless times, and it was Joe who first gave me the nod that the Swans were interested in me.

I had always dreamed of turning out for my hometown team and wearing that famous all-white strip, so imagine how I felt when he walked up to me after one game at The Vetch and said: "How would you like to play for Swansea when you leave school?"

Yorkshireman Joe had been a top performer for Swansea himself between the wars, joining from Sheffield Wednesday and then playing more than 300 games for the Welsh club as he developed into a hugely classy ball-playing centre-half. Now he was still serving Swansea nobly by passing on his tremendous knowledge to the kids and frequently offering much-needed emotional support when things didn't go according to plan. I learned so much from him about technical aspects of the game, like passing with the inside of the foot, how to head the ball without knocking yourself out, and how to time your runs to slip free of your marker. He was so generous with his time and I'll always think of him as one of the key influences on my career.

But for all Joe's fabulous input, the fellow who made the biggest impact on me on my first morning as a Swansea apprentice was Frank Barson. He was the first-team trainer and nobody messed with him. Nobody *dared* mess with him, because Frank was one extremely tough nut. It was a common saying at the time, one which carried a compelling ring of truth to my impressionable ears, that there were hard men in the game, and then there was Frank Barson.

Indeed, in those days there were some pitilessly flinty characters at Swansea, boys who'd been through the Second World War and witnessed some of the most terrible things imaginable. They looked at the world through a different perspective to green-behind-the-ears rookies like me and my mates; they had a grip on real life and what was really important. Certainly, having been on the battlefield with death and destruction all around them, they weren't going to be thrown by anything that cropped up on a football pitch or training ground. But even they wouldn't cross Frank Barson.

Sometimes people talk about larger-than-life characters, and that summed him up perfectly. He must have been a couple of inches above six feet tall, weighing about 16 stone, most of it muscle, and with battered, craggy features that you might call lived-in if you were wanting to be nice. Even now when I conjure up a mind's-eye image of that face, with its spectacularly

Put it there, Joe. I'm honoured to shake the hand of Joe Sykes, a coach at Swansea, a great man and a colossal influence on my football career. That's youth coach Bill Edwards in the centre.

busted nose and scar tissue everywhere, I experience a slight tremor of apprehension – and that's 65 years later!

As he lined up all the new apprentices that morning on the pitch at The Vetch, I gazed up in absolute awe at this man-mountain with a grisly reputation gained as a warrior centre-half with Barnsley, Aston Villa, Manchester United, Watford and Hartlepools United.

He began to speak: "Right boys, if you listen to me, you'll learn everything there is to know about football." Famously wary of people with education, he then asked if any of us had any qualifications. Gerald Griffiths piped up: "Yes, I've got four O-levels, Mr Barson – maths, English, history and geography." "Is that right, son. What position do you play?' demanded the great man, and Gerald informed him that he was a centre-half. At this the giant ex-stopper's eyes narrowed and they might have flashed fire as he replied: "Right, I'm going to tell you something now, and you'll do well to listen to it. When you've got some big, dirty centre-forward up against you, he's not going to be asking about what you did in school, or whether he can make an appointment to view your exam certificates. He's going to come at you and kick you right in the bollocks. Now if you listen to me you'll be able to do something about it. And you just might make a professional footballer."

That was our introduction to Frank Barson who, it was easy to believe, had once made his living as a blacksmith. Gradually we heard so many yarns about this tempestuous native of Grimesthorpe in Sheffield, how he was frequently sent off for violent conduct even though dismissals were comparatively rare in his playing day, how he was once banned for seven months and, perhaps a telling insight into a rather more complex character than was sometimes appreciated, how he reacted after being given the much-coveted landlordship of a pub as a reward for captaining Manchester United to promotion from the second tier in 1925. Apparently, when he opened his hostelry doors for the first time he was engulfed by back-slappers and so quickly grew sick of their sycophancy that he tossed the keys of the place to a waiter, then stalked out and never went back. What a man.

Knowing that the fearsome Barson might be looking over our shoulders at any moment, we apprentices went to work with a will. Apart from playing for the youth team, known as the Colts, we had plenty of other duties, menial but necessary jobs at any club. If you called us cheap labour, then you'd be right. Tidying the dressing room, cleaning the baths and toilets, sweeping the terraces, painting the stands, these and many other tasks were heaped upon us.

For instance, every close season our Scottish groundsman, Jock Fairlow, who was often at least three sheets to the wind, would re-seed the pitch and we had to help him. Then, as it grew, we had to cut the grass, but very carefully and painstakingly so the new blades wouldn't be dragged out by their roots before they could become properly established.

Now one of our directors happened to be a Welsh hill farmer, and one year he told Jock: "Don't bother cutting the grass, I'll sort it out for you." So the next day, up pulled this big wagon full of sheep and, at first, our groundsman was delighted. Surely, he reasoned, this flock of woolly, four-legged lawn-mowers would cut down on the work, enabling him to deploy the apprentices elsewhere, without costing a penny.

Well, to a certain extent it worked, in that the sheep did consume the grass. The problem was that when they re-boarded their wagon to head back to the countryside, they left behind them vast amounts of steaming manure, hardly the right treatment for turf about to be used for training and games. Jock was not happy, and neither were the groundstaff boys when we were deployed to clear up the muck. I'm pleased to say it never happened again, though you might say it was character-forming and might not do the comparatively pampered young players of today any harm at all.

Another by-product of the re-seeding operation might have been seen as hazardous in a different way. When the seed was scattered around The Vetch, it attracted large numbers of hungry pigeons and our Irish manager, Billy McCandless, liked nothing better than taking up station in the main stand, from which elevated vantage point he would attempt to pot the feeding birds with his shotgun. On such afternoons there was a marked lack of volunteers for extra training – nobody wanted to be filled full of lead. There can be few practices which illustrate the changing times more vividly than this. I've spent a lot of hours at White Hart Lane in recent times, and I'm yet to notice Mauricio Pochettino armed with a rifle!

Regarding the serious business of making my way as a player, my father used to watch me in action for the Colts as often as possible and soon he identified a shortfall in my game which eventually turned into one of my most effective attributes. He noticed that often I managed to beat a defender, but then lacked the pace to get away from him before he could get in a second challenge. Of course, if I had passed the ball quickly that wouldn't have mattered, but moving the ball on to a teammate was never going to be my forte.

Dad urged me to improve my speed off the mark, the first ten yards being of vital importance to an attacker like me. He had never given me bad advice, so I did what he said, staying after training sessions when most of the other lads had gone home, and practised short, explosive sprints.

I know that this wouldn't have worked for everybody. Some people just aren't built for extreme pace, but I had just the right sort of wiry build for running quickly and, sure enough, over the next six months I grew ever more nippy. It helped my game enormously and I was pleased with myself, but no sooner had I done that than Dad, a wise man who knew that good footballers never stop learning, saw something else I needed to do better – heading the ball. Clearly he was something of a prophet because he told me I'd score many more goals if I was more effective in the air and, after listening to him and working hard at the technique, down the years I reaped a rich harvest with my topknot. Later Bill Nicholson made the self-same observation and both were proved emphatically right.

When I arrived at The Vetch I was an inside-forward, seeing myself as both a maker and taker of goals operating alongside a main spearhead, and in that role I progressed smoothly enough through the junior levels before making my Second Division debut as a 17-year-old against Bury at Gigg Lane in October 1952.

To be honest, I didn't expect promotion to the first team quite so soon and was working at the docks, covered in oil and brandishing a hammer as I put together a torpedo vent, when out of the blue I received a heavy pat on my back. I heard the shout "Well done, Jonesy!" and a copy of the *Swansea Evening Post* was thrust before my eyes.

The big news was that I had been called up for my Football League entrance, and there was my picture staring up at me. I must admit I wondered if I was ready for senior competition, but reasoned that Mr McCandless was such an experienced football man, so if he had faith then so should I.

Lining up at inside-right, between my future Spurs comrade Terry Medwin at centre-forward and the excellent Harry Griffiths on the right flank, I had every opportunity to impress and I think I did all right. At any rate, we won 3–1 with two strikes in the last ten minutes, one shot home by Harry, who had also notched our first-half opener, and the other by inside-left Frank Scrine. I had made the pass to set up one of the goals and our happy boss, not a fellow to ladle out praise lightly, made my day by telling me: "Well done. I liked the way you worked."

Having been given my chance because the brilliant Ivor Allchurch had been away on international duty, facing Scotland at Ninian Park – in the 1950s they didn't call off League games because of internationals, the clubs just had to get on with it – I thought I'd be out of the team for the next match, but I was wrong.

The veteran Swansea trainer Frank Barson, looking a lot less fearsome than in real life!

Ivor returned to face Southampton at The Vetch, but it was Scrine who made way.

However, after we had lost 2–1 to the Saints and I had made precious little contribution to our cause, I was not so happy. During the game I had felt rather adrift from the action, which largely passed me by. Having been nowhere near my best, I could have no complaint when I was dropped for the next match, Billy McCandless having been far too wise to persist with a rookie who had looked out of his depth, albeit a promising one if I do say so myself.

The manager's priority was stabilising the club in the Second Division. Having been relegated to the third tier in the first season after the war, Swansea had bounced back up as champions in 1949, but the early part of the new decade had not proved easy, with demotion having been avoided by only a couple of points in 1951/52.

So during the next term, my entrance was part of an ongoing reconstruction process and I understood totally why I was left out in October and not recalled until April, when the team was safely ensconced in mid-table and there was a chance to experiment.

My comeback game was at home to Leeds United, and I was handed the number-eight shirt at the expense of my brother, Bryn, who had been enjoying a decent run in the side. That was a situation which McCandless handled diplomatically, explaining to Bryn that I needed a bit more experience and he needed to have another look at me.

Happily my brother was very understanding, not least because he realised I'd have been willing to stand aside for him if the positions had been reversed, and it turned out to be a memorable day in several respects.

For a start the Charles brothers, the mighty John of Leeds and our own Mel, were made captains for the afternoon and there's a lovely photo of the pair of them together before kick-off. What followed was an absolutely terrific contest in which George Meek put the visitors ahead early on, then Terry Medwin equalised before Big John put Leeds back in front about halfway through the first period.

The football from both sides flowed beautifully in front of 21,000-plus fans, who were treated to some wonderful entertainment for their money, and on a personal level I felt I was holding my own. Then, just around the hour-mark, things got even better for me. Terry delivered a delightfully floated corner from the right flank, I kept my eye on the ball all the way and I timed my leap perfectly. I caught it smack-bang in the middle of my forehead and it sailed past Leeds keeper John Scott for our equaliser.

I had scored my first goal in League football and felt like I was walking on air. To round off a glorious afternoon, Medwin grabbed our winner near the end, and when the referee blew the final whistle I walked off The Vetch feeling like a million dollars.

Understandably Billy McCandless used the last two games of the season to continue shuffling his pack, bringing Bryn back instead of me, but in view of my positive experience against Leeds it was hardly surprising that I was bright-eyed and bushy tailed, very much raring to go, at the outset of the 1953/54 campaign.

Alas, I had it rammed home to me unceremoniously in only the second match of the new term, in which we were hammered 6–0 at Birmingham, that football will always be a game of dramatic ups and downs. That afternoon at St Andrew's we had our trousers well and truly taken down, and our situation was made worse by the loss of our influential right-half Billy Lucas to an extremely nasty injury.

Now Birmingham were renowned as a physical side, with a fearsome half-back line of Len Boyd, Jack Badham and Roy Warhurst, though we were spared Boyd on this occasion, his replacement being another tough cookie, Keith Bannister.

Not that we were angels, of course! In fact, in all honesty, our Billy could be a downright dirty sod who positively relished a scrap. Mind you, he wasn't merely a hacker, being blessed with plenty of technical ability, but sometimes he gave the impression of kicking lumps out of an opponent just for fun. But this didn't turn out to be Billy's day.

Faced with Peter Murphy, an inside-forward who normally wouldn't say boo to a goose, our midfield destroyer absolutely stormed into a tackle, and in the split-second I had to think about it I genuinely feared for the Birmingham man's safety. But at the very last moment, perhaps spooked by the Lucas reputation, Murphy turned his shoulder and went right over the top of the ball. He really did for Bill, big time, leaving him on the floor in a hell of a state.

He had to be stretchered off, and as he came past me, he said: "Cliff, let that be a lesson to you. When you go on to the field, don't trust any of the bastards." It was so ironic that Billy, such a gnarled and streetwise professional, had been openly wary about Birmingham's acknowledged hard men but had not considered Murphy to be any sort of physical menace. The fact is that, sometimes, some sort of devil can take over any player and they can act out of character. The moral of the story was to expect the unexpected, which I did for the rest of my career.

The scene in the dressing room after the match was one of utter dejection, and Messrs McCandless, Barson and Sykes had to work exceedingly hard on the training ground during the following week to raise our spirits.

Around this time the manager suggested that he might try me as an inside-left as he thought it might turn out to be my best position, but this rather worried me because it meant that I would effectively be an understudy to Ivor Allchurch, who was rightly lauded as the golden boy of Welsh football, and that didn't do my prospects a whole lot of good.

Suddenly, from believing that I was making real progress towards a regular place, it felt as though I was drifting towards the periphery of the team, becoming one of those lads deemed expendable if ever changes were made.

Enter Joe Sykes, one of the shrewdest football men I ever met, with an inspired suggestion which was to alter the entire course of my career. Joe had always seen something in me and was always there for me when I was growing up in the game, definitely the most important individual in my early development as a footballer

On this blessed occasion, one evening when I was training at The Vetch and feeling a bit sorry for myself after a hard day's graft in the sheet-metal workshop, he pulled me to one side and, at first, mystified me by telling me something I already knew – that I was never going to get ahead of Ivor as a number ten. In addition, there were other gifted inside-forwards at Swansea, including my brother Bryn and Frankie Scrine, so becoming established in that position was always going to be tough.

But Joe was not one to preach a gospel of despair, he was always such a positive character, so I half expected a carrot to be dangled in front of my nose, and duly it appeared. "Look Cliff," he said, "you've got a turn of pace, you can run with the ball under control, so why don't you try playing on the wing? I really think you could make a go of it."

Despite my struggle to pin down a place, and my total respect for Joe's judgement, I have to admit I was very sceptical at first. After all, the Jones family had always produced inside-forwards, that was what we all did, and it had never crossed my mind to try my luck in another position. But Joe was persistent, pointing out that operating wide would give me extra space to show what I could do and stressing that the experience would do me good even if it didn't work out in the long run.

Intriguingly, although I was right-sided, he wanted me to have a go on the left flank, so I could cut inside and take a shot with my stronger foot. I pondered long and hard. The team was not doing very well and the number 11 slot was one of the problems, with Cyril Beech and Alfie Bellis both toiling to make an impact and the excellent, hugely versatile Harry Griffiths really needed in other areas.

Gradually the notion sunk into my thick skull. I said to myself that maybe Joe had a point – though why I should ever have doubted such a wise man, imbued with so much patience, understanding and deep-seated knowledge of the game, is completely beyond me as I gaze backwards with the benefit of more than 60 years' hindsight.

Thus I was deployed on the wing in a few reserve games, and must have done well enough in the unfamiliar role because on Boxing Day 1953 Billy McCandless called me up to partner Ivor Allchurch on the left flank of Swansea's attack in a home encounter with Stoke City. I didn't fully appreciate it at the time, but I had reached a crucial crossroads. A new, exciting and ultimately fulfilling direction was beckoning.

Love at first sight

Joan remembers . . .

When we first set eyes on each other, Clifford William Jones and I, was it love at first sight? Well, it was for me! I can't recall why I was in the Boys' Club in Townhill, it was probably some sort of Christmas function, but that's where I saw him for the first time. I was only 12 years old and hadn't had anything to do with boys at that point. But I can remember seeing him, quite vividly, and it might seem stupid now but I went home and I thought "I'm going to marry him." Mind, I hadn't consulted him! He would have been 14 and not interested in girls at the time. I think football was all that filled his head at that point.

To be honest, I didn't even know who he was, but I made it my business to find out, and discovered that not only had we attended the same primary school, but that he lived only ten minutes' walk from where I lived. So I took to strolling casually past his house – you might have called me the first stalker, before it became fashionable! – but years passed and it didn't come to anything. We spoke a few times, flirted a bit I suppose, and there was one occasion when he promised to take me to see a film but he never turned up. That wasn't very encouraging and there was nothing more for a long time.

Then, when I must have been about 15, I went along to a funfair on our local rec with a girlfriend. To my surprise I saw Cliff there with a crowd of his mates and we said hello, but that was all. Later I left the fair with my friend and when she parted from me to go home I didn't have far to go on my own. But Cliff must have noticed me leaving the fair because as she went he trotted up behind me – now he was doing the stalking! He asked if he could walk me home and I agreed. Then, when we got to my front door, he asked me to go to the pictures with him the next evening but I said: "No, because the last time you didn't turn up!"

But Cliff, who was on the groundstaff at The Vetch by then and playing occasionally for Swansea's first team while working at the docks as an apprentice, persisted in his efforts. He said he'd come and pick me up, all grown-up like, so I said OK but I still wasn't sure he would. At the time I was still at school, doing my O-levels, and I used to pop home for lunch. Next day I was still eating when there was a knock at the door and there was Cliff, nervously smiling at me and saying: "I just wanted to check that I was picking you up later on." That was more like it, and that was the start for Cliff and me.

It seems awful to admit it, but I can't remember which film we went to see, nor even at which cinema, though probably it was the Plaza or the Odeon. It's not easy to recall because in those days there must have been at least ten picture houses within easy reach of where we lived.

I did well in my O-level exams but I left school at the age of 16 – my sole ambition in life was to marry Cliff. My last day as a pupil was on the Friday, and I promptly started work in the local income tax office on the following Monday. It didn't enter my mind about having a holiday. If I'd said I wanted some time off people would have thought I wasn't right in the head. That's how it was in those days.

By then I was going to Cliff's house regularly, and when we reached the ripe old ages of 17 and 19 respectively, we decided to get engaged. The first thing Cliff had to do was ask my dad for my hand in marriage. I had already told my father what was happening, that we were going off to buy the engagement ring as soon as he gave his consent, but when we all met up Cliff bottled it as he was so nervous! I think my father actually came into the jewellers with us when Cliff bought the ring and he acted all surprised. I was the first one in my group of friends to get engaged, but it didn't seem so extraordinary then because people used to get married much younger back in the 1950s than they do now. There was

A quick cuddle with my lovely Cliff. We've been through so much together, and I have to conclude we were made for each other.

never any opposition to my determination to get married while still in my teens.

I was an only child, my mother and twin sister had died when I was four and I was brought up in a loving household of adults – my Nan and Grampa, Dad and my maternal Uncle Ivor. Then my Nan died when I was 14 and a year later Dad remarried, so when Cliff and I wed at St James' Church, Uplands, Swansea on 3 October 1955, we set up home in the house where I was born.

I was so happy, everything seemed so uncomplicated, and it was a truly wonderful time in my life.

Family has always been of supreme importance to both Cliff and myself, and in time we had four beautiful children – Steve, who was born in August 1956; Debbie, who came along in May 1958 and who we lost so tragically to cancer in 2006; Kim, who appeared in July 1959; and Mandy, who completed our set in June 1961. At the last count we have nine grandchildren and seven great-grandchildren. No question about it, we have been blessed.

CHAPTER THREE

Winging it

It would be lovely to record that the first day of the rest of my career started with an emphatic victory and a dazzling personal performance by Swansea's new left winger. What actually unfolded at the muddy Vetch on that brisk Boxing Day afternoon was a 2–2 draw, which was welcome enough after three losses in the last four games, and a satisfactory display from a number 11 who had enjoyed himself thoroughly.

Though it was natural to feel a wee bit of apprehension before kick-off, and a certain relief at being back in the team, I still retained my basic self-belief, and by the end of the game I was already blessing the shrewdness of Joe Sykes for coming up with the notion of changing my position. As a right-footer, I loved being able to swerve inside, beating my marker with a sudden injection of pace and then being perfectly placed to have a pot at goal with my stronger peg.

It was a pleasure and a privilege, too, to be part of such a high-quality forward line, which included the adaptable Harry Griffiths on the right wing, Len Allchurch at inside-right, Mel Charles leading the attack and, best of all, the scintillating Ivor Allchurch next to me at inside-left.

Ivor was an out-and-out thoroughbred, such an elegant performer bountifully endowed with every football skill imaginable. He had total command of the ball with either foot, he possessed a searing turn of pace, he was deceptively strong, he passed intelligently and instinctively, and he was a regular scorer of sensational goals from outside the box. In fact, he had a great deal in common with Bobby Charlton, one of the most special players

Wide-eyed, innocent and all ready to go in a spotlessly clean Swansea shirt at Goodison Park, where we faced Everton in the autumn of 1953.

of all time, right down to that wispy fair hair. He was a smashing lad, too, like Bobby very modest and unassuming, absolutely one of the boys despite his golden reputation.

It's sad that outside of Wales he doesn't always attract the recognition his staggering talent deserves. Ivor was five or six years older than me and, after making his debut in 1949, he quickly matured into a top player who probably lingered too long with a club which never looked really likely to win promotion from the Second Division.

Of course, conditions were different back then. Because of the maximum wage restriction, a rotten rule that held sway until Jimmy Hill led the successful battle to have it abolished in the early 1960s, a footballer couldn't better himself financially from a transfer, and anyway Ivor was essentially a home-town boy who was happy to remain with his mates.

During the mid-1950s there were plenty of huge clubs who wanted to buy him, notably Wolverhampton Wanderers, who won three League championships during the decade. Their boss, Stan Cullis, was desperate to sign Ivor, who would have given his hard-running team an extra dimension, but repeated offers were rejected by the Swansea board and he remained at The Vetch until the autumn of 1958, when he finally moved, to Newcastle United for £28,000.

By then he wasn't exactly past it, having recently sparkled for Wales in the World Cup finals in Sweden, but much of his prime had gone. Still, they loved him on Tyneside, where they really know the game, and he remained a favourite with the Geordies for four years.

I don't think Britain has produced many better players than Ivor Allchurch, and it's appropriate that there is a statue of him today outside the Liberty Stadium, the new home of Swansea City.

Back at the end of 1953, with the Swans frankly toiling in the wrong half of the Second Division, the very idea of raising a monument to a football man would have been deemed laughable, but at least when we walked off The Vetch after 90 minutes with honours even I felt there were genuine grounds for optimism that a radical improvement was on the way.

But, as so often happens, just when you think a corner has been turned, the game of football can kick you in the behind. Billy McCandless fielded an unchanged 11 for my second match as an outside-left, the return with Stoke City in the Potteries two days later, but we put in a terrible all-round performance and were trounced 5–0.

That set the scene for a dismal second half of the season which saw us escape only narrowly from relegation to the Third Division South. We managed only four wins after Christmas and finished just one place clear of the second demotion slot, which was occupied by Brentford.

It was difficult to see how a team containing so many excellent players – talented forwards like the Allchurch brothers and Terry Medwin; Mel Charles, who was equipped to shine at centre-half, wing-half or centre-forward; doughty defenders such as Tom Kiley and Dai Thomas; and utility man Harry Griffiths – could do so badly, but sometimes I think we might have been a bit rash in committing ourselves to all-out attack, which left us vulnerable at the back.

All dressed up – I'm sure I had somewhere to go.

On a personal level, though, I must have been doing something right because at the end of the season I was called up for my first full international cap. I was still only 19, and although Billy McCandless had told me that the selectors had had their eye on me since my switch to the left wing, pulling on that blood-red shirt for my country was still nothing more to me than a distant dream.

But shortly before Wales were due to meet Austria in a friendly in Vienna, I was working at the dry dock and had just stopped for my breakfast break when one of the crane drivers came running towards me brandishing a copy of the local morning newspaper, the *Western Mail*. He was clearly excited, shouting at the top of his voice even though he was only a few feet away from me, and when he thrust the sports page at me I could hardly believe my eyes. There was a massive headline telling me, and the rest of the world, that I had been picked for Wales.

Honestly, despite having received that hint from my Swansea boss, this was completely unexpected and I found it almost impossible to concentrate on sheet-metal for the rest of the day. I had only just finished my first full season in the Second Division and now things were moving so rapidly I could hardly keep up.

But if that all sounds like a fairy tale, there was to be no happy aftermath, at least not in the short term. Before kick-off at the Prater Stadium – now renamed after the great Austrian manager Ernst Happel – I lined up with incredible pride alongside goalkeeper Jack Kelsey, full-backs Stuart Williams and Alf Sherwood, a half-back trio of Bill Harris, John Charles and Ronnie

Burgess, and my fellow forwards Mal Griffiths, Derek Tapscott, Trevor Ford and Ivor Allchurch.

It was a tremendous boost for me to be operating next to my Swansea teammate and close pal Ivor, but even that didn't lift me to perform anything near my best. To be brutally honest, I just never got going and was very poor on my full international debut, although there were extenuating circumstances.

Austria were one of the best sides in Europe at the time, and in Ernst Ocwirk and Gerhard Hanappi they had two of the finest footballers to emerge in all of Europe. Walley Barnes, the old Arsenal full-back and later a successful broadcaster, was in charge of the Wales team, although without the official title of manager, and before the game he gave us a few tips. Most of all I recall him telling Big Trevor, our dreadnought of a centre-forward, that our hosts didn't go in for the physical stuff, so remember to take it easy.

Fordie, of course, was renowned for his rumbustious style, which often involved what might be termed these days as vigorous challenges on goalkeepers. So, as if poor Walley had never spoken, only a few minutes into the game the Austrian keeper cleared the ball, Trevor charged at him from about ten yards and hammered him into the back of the net. It was a pulverising assault which would have been penalised in the British game, even in the days when wholehearted contact between net-minders and attackers was allowed.

Instantly there was pandemonium all around the ground, with Austrian players and supporters going berserk. Trevor wasn't sent off and after that the game got completely out of hand, with terrible tackles flying in all over the place. Ocwirk, a tough and experienced operator, took it out on me a little bit and so it was hardly surprising that, as a green young lad, I made no discernible impact on proceedings.

When we went in at half-time, Barnes taxed Ford with his wild challenge, and Trevor's response was an absolute classic: "I never touched him, Walley!" said the abrasive Cardiff City spearhead. Thereafter the match disintegrated as a meaningful contest and we lost 2–0, which was probably just as well. If we'd won we might have been lynched. As it was I could look back on my international baptism with mixed feelings – pride at having been selected, but disappointment at failing to make my mark.

In the circumstances, I was less than stunned to be overlooked for Wales' next few games, even though I felt I was playing well for an improved Swansea team in 1954/55. McCandless was very much an old-school manager, always turning up at the training ground in a suit or sports jacket, certainly never a tracksuit, but he was a down-to-earth football character who much preferred to sit on the touchline at matches rather than the directors' box.

Generally speaking, he was a fair man who had the respect of his players, and he didn't need to be a particularly stern disciplinarian because he had Frank Barson to look after that side of the business. Frank's intimidating physical presence would keep order in virtually any situation, though underneath all that he was utterly steeped in football, knowing the game inside out. Still, it would be idle to deny that a huge part of his legendary status in the game was due to the fact that he would front up to any player, administrator, official or supporter whom he judged to be messing him around.

For instance, we had a goalkeeper named Danny Canning who used to fancy himself a little bit. He had joined us from Cardiff, eventually leaving for Nottingham Forest, and he was a big man, a decent enough performer between the posts but not a world-beater. One day he strode into the dressing room as the kit was being put out, and he was flexing his muscles, sticking out his chest as he told us "I could have been a contender" or words to that effect.

Somehow that got right up Frank's nose and he just hit Danny – smack! Right on the point of the chin. Danny went down like a sack of spuds. Frank glanced down at him, then looked round at the rest of us and said: "Yup, there's Danny Canning. He could have been a contender and now he's lying on the floor!"

Just imagine that today. It simply couldn't happen. There'd be lawyers all over the place. It's almost impossible for me to imagine Frank in the modern world, but in some way his approach was incredibly effective. Certainly nobody had the remotest chance of getting too big for their boots around him. I have to admit that, to an extent, I was afraid of him and so were the rest of the players. He was very much of his time, he had his ways and they got results, though I guess you have to say now that he could be a tad excessive.

Might he have made a manager? I don't think there was ever any question of that, either at Swansea or anywhere else, even in the much freer days of the 1950s. The job he did, as the iron fist alongside Billy McCandless' velvet glove, was ideal for him. You might say that Frank was not quite enough of a diplomat for higher office!

That thought is borne out by another colourful incident, this time when we were meeting Sheffield United at Bramall Lane. Frank was from Sheffield and had played for Barnsley, no doubt being involved in some feisty encounters with United, so as soon as we walked out on to the pitch the locals started having a go at him, calling him all the names under the sun.

At the end of the game, which we won, he turned to his tormentors and demanded: "How'd you like that then?" When he was greeted by yet another volley of catcalls, he picked up the bucket of water in which he kept his sponge, turned back to the fans who were still bating him and shouted: "Here you lot, have some of this then." And whoosh, he threw the whole bucket of water over them.

To be fair to those supporters, they took it pretty well, most of them trying to dive out of the way and having a laugh, but if such a thing happened in 2016 there'd be questions asked in Parliament, if not the United Nations. A few of them wanted to have a go at him, but that wouldn't have bothered Frank Barson. I reckon he'd have taken the lot of them on, and enjoyed doing it.

Not that Frank was purely an intimidator. He could be very droll, too.

Jumping to it for the Swans, nodding towards goal against Leeds United at The Vetch, with Townhill looming in the background. It's an exposed spot where, legend has it, people used to sleep in the bath so as not to be blown into the sea!

There was a time we lost 6–2 at Middlesbrough, with one Brian Clough scoring a couple of their goals. We had a centre-half called Dudley Peake, a tough local lad who would always have a go, and he'd had a right chasing from Clough in the first 45 minutes. Just before half-time, with Swansea already 4–0 down, the ball flew into the box, Dudley went up for it and there was a fearful collision of heads. Our big defender was knocked senseless, spark out, and was carried off. Soon afterwards we trooped into the dressing room and there was Dudley, stretched out on the floor with our manager – who was Ron Burgess by that time – trying everything to revive him. He had the smelling salts out, he was splashing water on his face and he was shaking him gently. Now Ron said to Barson: "Dudley, he's concussed, he doesn't know what day it is, he doesn't even know who he is." Frank had an instant answer: "Tell him he's f****** John Charles – we might have a chance then!"

Of course, that wasn't a great deal of help medically, but it did give everybody a damned good laugh. That was professional football in those days, it was no place for faint hearts. Anyway, Dudley was one tough cookie. He came round and played on in the second half, but I don't believe he thought he was John Charles. If he did then it was a bad day for Big Charlo because we were annihilated, although I suppose you could say we did draw the second half.

As for the new boss I've mentioned, Ron Burgess, his arrival at The Vetch from Tottenham, initially as a player in August 1954, was a tonic for everybody at the club. Though he was 37 when he joined Swansea, he had been one of the top footballers in the land ever since the war – witness his selection for Great Britain against the Rest of Europe in 1947 – and he had been the dynamic midfield dynamo at the heart of Arthur Rowe's magnificent push-and-run side.

With Burgess as a titanically inspirational left-half and captain, Spurs had lifted the championships of the Second and First Divisions in successive seasons at the turn of the decade, and many years later no less shrewd a judge than Bill Nicholson would describe the prematurely balding Welshman as the best midfielder Tottenham had ever known, thus placing him above such icons as Dave Mackay, Danny Blanchflower, Glenn Hoddle and Paul Gascoigne.

Soon Ron, a friendly bloke who fitted in brilliantly with the other lads, was proving that he had plenty of fuel left in his ageing tank. In 1954/55 he missed only a handful of games as we improved radically to finish tenth in the Second Division, but then in the following summer, as he contemplated starting the next campaign in his 39th year, fate took a decisive hand.

Billy McCandless, who had occupied the manager's seat at The Vetch since 1947, died suddenly one night at home at the age of 62. The club and everyone involved with it were rocked. Not only was Billy a popular figure with most people, he had also achieved a great deal with his youth system, bringing in and nurturing a whole crop of juniors who progressed to the first team, including myself.

But at least, in Ron Burgess, Swansea had an ideal man to pick up the gauntlet, initially as player-boss, though soon he laid aside his boots to concentrate on running and developing the side. He knew the game inside out, and had set a personal example on the field that few would be capable of following, but if he had a fault as a manager it was that he was perhaps a tad too nice and easy going with his lively charges.

To illustrate the point, on the first day he took over he got all of us together and said: "Okay lads, when you speak to me from now on it's either Mr Burgess or Boss or Guvnor." But the boys came back with: "F*** off, Ron, we're not calling you Boss, don't be so bloody daft" and he accepted it. You can be a top manager and still be a decent chap, of course, but I do believe a harder edge than Ron possessed is required. You have to have a certain distance from the players, which was what he was trying to achieve, but having formed so many close friendships over the previous year, it must have been extremely difficult for him.

Still, by no means did Ron Burgess do a bad job for the Swans, keeping them in the top half of the division (just) for two seasons, though it might be argued that he didn't draw the very best from a talented squad that included some wonderful footballers.

For starters, there were Ivor Allchurch, about whom I've waxed lyrical already, and Mel Charles, both world-class Welsh internationals. Mel was a terrific person and a marvellous footballer who didn't always get the credit he deserved. I used to room with him when we were on international duty and we became very close, having a fantastic time off the pitch as well as (sometimes!) on it.

Swansea Town in 1955/56, when we played some delightful football but lacked the consistency to push for promotion. Back row, left to right: Arthur Willis, Bobby Henning, Johnny King, Ron Burgess, my brother Bryn Jones, Dai Thomas. Front: Len Allchurch, Harry Griffith, Ivor Allchurch, Terry Medwin and me.

The biggest problem for Mel was that he was the younger brother to John Charles, one of the most wonderful players who ever lived, and he spent most of his own life being compared to someone who was simply, well, beyond compare. Mel even titled his autobiography *In the Shadow of a Giant* and that's just the way it was.

What made such treatment all the more inevitable was that there were so many similarities between the Charles boys, who had a marked facial resemblance to each other. They were both big, handsome, easy-going, gentle individuals and they were both capable of dominating games of football as both centre-halves and centre-forwards.

John, who I will talk about in detail later, was a genius, a veritable leviathan, but Mel also had so much going for him. Colossally effective in aerial combat, he also possessed amazingly intricate skills for such a huge fellow, he was as strong as an ox, nothing scared him and he was totally loyal to the cause.

Mel was a mountainous bulwark for Swansea throughout most of the 1950s, starting off as a wing-half, then switching to the middle as and when required. Being tackled my him must have been like being hit by an avalanche, but I always enjoyed seeing him up front because he was such a lethal finisher. Once he scored all four goals in a 4–0 thrashing of Northern Ireland at Cardiff and you don't do that without being a fair old predator.

When he eventually left Swansea for Arsenal in the spring of 1959, joining me in north London as I'd moved to Tottenham the previous year, I was convinced that he would kick on to genuine greatness as a Gunner. But he was so laid-back in his outlook that, probably, he took things a wee bit too easy at Highbury, where life was very comfortable. He always liked a drink and a smoke, to live life to the full as they say – that was his nature and there was no changing it.

Certainly there must have been pressure on him as the club's record signing – his fee was £42,750 with a couple of youngsters dispatched to The Vetch as part of the deal – and he arrived at a time when Arsenal were mired in a period of transition. Then he picked up a nasty knee injury and I'm not sure it was properly diagnosed at first. Whatever the truth about that, you have to work incredibly hard to regain fitness following such a setback and Mel wasn't someone who would necessarily apply himself to a rigorous training regime. Football had always come easy to him, he didn't like being out of his comfort zone and he wouldn't push himself unduly. For all that, he still enjoyed a long and successful career; it's just a crying shame he didn't maximise all that staggering potential.

Another of my best friends at Swansea – and we remain very close to this day – was Terry Medwin, whom I was destined to follow to White Hart Lane. He could play on the wing or at centre-forward – or in any attacking role – but I liked him best in the middle. He had pace and power, he was ready to work all across the front line, he had total command of a football with either foot and he was a superb team man, always on hand to receive the ball from a mate who was under pressure.

Playing centre-forward for the Swans might have jeopardised his place in the Wales team, which was one of the main reasons why he was ready to leave when Spurs came calling for him in the spring of 1956.

These days he lives back in our hometown and whenever I return there with my wife, Joan, usually the first people we go to see are Terry and his better half, Joyce. They have a beautiful family – six children, 17 grand-children and now some great-grandchildren, and Terry knows all the names infallibly. In fact, I have never met a man with a more astonishing recall of the minutest details of his football career. Ask him who played in any position in any game he ever took part in and he'll know the answer. I call him The Memory Man, and really it ought to be him writing a book rather than me!

I have mentioned the obvious stars of that Swansea side, but there were plenty of other cracking players, too. Len Allchurch, who could fill any attacking position but was probably at his best on the right wing, was a case in point. He would be the first to admit that he wasn't in the class of his older brother, Ivor – who was? – but he was a terrific performer who liked to drop his shoulder, then nip outside his marker and reach the by-line, from where he could deliver a precise cross. He had two good feet, and scored his share of goals, too.

Eventually he left the Swans to join Sheffield United, who he helped to gain promotion to the top flight in his first season at Bramall Lane. Later he won a Fourth Division championship medal with Stockport County, and later still he returned to The Vetch and was part of the team which rose to the Third Division under Roy Bentley in 1970. There wasn't much of little Len, but he made a big contribution.

Then there was my brother, Bryn, a delightfully versatile all-round footballer who was very much at home in the traditional Jones slot of inside-forward, but was equally adept at wing-half or full-back. He topped a century of games for Swansea before switching to Newport County in the summer of 1958, subsequently putting in stints with Bournemouth, Northampton Town and Watford, totalling more than 400 appearances before leaving the Football League in 1967, having enjoyed a tremendous career of which the family was terrifically proud.

The Swans at Rotherham in 1956/57, the season in which I realised that, despite being blessed with so many wonderful teammates, I'd be unlikely to reach the top flight with my hometown club. Back row, left to right: Arthur Willis, Tom Brown, Tom Kiley, Ken Evans, brother Bryn, Dai Thomas. Front: Len Allchurch, Harry Griffiths, Johnny King, Ivor Allchurch and me. That day Johnny King, usually a keeper, was tried at centre-forward after impressing in a practice match. The upshot? We lost 6-1 and he was never handed the number-nine shirt again!

Others who played an important part during the McCandless and Burgess eras include the exceptionally adaptable Harry Griffiths, who turned out in every position for the first team except goalkeeper and centre-half, though I'm sure he'd have done a tremendous job in those roles, too, if he'd been asked. I recall him most vividly as a tough, old-school defender who could put it about a bit, but he was also extremely skilful, comfortable with the ball on either foot and a lovely passer, and for my money he was unlucky to have collected only a single cap for Wales. Crucially, he would have done anything for Swansea, whom he went on to serve as coach, chief scout and manager.

Harry died at the tragically premature age of 47, while working in the treatment room at The Vetch.

There was the goalkeeper John King, who was brave and reliable; full-back Dai Thomas, a fearsome tackler and a tough Port Talbot character who you could bet your house on; and a trio of centre-halves, Tom Kiley, Ray Daniel and Mel Nurse. Tom was the old-fashioned type, like a column of granite at the heart of the defence, while Ray, who arrived towards the end of my time at The Vetch having made his name for Arsenal and Sunderland, liked to call himself the last of the ball-playing centre-halves.

This was a reference to the fact that in the very old days, before number fives were employed principally as stoppers, they used to venture forward on frequent attacking sorties, and this was a practice which had decreased in the 1950s. Even so, I think he was stretching a point in his description of himself, although there was no doubting that he was a brilliant footballer. That said, he was very full of himself, not the most modest man in the game, and he can't have been the easiest to handle at times. Eventually, after a few drinks, he upset some of the Welsh selectors on one occasion, which will have limited his total of caps considerably.

Mel was quite a few years younger and a lot more level-headed. He was big and powerful but also assured with the ball at his feet, while he was one of the most enthusiastic and loyal players Swansea ever had. He went on to serve Middlesbrough and Swindon before coming back to Swansea to conclude his career, then later he became a successful businessman and was involved in saving the club when it was struggling so badly for cash that it was in danger of going out of existence.

Finally, yet another smashing fellow whom I've never forgotten is Jim Pressdee, a full-back who made only a handful of senior appearances in mid-decade but who has lodged in my mind because he did make the grade as a cricketer with Glamorgan. I always adored the summer game, spending countless happy hours playing it on the lovely firm beach as a boy, and Jim made a fine fist of it as an all-rounder, a hard-hitting batsman, slow left-arm bowler and a spectacularly brilliant fielder. We knew him as Whistling Jim, because he never seemed to stop puffing out snatches of tunes, even when he was on the football pitch. It was an unusual habit which used to draw some funny looks from opponents who weren't ready for Jim's musical efforts.

I loved watching Glamorgan, and so many of my sporting heroes played for the only Welsh first-class county, the likes of irascible but inspirational skipper Wilf Wooller, wonderful batsmen like Gilbert Parkhouse and Bernard Hedges, and, best of all for me, the all-rounder Allan Watkins, who was an absolutely sensational close-to-the-wicket fielder and also played rugby for Swansea, the All-Whites.

Having sketched in a bunch of the characters who made my time in Swansea so special to me, I must return to my narrative at the start of the 1955/56 campaign, during which Ron Burgess led us to another mid-table finish. At our best we served up some marvellous stuff, but we weren't consistent enough to mount a genuine promotion bid, though on a personal level, that autumn threw up the most joyous moment of my career to date.

CHAPTER FOUR

"Leave it, Trevor!"

If my full international debut had been a damp squib, a sorry anti-climax by any way of reckoning, I like to think I more than made up for it in my second appearance for the Red Dragons.

Probably quite wisely, I had been left out for a few games after my disappointing afternoon in Vienna, when the encounter with Austria had descended into an unseemly scrap, but some 17 months later in October 1955, I had put together a run of decent form for Swansea and when the team to face England at Ninian Park was announced, I had been brought in to replace Len Allchurch on the left wing.

But even though this was clearly a golden opportunity, and a key landmark in my fledgling professional life, I somehow contrived to drop a clanger that must have had my international manager, Jimmy Murphy, mouthing the words 'Stupid boy' – or, knowing Jimmy's imaginative command of language, perhaps he coined a phrase that was rather more colourful!

At the time I was still serving my apprenticeship at the docks and I wasn't at The Vetch as much as the other players, so Swansea gave me the responsibility of looking after my own boots. Now bear in mind that a lot was happening to me at that point. I had been married for only a couple of weeks and now there was great excitement because I had been called up for my first full international on Welsh soil. So maybe my head was in the clouds when I went off to join the rest of the team at Cardiff, probably on the Tuesday before the game on the Saturday, and when I looked through my kit ahead of our first training session I realised I'd forgotten something quite important – my football boots!

I did have some training footwear so nobody else noticed and I rang Joan, at her desk in the Swansea tax office, with a plaintive request: "Can you do me a favour? Pick up my boots from home, bring them with you to the match on Saturday and meet me with them outside the dressing room in time for me to get ready with the rest of the lads."

Joan, as ever, was brilliant. She picked up the boots, then caught the train from Swansea with the rest of the family, who were all coming to watch me in action, but when she arrived in Cardiff she was faced by a daunting scene. There she was in a strange city – she didn't know Cardiff at all – and was confronted by thousands of people milling around the station and the surrounding streets. The queues at all the bus stops were massive and, fearing that she might be too late if she waited, she decided to walk. She had no idea where Ninian Park was and just followed the crowd, but during what seemed to be an endless trek she grew anxious that she might not make it on time and, showing bold initiative, flagged down a car. "Excuse me," said my gloriously determined wife to the surprised driver, "Are you going to the

match? Could you give me a lift because I've got my husband's boots and he's playing this afternoon." "Who's your husband?" she was asked, and when she replied "Cliff Jones" was told to hop in.

Now she thought her troubles were at an end, but no such luck. As they got closer to Ninian Park the traffic slowed almost to a standstill and time was ticking on. But now it was the driver's turn to take command, and he enlisted the help of a mounted policeman who provided an escort for the last quarter of a mile to the ground.

Meanwhile I'm pacing up and down outside the dressing room and

Even on my wedding day, football was never far away. Joan and I prepare to slice up the pitch!

The Wales team that fought like tigers on the greatest day of my international career, when we beat England 2–1 at Ninian Park in October 1955. Back row, left to right: Mel Charles, Stuart Williams, Jack Kelsey, John Charles, Roy Paul, Ivor Allchurch. Front: Derek Tapscott, Noel Kinsey, Alf Sherwood, Trevor Ford and me.

Jimmy Murphy is wondering what's wrong with me. "Come on, Cliff. Stop messing about, go and get changed now." I told him I had to see my wife and he imagined I wanted to give her some tickets, so he said: "Just leave them for her in the office, she'll pick them up safely. It's time you concentrated on the game." And that's when I finally had to come clean:

"It's not tickets, Jim."

"What is it then?"

"She's got my football boots…"

"WHAT!?"

"I forgot 'em…"

At that point, I thought poor Jimmy was going to explode: "What!? You're playing against England – Stan Matthews, Tom Finney, Nat Lofthouse, the lot of them – and you've forgotten your f****** boots? Are you f****** serious?"

Luckily, at that precise moment when Jimmy was probably about to murder his youngest player, Joan materialised with the boots. Not for the first time or the last time in my life, she had saved the day.

I can't say the manager was happy with me exactly, but now he could at least turn his full attention to what was a truly colossal occasion. It had been 17 years to the day since Wales had last beaten England, 4–2 on that same stretch of Cardiff turf back in 1938, with my Uncle Bryn scoring one of the goals, and now Jimmy was absolutely burning to put the record straight. Since then the world had been torn apart by conflict, but some things never changed – Stanley Matthews had netted in that historic pre-war contest and he was still in possession of his country's number-seven shirt when I ran out to earn my second cap.

For me it turned out to be such a momentous event that I'm going to name the two sides, both of which were bursting with tip-top talent. Wales lined up with Jack Kelsey in goal, Stuart Williams and Alf Sherwood at full-back, a middle line of Mel and John Charles, and captain Roy Paul, with an attack comprising Derek Tapscott, Noel Kinsey, Trevor Ford, Ivor Allchurch and myself.

In opposition were the great Wolves custodian Bert Williams behind full-backs Jeff Hall and Roger Byrne, half-backs Bill McGarry, skipper Billy Wright and Jimmy Dickinson, and a forward line of the future Sir Stan, Don Revie, Nat Lofthouse, Dennis Wilshaw and Tom Finney.

Not surprisingly given their attacking quality, England poured forward in the early minutes, with Matthews and Finney threatening to run amok. But gradually we turned the tide, with Mel and Roy Paul a pair of titans in midfield and Big John at his imperious best at the back, and it was no more than we deserved when Tappy raced through to put us in front with a powerful rising shot past Williams on 38 minutes.

Then 60 seconds later I was in dreamland. Our captain, performing fabulously, went on a typical surging sortie down the right touchline and delivered a deep cross which seemed to hang in the air. I had lost my marker and was sprinting in from the left, with Trevor Ford lurking in front of me.

CLIFF JONES
Swansea Town and Wales

I was always so proud to wear the blood-red shirt of Wales, and was fortunate enough to do so 59 times in full internationals.

In the brief moment I had to make a decision, I judged that it would be a stretch for our centre-forward to reach but it was in the perfect slot for me, so I yelled "Leave it, Trevor!" and kept running.

I wouldn't have been a bit surprised if he had ignored me, but he didn't. He left it for me, and I caught it sweetly on my forehead from round about the penalty spot. As soon as I made contact I was certain it was a goal and, sure enough, it arrowed just inside the far post. Williams was one of the most agile of all keepers, renowned for his athletic diving stops, but this time he didn't have a chance, he couldn't get anywhere near it. With all due modesty, it was a perfect header, the sort you score in your dreams, and I never met one better.

The whole place seemed to explode as I was mobbed by celebrating teammates. What a feeling! I had never experienced anything like it. Here we were 2–0 up against the mighty England side, complete with Matthews, Finney and all the stars, a whole raft of world-class players – and it was happening in front of our own people, the fans who stuck with us year in and year out no matter what the results.

We got a standing ovation as we walked off at the interval, but it wasn't all over and we had to guard against complacency. Predictably enough England fought back in the second half, though the nature of their goal after 51 minutes was totally unpredictable. The left-back Roger Byrne, destined to lose his life so tragically in Manchester United's Munich air disaster, lofted a seemingly harmless lob into our box and John Charles, of all people, leapt high to nod the ball crisply past an astounded Jack Kelsey. It looked a picture-book effort by Charlo, except that it was past his own keeper, which just goes to prove that even the very best can drop a clanger.

At that moment Mrs Charles, John and Mel's mother, who usually never went to football matches but was present on this occasion to see her sons play for Wales, jumped up and proclaimed that her lovely boy had just scored. But her husband, Ned, was quick to tell her: "Sit down, you silly bugger, he's just scored for England!"

After that, with our style cramped by an injury to Paul – no substitutes in those days, remember – England had the lion's share of possession, but the only time they really threatened our goal was when Revie hit the crossbar with a sensational back-heeled volley from a Finney cross.

When the final whistle went there were scenes of wild euphoria, with our ecstatic supporters carrying me off the pitch shoulder-high. I was surrounded by a sea of people, but there was nothing menacing about the situation, it was one of the happiest moments of my entire life. I felt particularly delighted for our veteran full-back Alf Sherwood, who'd been playing for Wales for what seemed like an eternity without ever tasting victory over England. Now his grin was as wide as Cardiff Bay. As for me, I was 20 years old, newly married, the scorer of the winning goal – my first for Wales in my first international on home soil – against our keenest rivals.

Even though I went on to play in the World Cup finals in Sweden in 1958, this afternoon in Cardiff represented the pinnacle of my Wales career. I felt at the time that I could never expect a better feeling than that while wearing the red shirt, and I was right. I was so delighted for Jimmy Murphy, too, especially after the pre-match drama over my absent footwear. Certainly that was something he never forgot, and ever afterwards, whenever we had a game in Cardiff, his greeting would be the same: "Got your boots, Cliff?"

However, if I needed to be brought back down to earth after all that euphoria, I didn't have to wait long. At the time I was in the last year of my apprenticeship at the dry dock and on the following Monday I went into work as usual. I was met by Dai Vaughan, my foreman, who greeted me with: "Well done on Saturday, Cliff, but now there's your tools, you've got a proper job of work to do. Get on with it!"

That shaped me, making me realise just how fortunate I was to be planning to play football for a living for the foreseeable future. Looking back now, it emphasises just how dramatically the world has moved on. Just imagine a Ryan Giggs or a Gareth Bale, having enjoyed their magical moment, then strolling into a workshop or factory to do their next shift. Yet I can recognise, too, that the experience for me was so wholesome, so grounded in reality, demonstrating that while there was a place for great achievement in sport, essentially it's a recreation.

That deadpan greeting by Dai also linked me inextricably to the fans. It reinforced a fact that I always appreciated, that I was one of them, no more and no less. Today's footballers are far removed from their communities. I wasn't, and I would never have wanted to be.

Later Bill Nicholson at Tottenham always made it clear to his players that the fans were the most important part of the football club. He stressed that without them there would be no club, and he always wanted to entertain them, to give them value for their hard-earned money.

That's what we always attempted to do at Swansea, too, with boss Burgess sharing the philosophy of his old Tottenham comrade. So we started the 1955/56 campaign with high hopes, and despite losing three of the first five games, we improved radically through the autumn, so that when we won 2–1 at Bristol Rovers in mid-October, thus ending the Pirates' proud unbeaten home record, we rose to the top of the table. That afternoon at Eastville – always an atmospheric ground with its flowerbeds at either end of the pitch and gasholders looming over the stands, now the site of a huge furniture store – we played some lovely flowing stuff, with Mel looking particularly fine in his favourite position of right-half and Ivor orchestrating attacks with typical flair and imagination.

When we built on that with successive victories over Hull City, Plymouth and Liverpool, we had the scent of promotion in our nostrils and I began to dream of playing for my beloved Swans in the elite division. But just as I felt we were gathering irresistible momentum, we lost our mountainous centre-half Tom Kiley to injury. Big Tom was our bulwark at the back, a dominant linchpin whose voice you could always hear on the pitch, and without him we suffered a string of debilitating defeats between November and March, which knocked us out of contention. Had we had the resources to bring in a high-quality replacement then the outcome might have been different, but all we managed was a young hopeful from Llanelli named Tom Brown, a promising lad but not what we needed at that moment. There was no question of Swansea splashing out, which rammed home to several key players that they would need to leave for the sake of their careers.

There was one fascinating diversion from this growing disillusionment, however, at Elland Road in February when the game against Leeds United featured three sets of brothers. John and Mel Charles were the two centre-forwards, Ivor Allchurch was our inside-left with Len on our right wing, while Bryn and I made up our left flank, he at number six and me at number 11.

We did pretty well that afternoon, holding Raich Carter's soon-to-be-promoted Yorkshiremen – who were unbeaten in 32 home games – to a 2–2 draw

The three pairs of brothers who took the field at Elland Road in February 1956. On the far left is John Charles, the only one of the half-dozen who turned out for Leeds, scoring from the spot in a 2–2 draw. The others are, left to right, Mel Charles, who also hit the target, Ivor Allchurch, Len Allchurch, Bryn Jones and me.

on their own patch, which didn't look to be on the cards when John Charles gave them the lead from the penalty spot, his 100th goal for the club. However, brother Mel struck a blow for family pride with the equaliser, and when Ivor put us 2–1 in front it looked like we might revive our season with an unexpected win, only for the excellent inside-forward Albert Nightingale – whose career would soon be terminated prematurely by a chronic knee injury – to level things up five minutes from the end.

Come the end of the season Swansea were in tenth position again, while I found myself doing duty for Queen and country, having been called up for my National Service in the Army, which had previously been deferred because of my apprenticeship at the docks.

I was very fortunate because I was sent to St John's Wood in London to join the King's Troop Royal Horse Artillery, a mainly ceremonial outfit responsible for parades, salutes and the like. The sympathetic commanding officer, who aspired to win the Army Cup, allowed me to have weekends off to continue to play football. A lot of lads weren't so lucky and plenty of careers lost crucial impetus because they were whisked away from their clubs for two years. Others, like Bill Foulkes of Manchester United, with whom I played in the Army, had to resort to elaborate subterfuge to get away from his barracks for matches. Poor Bill – rather a grumpy old sod in those days, though he mellowed appealingly as he grew older – had to disguise himself as a businessman and travel around the country on trains with the ever-present fear of being apprehended by the military police. Happily he got away with it, but I was just hugely relieved that I didn't have to go to such extreme lengths to play my football.

As for the principle of National Service, I think it did us no harm at all. We learned respect for authority, which I believe is always good, and we learned how to look after ourselves away from home, getting used to cooking, cleaning and ironing. It developed young boys and turned them into men. Certainly it did me a power of good. I came out of the Army a much more rounded person than when I went in, with a bit more discipline and capable of being independent.

Then there was the fantastic fun we had, the lasting friendships we made and the amazing scrapes we shared at times. I shall never forget one escapade with Barry Hughes, a player with West Bromwich Albion. Most of the troop were away from camp on exercise and we were ordered to whitewash the stables in their absence. We thought, wrongly as it turned out, that we were free from authority for the day, so we didn't shave or dress properly and our work rapidly turned into an uproarious session in which we sprayed the white stuff at each other, making one hell of a mess. Alas, we were witnessed by no less a personage than the adjutant, who hauled us over the coals and threatened me with an overseas posting which would have properly ruined my footballing aspirations, as well as proving massively disruptive to family life as my wife, Joan, was expecting a baby.

What had daunted me at first was that I was expected to work with the Royal Artillery's horses. I had never had anything to do with such enormous beasts before – I hadn't even ridden a donkey on the Swansea sands! – and I was more than a little terrified of animals which I now had to feed and clean. But I knuckled down, even began to enjoy it, and if I'm honest the tasks I was given were hardly onerous.

At certain times the whole camp would go down to Okehampton in Devon to enable the horses to relax and get back to nature. On one of our nights out Barry, his rugged West Bromwich teammate Maurice Setters and myself visited an inn specialising in scrumpy, which, to the uninitiated, is very strong but beguilingly tasty cider. The landlord saw we were Army boys and asked us if we had drunk scrumpy before. When we said "no" he replied, "Do yourselves a favour, lads, and have half pints," but unwisely we spurned his excellent advice. It was pints all round for us, but we found out soon enough that we should have listened

Would you really trust this man with a lethal weapon? Cleaning my rifle for inspection at St John's Wood barracks during my National Service with the King's Troop Royal Horse Artillery.

*Brothers in arms: Alex Parker and I were big mates in the Army, but later
the Scottish full-back put our friendship firmly to one side, with painful
consequences, when he was marking me for Everton against Spurs.*

to him. How we got back to camp I do not know. Reveille was sounded at 6am
and we had to take the horses out for what they called rough exercises. I found
myself on the horse of a Captain Saunders, who happened to be not too keen
on footballers. Unfortunately, in my delicate state, I came off his horse and it
galloped away into the distance. I made my way back to camp, not feeling too
clever, and was confronted by the captain, who said: "Where's my horse,
Jones?" I could only reply: "I've lost it, sir.'" Not surprisingly, he was incandescent: "What do you mean, you've lost my f****** horse? Well, you'd better go
and find it, otherwise I will transfer you so far away that your family, friends
and the whole world of football will never hear of you again!" Luckily for me,
horses are territorial animals and soon this one made its way back to camp,
albeit not in the best of states. Duly I returned it to the captain, who was not

impressed. He glared at me as if he could kill me and snarled: "Jones, if you ever touch my horse again I'll have you f****** shot." I think he meant it!

Clearly there was nothing for it but for Gunner Jones, National Serviceman 23306136, to mend his ways forthwith and throw himself into his duties instead of trying, ever so immaturely, to treat his Army stint as one long holiday. Eventually, I'm happy to report, I was allotted a cushy number in the stores.

Most importantly, I was given all the football my heart could desire. Apart from turning out regularly for the Swans, I found the Army game to be immensely enriching because I was playing with and against some of the most gifted players in the land.

Among the professionals I took the field with were Alan Hodgkinson, the Sheffield United goalkeeper who went on to play for England; his Bramall Lane teammate, the full-back Graham Shaw; Hibs defender Jackie Plenderleith, who made his name in England with Manchester City; winger Ian Crawford of Hearts and his teammate, a certain Dave Mackay, who was to become one of my most revered comrades later when I joined Spurs; centre-forward Dave Dunmore, who was already at White Hart Lane; my pal Maurice Setters, a real tough nut of a wing-half; Charlton goalkeeper Willie Duff; Wycombe Wanderers winger Len Worley, who made one appearance for Tottenham; a Scottish lad named Dougie Hall; and a star-studded contingent from Manchester United which included the aforementioned Bill Foulkes, an extremely rugged full-back at the time who became a top centre-half; Eddie 'Snakehips' Colman, one of the most delightfully gifted midfield men I've encountered; Bobby Charlton, destined to mature into one of the greatest footballers the world has ever seen; and a towering prodigy by the name of Duncan Edwards, who somehow contrived to be even more impressive than Bobby.

The highlight for me has to be playing alongside Duncan, who along with poor Eddie was doomed to lose his life at Munich a few years later. When you're talking about great players, Big Dunc was in a class of his own. I believe that but for the air crash he would have developed into the finest player who ever lived. What made him so special? Fierce commitment to the game, incredible fitness and physical prowess, and just about every skill I've ever seen performed on a football field. He was a fearsome powerhouse and I have no doubt that he would have gone on to captain United and England for many years.

Even before I met Duncan in the Army I'd heard so many stories about him from Jimmy Murphy, who ran the Wales team and was assistant to Matt Busby at Old Trafford. I had total respect and affection for Jimmy, and recognised that he was an astonishingly shrewd judge of football ability, but before I got my call-up papers, I did have the notion that he was exaggerating when he talked about Edwards, whom he made sound like a combination of Superman and Roy of the Rovers. But when I saw him in action regularly, I had to hold my hands up and acknowledge that Jimmy was dead right.

When he was in full flow, there was no more colourful speaker about the game than the Wales coach and, on occasion, no more humorous one. Before one game against England, Jimmy was giving us a team talk, running through the strengths and weaknesses of the men we were about to face. He went through ten names with his customary eloquence, but he didn't mention Duncan, which rather perturbed our inside-right, Reg Davies of Newcastle, who would be his direct opponent.

So Reg piped up: "Boss, that's all very interesting, but what do I do if Duncan Edwards brings the ball through from deep. Should I close him down and make a tackle, back off and protect our space, or what?" Jimmy glanced at him with a tolerant grin and replied: "Reg, if Duncan Edwards is coming at you, the best thing you can do is get out of his f****** way!"

That had the dressing room roaring, and did a lot to dissolve the tension. Of course, we were all professional footballers and we weren't scared of anybody, but we knew Duncan was a special case. Reg took it in good part and we all had a laugh, but the point had been made with typical Murphy eloquence and wit. If any further testimony were needed, it came when his close pal, Bobby Charlton, told me that the only player he has ever been in awe of on a football field was Big Dunc – and when you consider some of the performers Bobby has knocked up against, that's saying something.

Edwards' death was a tragic loss to the game at large, which he would surely have graced for another decade and more, but it was unspeakable, too, on a personal level because he was a marvellous character, a very grounded individual with whom it was a pleasure to spend time. He had extraordinary confidence in his ability, but that never teetered into arrogance or conceit.

Much the same, of course, can be said of Charlton himself, a delightfully

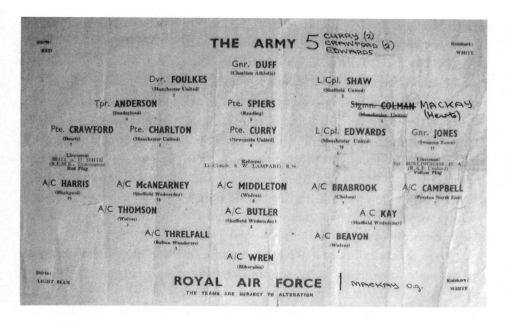

THE ARMY 5 ~~CURRY (2)~~ CURRY (2)
CRAWFORD (2)
EDWARDS

Gnr. **DUFF**
(Charlton Athletic)

Dvr. **FOULKES**
(Manchester United)

L/Cpl. **SHAW**
(Sheffield United)

Tpr. **ANDERSON**
(Sunderland)

Pte. **SPIERS**
(Reading)

Stgmn. ~~COLMAN~~ MACKAY
(Manchester United) (Hearts)

Pte. **CRAWFORD**
(Hearts)

Pte. **CHARLTON**
(Manchester United)

Pte. **CURRY**
(Newcastle United)

L/Cpl. **EDWARDS**
(Manchester United)

Gnr. **JONES**
(Swansea Town)

Linesman
W.O.1 A. D. SMITH
(R.E.M.E. Donnington)
Red Flag

Referee:
Lt.-Comdr. S. W. LAMPARD, R.N.

Linesman
Sgt BURLINGHAM, D. A.
(R.A.F. Cosford)
Yellow Flag

A/C **HARRIS**
(Blackpool)

A/C **McANEARNEY**
(Sheffield Wednesday)

A/C **MIDDLETON**
(Wolves)

A/C **BRABROOK**
(Chelsea)

A/C **CAMPBELL**
(Preston North End)

A/C **THOMSON**
(Wolves)

A/C **BUTLER**
(Sheffield Wednesday)

A C **KAY**
(Sheffield Wednesday)

A/C **THRELFALL**
(Bolton Wanderers)

A/C **BEAVON**
(Wolves)

A/C **WREN**
(Hibernian)

Shirts:
LIGHT BLUE

ROYAL AIR FORCE | MACKAY O.g.

Knickers:
WHITE

THE TEAMS ARE SUBJECT TO ALTERATION

The strength of forces football is made obvious by this teamsheet.

unassuming lad with a wicked sense of humour when you got to know him well. With me a left winger and Bobby an inside-forward, we played in tandem often and he was a dream to link up with. Even at this early stage of his career it was obvious that he was destined for the very top, and his star was firmly on the rise when a group of mates from the Royal Artillery turned out to see him play for United at The Valley against Charlton Athletic, for whom another chum, Willie Duff, was standing between the posts. Poor Willie had to pick the ball out of his net five times that afternoon, with Bobby plundering a tremendous hat-trick. But afterwards there was no crowing from the United man – there has never been a scrap of big-headedness about him.

During my period of service the British Army team played against their French, Belgian and Portuguese counterparts, and one particularly treasured memory is of our celebration after beating the French in Paris. That evening Dave Mackay, Eddie Colman, Willie Duff, Maurice Setters and myself repaired to a very welcoming café on the Champs-Élysées for some liquid refreshment. We had a high old time, but when the bill came at the end of the night we suddenly realised we didn't have enough money to pay it. Of course, Mackay, always a leader, knew what we must do. Very quietly he told us: "When I say RUN, f****** run!" With that, he said "RUN!" and we did. We put on a terrific turn of speed and although we were pursued along that famous boulevard by four or five waiters, they had absolutely no chance of catching us!

Not surprisingly with such a collection of wonderful players, we in the Army's full representative side won the Inter-Services Shield in both seasons I was in uniform, something I still gaze back on with a sense of achievement. But even without that to stir the memory, I would be an enthusiastic advocate of National Service. I don't think it would be a bad thing if it were brought back today, but I can't see it happening – there would be an absolute outcry if any government attempted to introduce it.

I guess my perception of it is coloured by the fact that my input to Swansea was virtually uninterrupted. At the time, in the second half of the 1950s, I would say that the magnificent Ivor Allchurch was at his very best, and I would have hated to have missed out on that. I like to think we combined well together and for some unknown reason I still carry images in my mind's eye from a seemingly run-of-the-mill home encounter with Doncaster Rovers when nearly everything we tried came off. That afternoon at The Vetch our passing and movement just seemed picture-perfect as we won 4–2, with Harry Griffiths bagging a hat-trick and Mel Charles scoring the other. One journalist was kind enough to write of the display by Ivor and myself: "Only the brilliance of Allchurch and Jones separated the two teams. Both players electrified the crowd with as fine a display of football as one would wish to see."

One other deathless impression from that contest in October 1956 is of a man I rate as one of the most dominant goalkeepers I have ever seen. I'm talking about Harry Gregg, the Northern Ireland international who went on to an illustrious career with Manchester United and was voted the best netminder at the 1958 World Cup finals in which both our teams reached the last eight.

I have never seen a footballer braver or more fearsome than this big, redhaired Ulsterman who seemed to breathe fire through his nostrils. When he was going for the ball he would charge off his line and go through – and I do mean through – friend and foe alike to get it. But for all that ferocity, there was a tremendous warmth about Harry, and he had a wicked sense of humour, far more subtle than most people realised.

Once when I was playing for Spurs against United, there was a chaotic scramble in his goalmouth, in which he ended up lying on his stomach with his hand pressing down on the ball. I was close by and I fancied I had a chance of getting it off him, but when I moved towards him he just glared at me with an expression that was worth a thousand words. He might have said, 'I wouldn't, wee man, if you know what's good for you' but he didn't have to. I understood his intention fully, and when he twigged that the unspoken message had been understood, he grinned as if to say, "Good decision, Cliff, at least you'll go home in one piece!"

The British Army was a grand old team to play for, packed with plenty of fabulous footballers. Back row, left to right: Alex Parker, 'Tosh' McIntosh, Willie Duff, Johnny Williams, Dick Spiers and Freddie Sharpe. That's me and Ron Newman crouching in the middle, with Brian Harris, Gerry Hitchens, Bill Curry and Bobby Charlton at the front.

Probably Harry was too brave for his own good because he suffered horribly with injuries, often playing when he was not really fit enough, something that wouldn't be allowed today. Lots of players did that in the 1950s and '60s, being sent into battle pumped full of cortisone, which deadened the pain at the time but often allowed lasting damage to be done to joints, causing untold misery in later life. I've been very fortunate in that respect. I've had my share of painkilling drugs down the years but seemed to have escaped any unpleasant consequences.

Regarding Harry, I will always remember him as one of the very best. He was a hero, too – though he never sought that label, for he was always an engagingly modest fellow – when United's plane crashed at Munich, rescuing fellow passengers from the wreckage. Quite a man was Harry Gregg.

As the 1956/57 season wore on, it became obvious that we were not going to mount a genuine push to reach the First Division. My pal Terry Medwin had left to join Spurs in the previous spring, the team was much the poorer for losing him and, even though we managed the score the tremendous total of 90 goals, we conceded the same number and finished tenth for the third successive year.

Meanwhile the fact that I was meeting lots of players from other clubs during my National Service was giving me itchy feet. They told me a lot about the wider world, opened my eyes to the opportunities that were out there, and made me ponder that perhaps my future lay away from Swansea, a notion that for a long time had been unthinkable to me.

The truth is that, much as I would always love my hometown club, I felt I'd gone as far as I could at The Vetch. We'd had one or two sniffs of rising to the big league, but every time we got anything like close to that dream, it became apparent that the club had no intention of spending the necessary money to make that last vital step up. I understand perfectly well that smaller clubs have always had to be careful with their finances, but it's also true that sometimes there comes a moment where boldness and decisiveness can change the landscape. The injury to Kiley and the consequent problem in defence was a case in point. That brought it home to me that I was never likely to get top-level football with Swansea, that I owed it to myself as a professional, and to my family, to branch out in a fresh direction.

Not surprisingly there was always speculation that certain players would soon be on their way. Rumours about the likes of Ivor Allchurch, Mel Charles and others, including myself, never stopped swirling around, in the press as well as the pubs and clubs, and it was in this uncertain atmosphere that we started the 1957/58 campaign with a goalless local derby against Cardiff City at Ninian Park. There followed a dismal autumn with far more defeats than victories, and after a 1–0 home reverse in the return with the Bluebirds shortly before Christmas we were bottom of the table, seemingly with little hope of escaping relegation.

There was a shaft of light and a dose of yuletide spirit on Christmas Day itself, when we beat Bristol Rovers 6–4 at The Vetch, a ten-goal thriller to which I contributed a hat-trick, but any feel-good atmosphere was dissipated by a 3–0 drubbing in the Eastville return on Boxing Day.

People outside the game often expressed amazement to me that footballers should be asked to leave their families to go to work on Christmas Day. But although my son, Steve, was only two years old at that time, it wouldn't have occurred to me to feel hard-done-by. Playing over Christmas was part of the professional game, something you got on with automatically, not something you questioned or militated against. After all, we were part of an entertainment industry, so it was our job to put on a show when the majority of folk were on holiday and had the chance to watch us. Of course, it meant the players couldn't really let themselves go with their Christmas celebrations like most other people but, trust me, we tended to make up for it afterwards.

I always enjoyed the buzz around the grounds at Christmas, with crowds in the mood for fun, but Easter always seemed like more of a genuine football festival to me. By then it was showdown time for many teams, who were on the run-in to promotion or engrossed in relegation battles, and playing three games in four days could change the picture dramatically. Imagine that sort of fixture programming now – it just wouldn't be countenanced, but we had to get on with it. Usually the pitches weren't too clever by that time of the season, and almost inevitably you were carrying a few niggles accumulated over the previous seven or eight months of action, but you just had to be resilient. Quite simply, that was the English game in the 1950s.

However, by the time the Easter bulbs were springing up in 1958, I was no longer playing my football for Swansea Town.

The Welsh Gento

Bobby Charlton remembers . . .

For me National Service was more than anything an unwelcome inter-ruption to what I'd always felt I was born to do... play football at the highest possible level I could. Sometimes I would see an airliner passing over my Army camp in Shropshire and I would think wistfully that it might just be carrying my Manchester United teammates to some exotic location for European Cup action. I yearned to be with them. But there was a consolation in that the Army wanted to use its young professional footballers as much as it could and this meant I played a lot – and in some very good company.

For a while I shared a barracks dormitory with my prodigious clubmate Duncan Edwards, but when he returned to civvy street some time before me it was not as though I was suddenly without a star teammate. I played quite a number of representative games with the great Cliff Jones of Spurs and Wales.

Over the years I would marvel at the quality of Cliff's game – and not least when he joined with such greats as Dave Mackay, Danny Blanch-flower and John White to win the double so brilliantly in 1961. At United we were attempting to rebuild on the tragic ruins of the Munich air crash and if we had to set ourselves the highest ambition we could do no better than consider the level of that beautiful Spurs team.

We thought we were making some progress the season after the Tottenham double but when we faced them in the FA Cup semi-final we found out how much we still had to do. They beat us 3–1 and Cliff was one of the scorers.

Of course, by then I knew all about him. In the Army days he was a pleasure to know and to perform alongside – when I played against him it was a somewhat different sensation, but it was always coloured by the knowledge that he was a great lad and a truly tremendous player.

He had searing pace and a wonderful touch. In some ways I suppose he was the Welsh Gento, a winger who at times was simply unplayable. Cliff had that smoking speed but also the most acute, hard skill of wonderful judgement in deciding when to deliver the ball to the point of maximum danger. It also helped that he was such a grand, unassuming person.

CHAPTER FIVE

Spurs fork out a fortune

I have always loved Swansea, the place and the football club, and I always will. In many ways, despite all I was fortunate enough to achieve with Spurs, the most enjoyable days of my football career were spent at The Vetch. The majority of the boys were local, the crowd responded magnificently and the game came very easy to me. To a certain extent I could play in a carefree way, though obviously always working hard and maintaining professional standards.

On top of that, while still a Swansea player I had married and started a family. Looking back, it was an idyllic time of my life and my memories of it are treasured. But having said all that, in February 1958 I knew it was time for a change if I was ever going to achieve my ambitions. The Swans were toiling horribly, and while I would be delighted when they pulled narrowly clear of the trap door to the Third Division by taking seven points from a possible eight in their last four games of the season, I had made my second transfer request – the first had been rejected a year or so earlier – and was concentrating now on the interest my intentions generated, which was very flattering.

Arsenal came in strongly to secure my signature, Chelsea were extremely interested and actually thought they had tied up my transfer at one point, Wolverhampton Wanderers were mentioned, so were West Bromwich Albion, Birmingham City and Sunderland, every one of them a colossal footballing institution.

I was even linked with Manchester United, perhaps not surprisingly as, in the aftermath of the Munich tragedy in which eight players lost their lives and two more were so badly maimed that they never played again, the

Old Trafford club was urgently in need of reinforcements. There was an obvious close connection, too, because my international boss, Jimmy Murphy, had taken over the reins of United, fighting fires and keeping the red flag flying while the manager, Matt Busby, was still battling for his life in a German hospital.

Jimmy knew me well, and I had all the respect and affection in the world for him, but by the time of United's crash on 6 February I was already committed in my heart, and by gentleman's agreement, to Tottenham. Part of the reason I was so keen on White Hart Lane was that my fellow Swansea Jack, Terry Medwin, was telling me constantly what a marvellous club he had joined. Then there was Ron Burgess, one of the greatest Spurs of all time and now my boss at The Vetch, telling me that if I was absolutely committed to leaving Swansea, then to do myself a massive favour by throwing in my lot with his former employers.

Ron told me: "Whatever you do, don't sign for the Arsenal!" Obviously, old allegiances die hard but he needn't have worried because although the Gunners did pay court, and quite persuasively, they pulled out in the end because they didn't like the way Swansea were handling the situation. It seemed to Arsenal that the Swans had put me up for auction – and, to be fair, there was no reason why they shouldn't strive for the best deal possible – but that was not the way the famous Highbury club liked to do business. Plenty of observers had expected Arsenal to

Critics accused Swansea Town of conducting an auction when they decided to sell me, as reflected by this 1958 cartoon by the brilliant Roy Ullyett.

Unleashing a shot in one of my final outings as a Swan.

use my Uncle Bryn to lure me to their ranks because he was still very close to a club which had looked after him well. But that was never the case. True, he would have liked me to follow in his footsteps because he did love and respect Arsenal, but he never applied the faintest bit of pressure, understanding that it was important that I made up my own mind on such an important issue.

The Chelsea approach proved quite tricky for me and led to considerable ill feeling and even controversy. Their manager Ted Drake, a gigantic name in the game for his playing achievements with Arsenal, came to see me at my Army barracks in St John's Wood, along with Jimmy Thompson, their chief scout with a silver tongue, and they were offering money in large amounts. Now I was just a young boy from a working-class community where people were never too flush with funds, so it's hardly surprising that they turned my head a little when they arrived at the camp, saying I could have this, I could have that. The main inducement, to be paid in one fat lump, was several thousand pounds, which might not seem too much now, but represented riches beyond measure in 1958.

Of course, it wasn't legal – vast signing-on fees were not sanctioned and certainly Spurs were not offering one – but I know this sort of thing was common in football. I had not long been married and although money wasn't everything, it was very important, as it would be to any young couple. To sum it all up, they said they would set me up very nicely indeed, and I was wavering.

When I went back to Swansea and told the club that I was considering a late change of mind and a move to Stamford Bridge, they were extremely upset with me because their deal with Spurs had been practically done, and I had also indicated my agreement. There had even been a signing ceremony arranged at White Hart Lane, but I hadn't turned up, and that inflamed an already delicate situation. I had even done a newspaper interview in which I talked about my impending switch to Spurs.

Understandably enough Ronnie Burgess wasn't best pleased and the chairman, Philip Holden, who was basically in charge of the Swans' finances, was well nigh apoplectic. I guess they needed the money from my sale very badly and I was told: "You can't pull out now. You're going to sign for Tottenham."

Having taken on board Swansea Town's point of view, I chatted to my brother Bryn, my wife Joan and other family members, who all reckoned it wasn't right for me to go back on my word.

Looking back, I'm perfectly aware that this was no way to do things, but I was in a state of youthful confusion, and this at a time when footballers' earnings were limited by the totally unjust maximum wage rule, which was still several years away from being abolished thanks largely to a brilliant campaign led by Jimmy Hill.

In the end I saw sense, went back to White Hart Lane and put my name on the dotted line. It was all rather messy and, in retrospect, I was sorry for that without ever regretting my eventual choice. The deal was for £35,000, which made me the most expensive player to move between British clubs, taking over from the England inside-forward Jackie Sewell, who had been sold to Sheffield Wednesday by Notts County in March 1951 for £34,000.

I finished up with a £20 welcome fee from Spurs, an accrued share in my benefit which came to £100, and that was it. On one level you could ask the legitimate question: why should Swansea, who had acquired my services for a £10 signing-on fee all those years ago, pocket £35,000 for me while I got next to nothing?

But when I'd thought everything through, I never wanted to get bogged down in the financial considerations. Okay, Swansea came out of it smelling of roses because they received a huge parcel of money for very limited investment, but I also came out of it fabulously because I joined a wonderful club with whom I was rapturously happy and fulfilled for more than a decade.

So I had no regrets, not a single one. These days, of course, in a similar position, with the career I had I'd be a multi-millionaire. But so what? It's only money! I had a part in Spurs' glory years with the best teammates imaginable and guided by Bill Nicholson, one of the wisest and fairest football men on the planet. That was something that no amount of money could buy.

In fact, although Bill Nick was very much part of the White Hart Lane set-up when I arrived from Swansea, he was not the manager who signed me. That was Jimmy Anderson, who had replaced the incredibly successful Arthur Rowe at the helm and had begun the difficult task of rebuilding the team following the decline of Rowe's great push-and-run creation, which had won the Second and First Division championships in successive seasons at the start of the decade.

However, it fell to Bill, as Anderson's number two, to meet me ahead of my Spurs debut, which just happened to be the north London derby against Arsenal at Highbury. I was told to be at the Gunners' ground at 1.30pm and left plenty of time to travel from St John's Wood, where I would continue to be based until my National Service ended in the May. All went well until I presented myself outside the players' entrance, where I was confronted by a steward who didn't recognise me and downright refused to be convinced that I was Tottenham's new signing. Now the minutes were ticking by and I was getting worried. Eventually, after much discussion, the fellow did condescend to send in a message, and soon Bill appeared, shook my hand and assured the dumbfounded steward that I was actually who I said I was. Then he turned to me, fixed me with his steely gaze and said: "You're late!"

What a start to my life as a Spur – first denied access to the stadium where I was due to play in little more than an hour's time, then told I was dragging

*I scribble the most important 'autograph' of my football career. Swansea boss
Ron Burgess (left) and Spurs manager Jimmy Anderson are my witnesses as
I become the costliest player in the land in February 1958.*

my feet, all before I had even kicked a ball in anger for my new employer.
Well done, Cliff, and welcome to the First Division!

I guess all that might have thrown some people, but I was a philosophical
type of lad, always ready to take life as it came, so I wasn't upset in the slightest. Still, the gravity of the occasion was emphasised by Bill when he took me
to one side, spelling out that there were plenty of big derbies in English
football – Liverpool-Everton, United-City in Manchester, Newcastle-Sunder-
land – but for him the biggest of the lot was the north London clash between
Spurs and Arsenal. He really marked my card, made me aware of the tradition attached to the game, and that was something that I relished.

I couldn't wait to join the rest of the team in the dressing room, then get
out on the pitch to do battle with our local rivals, but while I think Bill liked
my obvious enthusiasm, his face clouded over when he saw what I was

carrying. "Those boots," he grated. "You really intend to play in them? You can't be serious?" At least, that's the family-friendly version of his remarks, which actually were rather more colourful.

The truth is that I was very attached to my faithful boots which had served me so well for Swansea and Wales, and I looked on them as old friends. True, one of the studs was loose and couldn't be tightened, but they were so comfortable and I trusted them, which is worth a lot. Clearly Bill wasn't impressed, telling me that they would have to do for that day but that Spurs would be handling my footwear in future. Not for the last time in my Tottenham tenure, he was to be proved spot-on in his judgement.

Despite everything, I felt confident when I ran out at Highbury, proudly sporting the famous cockerel on my chest for the first time, but I have to admit that I didn't do myself justice in what turned out to be a nerve-tingling 4–4 thriller, and I could hardly blame Spurs fans if they were wondering exactly what they had got for their money.

I had been drafted in on the left wing to replace the much older George Robb and I quite fancied linking up with the inside-left, the skilful Johnny Brooks. Though both teams were in mid-table, we were five points better off than an Arsenal side which was also going through a period of transition, so our hopes seemed a lot brighter than the dismally misty afternoon. Alas, an early own goal by Ron Henry got us off on the wrong foot, and with about a quarter of an hour left to play we were 4–2 behind. Then, with flakes of snow beginning to swirl around our heads, I had my chance to make a meaningful impact.

I broke away down the left touchline, flicked the ball inside my marker, the full-back Stan Charlton, and then sprinted towards the penalty area, where I was confronted by the lanky Scottish centre-half Jim Fotheringham. Using one of my favourite tricks, I feinted to pass, then started to swerve past him and as I reached the edge of the box I had a clear sight of my Welsh teammate, Jack Kelsey, on his toes between Arsenal's posts. Now I could smell a goal, but as I drew back my right foot to shoot I slipped on the greasy turf and tumbled headlong in the Highbury mud. In that split-second it flashed across my mind that a golden chance had been wasted and that I was to blame for wearing dodgy boots.

I'm concentrating fiercely as I attempt to outwit Arsenal defender Jim Fotheringham during my Tottenham debut, a 4–4 draw with the Gunners at Highbury in February 1958.

Fortunately Tottenham surged back to claim a point through a Tommy Harmer penalty and a Bobby Smith strike only three minutes from time, but as I trudged off the pitch I was all too uncomfortably conscious of the fact that our dreadnought centre-forward's late effort would have been a winner rather than an equaliser if I had been able to convert my own opportunity.

Afterwards Bill Nick was quick to emphasise the point: "That was an excellent chance that you created for yourself, Cliff. You'd have had your first goal but for those bloody boots." Not that I want to make excuses.

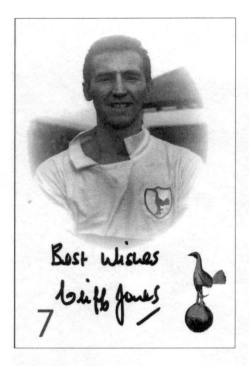

Best wishes
Cliff Jones
7

The shirt might be a tad baggy, but I was so proud to pull it on. For me, the Spurs cockerel has always been an emblem of all that is fine in our national game.

I wasn't at my best, simple as that. Even so, if I had been that bit more professional Spurs might have won, so that was a valuable lesson for me and a perfect example of how shrewd an operator Bill Nick was. He had pointed out the problem before kick-off and he had been proved right. It made me realise that attention to the tiniest details is vitally important and that nothing that is within your power should be left to chance.

But even though I had not sparkled on debut, my performance couldn't have been disastrous, as *Sunday Times* reporter John Sellers told his readers: 'How can any man show in one game that he is worth a transfer fee of £35,000? Cliff Jones, making his entry into the strife of the First Division on Spurs' left wing at Highbury yesterday, saw too little of the ball to offer any kind of answer. But his quality was obvious. He did not use all of his few opportunities quite as well as he can, nor did he move the ball as finely as he clearly will learn to do. But his value to Spurs' forward line should be immense.'

In the circumstances that was kind of Mr Sellers, but I'm afraid my rather faltering start did not end there. Though Spurs ended the season strongly, losing only one of their last 14 games and finishing third in the title race behind champions Wolves and runners-up Preston North End, I was a shadow of my real self. There was no shortage of pundits who reckoned I was overawed by colossal expectations through becoming the most expensive footballer in the land, but I never bought that theory. I think I've always been essentially level-headed, and I never worried about the size of my fee, almost feeling it was irrelevant to me, basically just a piece of business between the two clubs which took place above my consciousness.

I couldn't put my lacklustre form down to fitness difficulties, either. I was just completing my National Service, having played an enormous amount of sport of all descriptions in the Army as well as turning out regularly for Swansea, and was in physically excellent shape.

No, with the wisdom of hindsight I would ascribe my problems to being mentally stale. After all, there had been an awful lot going on in my life and I reckon the non-stop activity got a bit too much. There had been the strain of what became a complicated transfer, the step up from Second Division to First, the move from my homely community in South Wales to the Big Smoke, which was a gigantic adventure in itself; then there were my burgeoning family responsibilities and my ongoing duties with the Royal Artillery, not to mention an unexpected involvement in World Cup qualifiers with my country. Put all that lot together and I think it becomes obvious why I was a little bit jaded in the spring of 1958.

In those trying weeks towards the end of the season I played ten times and managed only one goal, though that was a satisfying one, a bullet header from a pinpoint Harmer cross in a 3–1 victory over Leicester City at Filbert Street. I slipped past a defender on his blind side and met the ball perfectly. Bill Nick was highly complimentary afterwards, which made me feel ten feet tall. At last I had shown a flash of the performer Spurs had expected me to be when they shelled out that fortune. I was getting on marvellously with my teammates, too, and felt it was only a matter of time before I came good. Before then, though, there was the little matter of the World Cup to contend with, followed by a setback which was agonisingly painful and frustrating when it happened, but in the long run might actually have been a blessing in disguise.

CHAPTER SIX

The Red Dragon roars

For Wales, earning an eleventh-hour place in the 1958 World Cup finals in Sweden was a windfall from the football heavens. During the qualification competition we had faced formidably tough opposition in Czechoslovakia and East Germany and, although we'd had our moments, we just came up short, finishing second behind the Czechs and therefore, apparently, being eliminated.

Undreamed-of salvation was at hand, but first let me set the scene by introducing some of my core international teammates and recalling our tense encounters with those daunting Eastern Europeans.

We had several world-class performers in our ranks, but in the spring of 1958 the man everybody wanted to know about was John Charles, our amiable colossus who, I can state without fear of contradiction, was one of the finest all-round footballers there has ever been. You can trot out all the exalted names you want – Di Stefano, Puskas, Pele, Eusebio, Matthews, Finney, Edwards, Charlton, Best, Maradona, Cruyff or, in the modern era, Messi and Ronaldo – and I would contend that our boyo from the Welsh Valleys was fit to stand comparison with any of them.

People always ask me what was his best position, centre-half or centre-forward, and I reply that I wouldn't like to be specific about that – but then I add that he was the best centre-half I've seen, and also the best centre-forward. John was truly remarkable, a master of virtually every aspect of the game, his spectacularly muscular physique and commanding, charismatic presence matched by a lightness of foot and delicacy of touch which seemed at odds with that gigantic frame.

Swansea had him on their groundstaff when he was a kid, but somehow let him slip away to Leeds United, for whom he proved a brilliant success, first in defence and then as the spearhead of the Yorkshiremen's attack. In one Second Division season he scored 42 goals, then after starring as they earned promotion, he hit another 38 in what proved to be his only campaign in the English top flight – a fantastic feat in any era.

That prompted the mighty Italian club, Juventus, to break the world transfer record, paying £65,000 to take him to Turin in April 1957, which was a bold and courageous move for John to take given that few British footballers to that point had managed to flourish overseas. Of course, the big fella took it all in his stride, plundering 28 goals as Juve won the league title, being voted footballer of the year into the bargain.

More than that, he enchanted everybody, fans and players alike, with his lovely nature. Given his height and power, if he had been a ruthless individual, he would have been an absolute monster, but he was an easy-going charmer on the field and off it, so much so that they christened him *'Il Buon Gigante'* ('The Gentle Giant') and the Italians took him to their hearts.

It was against this background of untrammelled admiration and achievement that John strode into the World Cup qualifiers. Our mate, who was as engagingly unassuming and self-deprecating as ever despite his incredible success, had truly become one of the first global superstars.

Not that we were a one-man team, or anything like it. Also up there with the best on the planet was the man between our goalposts, the Arsenal keeper Jack Kelsey. He was immensely strong, phenomenally agile, unbelievably brave and he had a brilliant pair of hands, which were very large and to which everything seemed to stick. In fact, the Brazilians called him The Cat With Magnetic Paws, and that summed him up pretty well. That said, Jack was no show pony, never jumping about all over the place if it wasn't necessary. Instead he tended to make his job look deceptively easy most of the time by his canny positioning, a fundamental but all-too-rare knack based on intelligent reading of the action.

The only flaw in the Kelsey footballing make-up was his kicking. You really didn't want to see the ball at Jack's feet because so often he would scuff it hopelessly, which used to annoy him intensely as he fancied himself as an outfield player. When we played five-a-sides he always volunteered to be a centre-forward, and nobody wanted him on their team because he couldn't hit a barn door from five yards. Had he been playing in the modern era, in which there is a far greater emphasis on a keeper's work with his feet, then he would have had to improve dramatically in that respect, but I'm sure he would have done so because he was such an avid competitor

The other memorable characteristic about Jack was his love of practical jokes. He once wound Mel Charles up to fever pitch, which was no mean feat given what a laid-back individual Mel has always been. Jack caught him out with a hoax telegram which carried the offer of a £3,000 boot sponsorship, which would have been a staggering bit of business back in the 1950s. Mel hit the roof when he found out that Jack had made it all up while the rest of us had a huge laugh, though most of us had been caught out by the wicked prankster at one time or another.

My turn involved being duped into ranting and raving at Henry Rose, the northern reporter for the *Daily Express* and a completely trustworthy guy, for supposedly breaking a confidence. After I had chatted at length to Henry, giving him background information about a PFA issue, Jack grabbed me and said he had heard Henry passing on the news to his sportsdesk. "You can catch him now," said my tormentor. "He's just round the corner in a phone booth, spilling the beans." I felt betrayed and was so furious that I stomped up to Henry, grabbed the phone from his hand and starting shouting into the mouthpiece, demanding to know who I was addressing and saying they had no right to the story. Imagine my embarrassment, then, when it transpired that poor Henry had been innocently engaged in a private conversation, nothing to do with work, leaving me looking like a right Charlie. Jack had struck again, but really it served me right because I should have known that the *Express* man would never have double-crossed me. Happily, he saw the funny side of it but, of course, nobody was guffawing louder than the infuriating Mr Kelsey. Not that I really minded, it was all part of the excellent team spirit that had built up under the management of Jimmy Murphy, and we all benefited from that.

Also with a key part to play in the camaraderie was the skipper Dave Bowen, another Arsenal man and another exceptionally passionate motivator from his position of left-half. I've heard it said that when Dave was at full

Wales boss Jimmy Murphy (centre), one of the most passionate football men ever to walk the earth, holds forth in typically eloquent fashion to skipper Dave Bowen (left) and myself during an international training session.

throttle he could make as much noise as a dozen fans, but there was far more to him than mere commitment to the cause. He was also a perceptive passer, and I enjoyed playing directly in front of him as he had a knack of sliding the ball inside my full-back for me to run on to, a ploy which could often break down an opposition defence.

The raiding Allchurch brothers, winger Terry Medwin and defender Dai Thomas I've already highlighted when discussing my Swansea days, then there were also such reliable full-backs as Stuart Williams, Ron Stitfall, Trevor Edwards and the outstanding Tottenham man Mel Hopkins. Reserve goalkeeper Graham Vearncombe never let anyone down, nor did doughty wing-halves Derrick Sullivan, Colin Baker, Alan Harrington and Bill Harris, while rounding off the squad were forwards Derek Tapscott, Colin Webster, Roy Vernon, Ron Hewitt and Des Palmer.

They weren't all world-class, naturally, but they all shared a burning desire to serve Wales, to wear the red shirt with all-consuming pride, a typical example being Tappy, who was a Highbury colleague of Kelsey and Bowen at the time. Having sprung to notice through his strenuous efforts for non-League Barry Town, he was picked up by the Gunners and went a very long way on sheer enthusiasm and energy, basically barging his way around and scoring plenty of goals along the way. He had rivals with more sheer quality – Vernon, for example, who could penetrate a defence with rare stealth, like a stiletto slicing through a feather pillow – but he was never outstripped for desire.

Thus it was with such a diverse collection of individuals that Jimmy Murphy, our voluble, irrepressibly excitable but matchlessly knowledgeable mentor, himself newly appointed to his task, led us into our first qualifier on May Day 1957, against Czechoslovakia at Ninian Park.

I'm happy to report that I gave arguably the best performance of my international career, one in which nearly everything came off. I say 'nearly' because the margin of our victory was only 1–0, courtesy of a goal by Roy Vernon. I had the chances to stick away several more but somehow they eluded me.

My principal marker that day was Jan Hertl, who was big and skilful but decidedly ponderous on the turn, so I was able to repeatedly push the ball past him, then dart away before he could recover. Their most imposing players were the majestic wing-half Josef Masopust and the defender Ladislav

Novak, their skipper, but our half-back line of Mel and John Charles and Dave Bowen was in particularly dominant mode, and we thoroughly deserved our win. Even so, we had to work hard for it, with Roy's goal not coming until the 71st minute.

It was always a pleasure to see Mel and John operating so closely together on the pitch in such glorious harmony. They melded effortlessly, almost seeming to read each other's minds, which I suppose is not surprising since they had been playing football together since they had been in short trousers. What a phenomenal experience it must have been for brothers to perform together on the international stage, having come all the way from makeshift pitches on the streets of Swansea to the grandest stadiums in the world.

Beating the Czechs, and playing so well in the process, should really have set us up for the rest of the group matches, but the wheels threatened to come off our bandwagon as we lost twice in Eastern Europe, 2–1 to East Germany in Leipzig and 2–0 to Czechoslovakia in Prague. That was the trip on which Ray Daniels upset the selectors and thus ended his Welsh career.

Now we were left with one more game but little hope of making the cut as the Czechs were expected to beat East Germany and top the group, which they eventually did. But that didn't stop Jimmy from demonstrating his passion as an arch-motivator before our second meeting with the Germans in Cardiff that autumn. He strode purposefully into the dressing room, and his team talk was both sharp and to the point: "Lads, you know these bastards you are playing today. Don't forget they bombed your mothers and your fathers." With that he turned on his heel and walked out, knowing precisely the profound impact he had achieved, given that the war had ended only a dozen years earlier. Duly we beat East Germany 4–1 – the Swansea striker Des Palmer got a hat-trick, I chipped in with one goal, only my second for my country, and Mel Charles put in a titanic display at centre-half – but it was only enough to finish second behind Masopust and company in our league table of three.

With only group-toppers going through to the finals in Sweden, it seemed certain that we were out, and we resigned ourselves to having another bash at reaching the finals in Chile in 1962, but that was when a gift fell from the skies and landed right in our lap. For political reasons in the Middle East, Indonesia and Turkey had withdrawn from the Asia-Africa qualifiers to avoid

This is the side that beat Israel 2–0 at Cardiff in February 1958, thus qualifying Wales for that summer's World Cup finals in Sweden. Back row, left to right: Alan Harrington, Stuart Williams, John Charles, Jack Kelsey, Mel Hopkins, Ivor Allchurch, Mel Charles. Front: Terry Medwin, Ron Hewitt, Dave Bowen and me.

encountering Israel, so it seemed that Israel would be handed a walkover. But FIFA decided it would be deeply unsporting for any country to progress without playing a single match, so they decreed there would have to be a play-off. Thus they put the names of all the group runners-up into a hat to decide who would face the Israelis on a home-and-away basis, and our luck was in. Out of the blue we had been reprieved, and had a second shot at joining England, Scotland and Northern Ireland in Sweden.

We didn't know an awful lot about our opponents, only that they consisted mainly of amateurs, so we were confident without being complacent. That feeling grew as Juventus rather grudgingly agreed to release John Charles for the play-offs. He had become their star player and they had invested a great deal of money in him, but it wouldn't have been right to prevent him from representing his country in such crucially important games.

We travelled to Israel for the first leg in January 1958, leaving behind a typical perishing British winter, and to land in the stifling heat of Tel Aviv felt bizarre in the extreme. We were surprised by the levels of poverty we witnessed among folk living near the airport, and also by the state of the ground, the Ramat Gan Stadium, which appeared to be roughly half-built.

Our prospects were improved by the return of the influential Ivor Allchurch, who had suffered a succession of niggling injuries, and sure enough he played superbly and scored, as did Dave Bowen, in a comfortable 2–0 victory. We prevailed by the same scoreline in the Ninian Park return, with Ivor on target again. I also managed to find the net, which was probably just as well as this was at the height of my transfer kerfuffle and I was very much in the shop window. In fact, because so many managers and scouts turned up to watch me that evening, the contest was labelled by critics of Swansea's methods as 'The Auction.' As for the game itself, it was marred near the end by an accident to the Israelis' brilliant goalkeeper Yaakov Chodorov, whose heroics had prevented a rout. He was stretchered off to a standing ovation after an accidental collision with John Charles and spent the night in hospital as we celebrated our qualification for the World Cup finals with a few beers in a Cardiff hotel.

On the day after our triumph, however, the happy grins were wiped from our faces by news of Manchester United's calamitous aircrash at Munich on the way back from a European Cup tie in Belgrade. A total of 23 people perished in the disaster, and we all knew the eight footballers who died, including the incomparable Duncan Edwards, who I had grown to like and admire when we were in the Army together, and who lived for 13 days before succumbing to his horrendous injuries.

Of course, the disaster had the most devastating impact on poor Jimmy Murphy, to whom the victims had been like sons. He had watched them grow up, nurtured their development, shouted at them, laughed with them and, above all, loved them. But for taking charge of Wales' qualifiers, Jimmy would have been on that plane, so for him it had been a miraculous escape, but it must have been incredibly difficult for him to think positively at the time. He had to, though, because with United manager Matt Busby at death's door in a German hospital, Jimmy had to keep the Red Devils' flag flying. It was a huge ask but he met the challenge inspirationally, as his patchwork

Duelling with Tottenham clubmate Johnny Brooks at Wembley in November 1956. Johnny had the upper hand that day, scoring in his side's 3–1 victory as Wales continued to build a team for their 1958 World Cup campaign.

team consisting largely of untried youngsters embarked on an emotional rollercoaster ride which took them all the way to the FA Cup final. At Wembley they lost to Nat Lofthouse's Bolton Wanderers, but Jimmy had performed a sporting miracle in getting them there. No wonder that team, which included another of my National Service pals, Bobby Charlton, will always be remembered as Murphy's Marvels.

Of course, Jimmy bore the mental scars of Munich for the rest of his life, but he was more than up for the fight when we headed for Sweden to take our place in the biggest tournament on the planet.

These days when a country qualifies for the World Cup finals, there is blanket coverage in all branches of the media, with every tiny detail of their progress being scrutinised minutely, but it wasn't quite like that in the summer of 1958. In all honesty, our preparation to face our immediate opponents, Hungary and Mexico followed by the host nation, was negligible in the extreme, which is hardly surprising given Jimmy's mammoth workload with United throughout a troubled spring. In the circumstances it might have been expected that the Welsh Football Association would take charge of the practical arrangements, but that was far from the case. We were given next to no information about the teams we would meet, and there weren't even any training facilities lined up for us in London where we gathered before flying off on our adventure. So hand-to-mouth was the situation that, instead of working out at one of the local stadiums, we trained in Hyde Park, in an area where no ball games were allowed! It became so ridiculous that after throwing down tracksuits and jumpers for goalposts, then starting a practice game, we were accosted by a furious park-keeper who ejected us unceremoniously. Can any World Cup final-ists ever have got their campaign off to a crazier start? I don't think so.

Happily, we were an easy-going bunch and just got on with our jobs. I must stress, too, that although there wasn't the intense public interest in the com-petition that there is in modern times, we were fiercely committed to giving a good account of ourselves – it could hardly be otherwise with a fellow like Jimmy guiding our fortunes. He was very much a hands-on boss, used to dealing directly with the players at Manchester United, where Matt Busby was happy to let him get on with it, and with us he was no less involved.

Jimmy was a compulsive talker and he had to have someone to listen to him. Jack Jones was our trainer and poor old Jack was subjected to some marathon sessions. Especially when Jimmy had had a drink – and he did like a drink – he was happy to talk football into the early hours of the morning, pretty well every morning! Jack had to be there to give him a sounding board, and every time he went home after a Wales trip, he was absolutely shattered. He was a lovely, friendly bloke who worked for Wrexham, got on excellently with the players from both club and country and did his job very well, but sometimes he did have to dig deep to find the stamina to keep up with Jimmy.

Not that I would ever hear a word of criticism about Jim. He knew everything there was to know about football and was an expert at commu-nicating all that knowledge. He had been one of General Montgomery's Desert Rats in the Second World War and his creed was simple – fix bayo-nets, up and at 'em, over the top – but he was very shrewd as well. Matt Busby would never have employed a man who was less than that. Marching on together, shoulder to shoulder, they were the perfect combination, though the 'good cop, bad cop' image which is often purveyed was mis-leading. Jimmy was tough all right, but beneath that benign, avuncular exterior, so was Matt. You don't achieve what he did in the face of such overwhelming adversity without being one extremely steely character.

The size of the task facing Jimmy and the rest of us in Sweden was immense, but we were not overawed, rather we felt privileged to be the first to represent our country in the world's biggest football festival. Once again there was doubt over the presence of John Charles because Juventus were so protective of him but eventually he did join us, albeit a few days late, at our base in the pretty little town of Saltsjobaden, situated among a cluster of picturesque lakes just outside the capital, Stockholm. The locals took us to their hearts, making us so welcome that we became their team. Crowds of people turned up just to watch us train and we had practice matches against local sides. I remember we won one game about 25–0, which makes it sound daft, but while it was all very pleasant and sociable, Jimmy made sure that we got on with the real business in a rigorously professional manner.

All along we knew we were out-and-out underdogs who had embarked on a huge adventure, but that was not a bad way to travel into the unknown and we were determined not to be whipping boys as we went into our first group game against Hungary in Sandviken. We knew that they were not the equals of the legendary Magnificent Magyars, the great side which had humbled England twice in 1953 and 1954, hammering Billy Wright's men 6–3 at Wembley and 7–1 in Budapest and furnishing clear evidence for all with eyes to see that the old-fashioned British approach to the game was outmoded. But they were still a very fine side, which included fabulous players such as their swashbuckling goalkeeper Gyula Grosics, the magisterial wing-half and captain Jozsef Bozsik, and the subtly creative, deep-lying centre-forward Nandor Hidegkuti, who had all made outstanding contributions to England's evisceration.

When Bozsik combined smoothly with the 36-year-old Hidegkuti to put his team in front after only five minutes, most neutrals expected an avalanche of Hungarian goals to follow, but they reckoned without the fighting spirit of the Welsh Dragon. John Charles, operating as our attacking spearhead, had been a marked man from the opening whistle but after 27 minutes he escaped his gaoler to meet my corner-kick with a typical towering header and we were level. Suddenly there was all to play for, and we looked as likely to win as did Hungary, but both defences held out for a draw which we would certainly have taken before kick-off.

Next up we were in Stockholm to face Mexico, who since being seen off 3–0 by Sweden were regarded as eminently beatable. Certainly Jimmy was dismissive, telling us that they were "only good for riding horses", which did not actually indicate a lack of respect. He was trying to build up our confidence and, with film and TV Westerns so popular in those days, was merely using current culture to illustrate his point.

In the event Ivor Allchurch gave us the lead after half an hour with a perfectly judged volley from a Terry Medwin set-up, and we expected to kick on from there. But the Mexicans refused to roll over, dominated much of the

A 1958 World Cup postcard autographed by Juste Fontaine, the lethal French marksman who scored 13 goals in the tournament, setting a record that seems unlikely ever to be beaten. It's one of my most treasured mementoes from our expedition to Stockholm.

second half, and grabbed what was a frankly deserved equaliser when their right winger, Belmonte, nodded past Jack Kelsey in the last minute.

That was a sickener for us, and I felt particularly bad because I had not thrown off the indifferent form which had weighed me down during my first couple of months with Spurs. On a more positive note, we were still undefeated and I felt I couldn't play any worse – but I was wrong.

In our third game, again in Stockholm, we took on a confident Sweden side with two wins already under their belt and, in truth, we were extremely poor. Somehow we got away with a goalless draw because the hosts, who had rested some of their top players, missed several inviting chances to score, and Jack Kelsey was in superb nick, making a string of exceptional saves. As for me, I spent most of the match in the pocket of a pacy, powerful full-back named Orvar Bergmark, one of the most efficient opponents I ever faced.

Jimmy had told us beforehand that a draw would be enough to earn us a play-off against Hungary, and he planned accordingly, employing safety-first tactics which, while not popular with folk who paid to watch the proceedings, paid off. We drew 0–0, took a thick-skinned attitude to the press criticism which came our way and looked forward to our decisive knock-out encounter with the Magyars, our third successive game in Stockholm.

Probably because of our dull showing against Sweden, only 2,832 people turned up to watch this showdown, and I can understand why so many stayed away, but those who did make the effort witnessed one the top achievements in Welsh football history. Sadly, and rather bafflingly for a team packed with talent, Hungary opted to make it a physical contest, targeting our best player, Big John, with outrageous cynicism.

With so few people inside the stadium the atmosphere seemed almost surreal, especially when the Russian referee refused to give us penalties when John was twice blatantly hacked down in the box. They kicked him from pillar to post but, typically of the Gentle Giant, he wouldn't retaliate despite being the most powerful individual on the pitch. That seemed to anger his tormentors even more and they redoubled their assaults on him, with the officials criminally turning a blind eye.

Our situation took a turn for the worse after 33 minutes when their star front-runner, Lajos Tichy, scored a tremendous goal and, under continued provocation, many a side would have lost their discipline. But Wales, with

Wales' talisman, the mighty John Charles, in full-blooded action against Hungary in the World Cup finals. Sadly, although we beat the muscular Magyars in a play-off for a place in the last eight, they kicked Big John so mercilessly that he missed the quarter-final showdown with Brazil.

Dave Bowen playing like a titan and urging us on, refused to buckle and we drew level ten minutes into the second period when Ivor Allchurch netted with a sensational looping volley from all of 30 yards. Very few players would have had the technique to pull off such a strike, especially against such a brilliant keeper as Grosics, and I'd have said it was the goal of the tournament, but for Pele's sublime effort for Brazil in the final against the Swedes.

Shortly after that Mel Charles dispatched a long, raking ball from his own half, and I judged correctly that it was going to bypass the Hungarian right-back, Matrai, so I darted past him, took the ball on my chest and had the goal at my mercy. Glory beckoned but somehow, in the heat of the action, I got it wrong, driving the ball well wide of the far post with my right foot.

At that moment I wished the ground would open and swallow me up, but with only a quarter of an hour left, my mistake was rendered irrelevant by a cheeky piece of opportunism from my old Sandfields mate Terry Medwin, who took advantage of a slack touch by Grosics to snatch what proved to be the winner.

Now the frustrated Hungarians grew even more disgracefully violent. Their technically superb but, on this occasion, totally reprehensible defender Ferenc Sipos was dismissed for kicking down poor Ron Hewitt, while John Charles continued to take so much stick that he was carried off and forced to miss the quarter-final against Brazil.

Jimmy Murphy was so proud of every one of us and, wearing his heart on his sleeve as ever, he kissed every man as he came back to the dressing room. All he had asked us was that we match Hungary for effort, and that we did. If you gave your all for Jimmy then he was happy, no matter what the outcome. What he wouldn't tolerate at any price was a shirker, and there were none of those in our ranks. To some people Jim might have come across as a yapping yard-dog, a real sergeant-major who demanded the kick-bollock-and-bite approach, but that was a ludicrously superficial judgement which didn't even begin to scratch the surface of the man.

There was a deep intelligence about him, too. He understood the game in all its complexities and did not harbour unrealistic expectations. He knew perfectly well that although he had several world-class players in his team, not everybody was at that level, and he was ecstatic that Ivor and one or two others had supplied that extra bit of quality which took us through to the last eight.

CHAPTER SEVEN

"Had a good holiday, Mel?"

Before we turned our minds to the little matter of a World Cup quarter-final against the impressively emerging Brazil, who had beaten Austria and the Soviet Union and come through a goalless draw with England, it was deemed acceptable – at least it was back in the 1950s – to let our hair down at a nightclub a couple of days before the game in Gothenburg.

Nothing excessive or in the slightest bit unseemly was planned for our evening at The Copacabana. We merely intended to relax after four hard matches and celebrate our progress to date in a restrained fashion. Alas, it didn't quite turn out like that.

While most of the lads were sensible enough to limit themselves to a couple of pints, one member of our team, whom I won't name, went a little bit further. He was a decent fellow at heart – fundamentally there was no harm in him – but he was inclined to get a bit lively, shall we say, and become rather a rascal when he'd had too much to drink.

As the evening developed everybody was pleasantly merry, but it was evident that this chap was in danger of getting carried away when he climbed up on stage, grabbed the microphone from the singer and treated us to a few of his favourite tunes.

So far it was merely slightly embarrassing, but suddenly things threatened to turn ugly when a waiter started to serve the people on John Charles' table ahead of those on our crooning teammate's. That wasn't to his liking, and when it became obvious that John was going to be prioritised as the

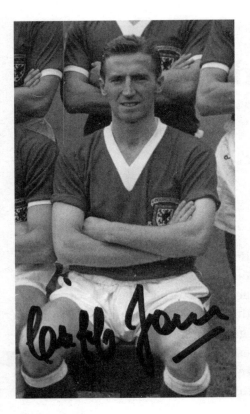

With the Welsh dragon on my chest and the adrenaline pumping, I'm impatient for the kick-off.

most famous individual in the party, suddenly our inebriated friend punched the waiter – hard.

The poor man went down, glasses went flying all over the shop, along with a couple of the unfortunate waiter's teeth, and in the blink of an eye an enjoyable, good-natured gathering had been transformed into a disturbing incident.

John was absolutely livid. Though usually he was slow to anger, this time he grabbed the individual concerned by the scruff of his neck, as if he was some badly behaved puppy, and hurled him bodily out of the door. Needless to say the celebration broke up in disarray and it was left to the players to make a cash collection the next day to pay for urgently needed dental surgery. The Copacabana management could easily have raised a stink, called the police and made a fuss in the newspapers, but I think they were impressed with John's prompt action and the sincere apologies forthcoming from pretty well all of us in the Welsh group.

If such a thing happened today it would be plastered all over the media, probably it would have been filmed on someone's phone, then circulated on the internet, and the proud name of Wales would have been thoroughly sullied. But those were different days – so different that the football reporters who had been drinking with us agreed to hush it up in the interests of our World Cup bid and of not souring relations with the men they wrote about. Can you imagine that happening today? Neither can I!

It's a massive tribute to the management skills of Jimmy Murphy that he didn't allow the Copacabana fracas to put us off our stride ahead of the game with Brazil. He just had a quiet word with the offending player – I'm sure it must have been a firm one, too – and got on with preparation for the biggest game of all our international careers.

Colin Webster, a rumbustious customer who could play anywhere across the forward line but essentially one of our fringe players, was going to be needed against the South Americans because John Charles, our top man and the team's touchstone, was not going to recover in time from the brutal treatment he had received from the Hungarians. John was a phenomenally strong man and normally was able to soak up the physical punishment handed out to him routinely by defenders who just couldn't cope with him in any other way. But now he could hardly walk and there was never any question of him making the game. It was a fearful blow to our hopes, but we just had to get on with it. At least we were better off than Scotland, who had failed to progress beyond their group, and England, who had lost a play-off to the Soviets, leaving gallant Northern Ireland to accompany us into the business end of the tournament.

By now Brazil were the hot tip to lift the Jules Rimet Trophy, and no wonder. They boasted a brilliant goalkeeper in Santos Gilmar; outstanding full-backs in the two Niltons, Santos and De Sordi; a formidable half-back line of Zito, Bellini and Orlando; and fine forwards such as Altafini and Zagalo. That lot would have been enough to give any side a good game, but then we came to the three jewels in the Brazilian crown. Pulling the strings from midfield was Didi, one of the cleverest playmakers of all time, while on the right flank was Garrincha, 'The Little Bird', who made light of deformities to his spine and both legs to establish a reputation as arguably the most bewildering dribbler and dead-ball expert in football. Finally, of course, there was the boy wonder Pele, collecting his seventh cap against us at the age of 17 and destined to become the best footballer the world has ever seen.

That was quite a line-up, but while ours was hardly in the same stellar category, it was not too shabby either, consisting of Jack Kelsey in goal, Stuart Williams and Mel Hopkins on the defensive flanks, a middle trio of Derrick Sullivan, Mel Charles and Dave Bowen, with Terry Medwin, Ron Hewitt, Colin Webster, Ivor Allchurch and myself forming the front line.

For all Brazil's attacking riches, Jimmy had organised us soundly at the back, believing that we had the knowhow, power and skill to resist our illustrious opponents for long periods, and we knew we were always capable of hitting anybody on the break.

In fact, we made a bright start and I managed to set up a presentable chance for Colin in the first minute, but he shot into the side netting. Soon afterwards both Ivor and I went close with efforts on Gilmar's goal and Brazil knew they were in a game. Of course, they had the majority of possession and territorial advantage, but we knew we could bother them with our pace and penetration. On more than one occasion each, Terry and I skinned our markers in wide positions and delivered crosses which parted Colin's hair, but he didn't quite have the stature and timing to convert them.

I don't want to be critical of Colin, because he was a good player in his own right and tried his socks off, but there was only one John Charles and he was irreplaceable. His head used to stand out like a beacon in the opposition's box and we knew that if we fired the ball over in the air, he would always have a tremendous chance of scoring. Given the way the game developed, with the scoreline remaining blank until 20 minutes from time, I'm convinced that we could have won with John in the team.

Brazil threw everything at us but with Jack seemingly impregnable in front of our net, Mel Charles a colossus at centre-half and the dreadnought Dave Bowen doing so much to neutralise the wondrous wiles of Didi, they must have wondered if they were ever going to break through. For more than an hour, even the remarkable Garrincha was stymied, thanks to the close attentions of the oft-underrated Spurs full-back Mel Hopkins. 'The Little Bird' liked to fly down the touchline and that suited Mel, who would let him start to run, then sweep out a long left leg to nick the ball away. He would time his challenges perfectly, often taking the ball and the player at the same moment. The Hopkins method was completely fair, but not much fun to play against – I know I wouldn't have wanted to swap places with Garrincha that day.

However, the Brazilian wing maestro was a true thoroughbred and after 70 minutes he finally found some space to induce mayhem in our defence. The ball was dinked into the box, Pele took it on his chest and swivelled past Mel Charles with a piece of characteristic magic before shanking his shot into the corner of the net from about eight yards. Let's be fair, the youngster had shown fabulous quality to squirm himself into a scoring position, but then his miskick took a slight deflection off Stuart Williams, thus wrong-footing the helpless Kelsey and creeping over the line. It would have been an agonising goal to concede at any time, but so near the end of a World Cup quarter-final it was an absolute killer. Stuart and Mel were blameless, but I felt so sorry for them as they had performed superbly in keeping the Brazilians at bay until that point.

In those days extravagant goal celebrations were not common, but the jubilant Pele was so overjoyed, and perhaps relieved that the underdogs' grip had finally been loosened, that he slid into the net on his knees and kissed the ball before he was engulfed by celebrating teammates.

After that we tried our best to push for an equaliser but we never really came close. Afterwards, despite the natural flatness which follows any defeat, there was a general feeling of pride that we had done so well, coupled with regret that Big John had missed out on the most important game of all. Mind, he had not moped, rather he roared us on from the touchline, and he reminded us at half-time that he would be fit for the semi-final! As for Jimmy, he knew the team had pushed itself to its limit and there was no need for regrets or recriminations. We had started the tournament as no-hopers who had been lucky to be still in the World Cup and we finished it by bowing out only narrowly to the side about to be recognised as one of the finest there had ever been.

The scale of our achievement was emphasised by what happened in the remainder of the competition.

Rising to the biggest occasion of my career to date. Helped (marginally, honest!) by a hand on the Brazilian's head, I beat my marker Bellini to the ball during our World Cup quarter-final clash in Gothenburg.

Undone by a teenage genius and a touch of ill fortune. Brazilian wonderkid Pele squeezes a mishit shot past his close marker Mel Charles and full-back Stuart Williams to knock Wales out of the World Cup.

After scraping past us, Brazil went on to thrash the highly fancied French – Raymond Kopa, goal machine Juste Fontaine *et al* – 5–2 in the semi-final with the *wunderkind* Pele notching a hat-trick. Then they rattled another five past Sweden in the final, with the young man delivering a goal for the ages and generally captivating everybody with his comprehensive range of skills.

What made him so special? The lad was an all-round genius and I've never seen anybody to equal him. Just watching him move and control the ball made me realise I was in the presence of something extraordinary. He could go past players at will, he was brilliant with both feet, he could shoot like a cannon or stroke the ball goalwards with the most delicate of caresses, he was unstoppable in the air, he had all the strength in the world... the list of his attributes is endless. Certainly I view it as a privilege to have shared a pitch with such a fantastic footballer.

Also it meant a lot to me to witness the start of such a glittering career. It was the same when I first laid eyes on the young Ryan Giggs when I was working at a school in Islington, north London. He had come to town with Salford Boys for the quarter-final of the English Schools Trophy and I had been told to expect something exceptional. The lad didn't disappoint, picking up the ball and zooming past a whole posse of defenders as if they were fenceposts. Sir Alex Ferguson later compared him to a frisky spaniel chasing a piece of silver paper in the wind, and that told the whole story. But although Ryan was soon to embark on a phenomenal two decades at the pinnacle of the game with Manchester United, and I was overjoyed to note that he was Welsh, not even he could hold a candle to Pele, who was nothing less than a force of nature.

After our elimination we didn't hang around in Sweden for the rest of the tournament, but made a hasty return to Wales, where it's safe to say we didn't receive the kind of euphoric greeting that we would if we reached the latter stages of the World Cup in the twenty-first century.

On the day after we lost to Brazil, the back-page lead story in the *South Wales Evening Post* was a progress report on the second day's play between Glamorgan and Essex in a county championship cricket match at Llanelli, which told us all we needed to know about where we stood in the national sporting consciousness of the time.

If any further confirmation of our status was required, when Ivor Allchurch, Terry Medwin, Mel Charles and myself got back to Swansea, a ticket collector of his acquaintance walked over to Mel and asked: "Where have you been, Mel? Away on your holidays again? Hope you had a good one."

At first we thought he was just having a giggle, but quickly it became obvious that he didn't have the faintest clue that we had been making a fairly decent fist of battling for the top prize in world football. Mel was outraged and replied: "What are you talking about, you silly sod? We've been at the bloody World Cup." But really it didn't matter. We knew what we had done, and that was enough.

CHAPTER EIGHT

A sickening crack

When I returned to White Hart Lane in the wake of the World Cup, it felt rather like I was starting my career all over again. In Sweden I had played my part in Wales' success without ever quite managing to hit my best form, certainly not in every match. In truth, I knew I hadn't performed anywhere near my full potential, and that was on top of a series of distinctly lacklustre displays towards the end of the previous season as I strove to settle into the Tottenham team following my expensive transfer from Swansea. Now I was determined to buckle down in training and do my utmost to show everyone at my new club – the manager and coaches, the other players and, not least, the all-important fans – exactly what I could do.

There were huge grounds for optimism, too, because I felt I was finally coming to terms with what was needed to compete at the right end of the First Division, I had completed my National Service and so had no Army commitments to fulfil either on or off the pitch, and I felt I was fitting in well with my new teammates in north London. But just when I thought everything was about to come together in perfect harmony, fate stepped in with a very low blow.

It was the last day of July, only a little more than three weeks before our season opener at home to Blackpool, a game to which I was looking forward with intense anticipation. I was really enjoying myself towards the end of a practice match on Spurs' beautiful, tree-lined training ground at Cheshunt in Hertfordshire. Having already scored three times, I was in an expansive mood when a stray clearance landed at my feet near the halfway line.

To me there has always been a certain magic about White Hart Lane, even when it's empty. Here I'm soaking up the atmosphere of my new footballing home shortly after my arrival from Swansea.

I was confronted immediately by Jeff Ireland, who was playing on the right wing on the opposing team. The most obvious thing to do would have been to play a safe pass back to Ron Henry, who was operating behind me at left-back, before racing into space to receive a return. Instead I tried something clever, flicking the ball over Jeff's head, then nipping past him, and my intention was to cut inside Peter Baker, the full-back who was looming to challenge me, and perhaps try for a fourth goal.

I was up to full speed as I approached Peter, but probably had allowed the ball to run a fraction further ahead of me than I would have liked. As I swerved suddenly to go past him, I lost my balance slightly, and instead of leaving him in my wake I was hit by his full-blooded tackle.

There was an almighty collision and, as we both went down, there was a sickening crack that could be heard all around the ground. It was like a dry piece of wood being snapped and it was clear that a bone had been broken.

Ready for anything: a young man with plenty to prove at White Hart Lane in 1958.

For a few seconds, as we both lay flat out on the turf, I don't think either of us knew which one had come off worst from the impact. Peter was in loads of pain and must have feared to look at his leg, whereas I just felt a certain numbness. When I did glance down at my right shin there was no outward sign of injury, no worrying bulges through the sock, and that gave me fleeting hope that I had had a lucky escape.

Bill Nicholson, who had sensed a serious problem and had arrived quickly at the scene, rolled down my sock and gave me further encouragement. "Doesn't look too bad," he said. "Get up and see if you can walk." But after only one or two steps, the pain burned through me and I knew something was seriously wrong.

When I managed, through clenched teeth, to explain to our trainer, Cecil Poynton, that I was feeling weakness as well as pain, he looked extremely worried, which I took as a bad sign. Dave Dunmore, our strapping inside-forward, helped Cecil to carry me off the pitch and I was rushed by car to the Prince of Wales Hospital in Tottenham, a splendid institution which has long since ceased to exist. The doctor who examined me offered initial optimism, saying he didn't think it was a break, but all too soon an x-ray revealed that he had got it wrong. I had a transverse fracture of my right tibia and I was plastered all the way up to the top of my thigh. Cecil reckoned I might be out for 12 weeks, but maybe he was trying to cheer me up because it was more than four months before I was back in the team, though it seemed more like an eternity.

At first I felt sorry for myself, but the support I received from family, friends, teammates and fans soon lifted my spirits. I had get-well-soon mail from all over the country, and there was some canny advice from the Chelsea left-winger Frank Blunstone, who I bumped into – not literally, I'm happy to say! – when I visited Stamford Bridge to watch Spurs face the Pensioners. Frank was on the long road to recovery from his second broken leg and he told me my troubles would really begin when I tried to get match fit. "You might be feeling fine," he said, "and you'll think you are fit to play, but when you get out on that field again you'll realise just how much more work you have to do."

Thanks Frank, that was just what I needed! Actually, it really was, because it saved me from unrealistic expectations, which would have been shattered anyway when my plaster finally came off. As I took in the shape of my mended limb, I was shocked by the wasted state of it. My legs could never have been described as tree-trunks at the best of times, but now my poor little right peg was more like a matchstick. It didn't look too clever at all for a professional footballer and I had to start the lengthy process of putting muscle back on to bone, building it up to face the rigours of top-level contact sport.

Now I faced a lengthy period of rehabilitation. Hard graft was demanded, there was no substitute for that, and the effort had to come from me. If I didn't put it in now, if I shied away from the necessary hours of sweat and boredom, then I could be throwing away my career, just when it felt like it was taking off in a big way. There was no way I was going to let that happen, so I worked my way through all the mind-numbing repetitive exercises, the wearing of a weighted boot, the cycling on the spot, the squats with a bar across my shoulders – these made me feel that amputation might be the kinder option!

What made this taxing period somehow acceptable was that I was not labouring on my own. Unluckily for him, another young Tottenham flankman, a lovely east Londoner name of Micky Dulin, was also striving to regain fitness after busting a leg – in his case against Birmingham City at St Andrew's – and he was first-class company. We got on so well and we helped each other through the ordeal, though demoralisingly for Micky, the outcome in his case was anything but positive. All the time I was progressing, seeing my leg grow more muscular as I gradually inched up the exercises, poor Micky's condition was just not responding to the rigorous regime. In the end he had to call it a

Leg in plaster and in an agony of frustration, I watch the action from the Stamford Bridge dugout as Spurs face Chelsea in the second game of the 1958/59 season.

day in professional football which, in sporting terms, was a tragedy because he was such a promising performer, having impressed enormously in his dozen or so senior games for the club. Clearly his injury must have been worse, or at least more complicated, than mine because ever since he has suffered pain in his leg, while mine returned to normal very rapidly, just one of the many illustrations of how Dame Fortune smiled on me throughout my association with the game.

Eventually, on a gloriously sunny day at Cheshunt, Cecil had me running again. I started gently, of course, and I felt a little sore, but gradually the strength began to filter back and I felt on top of the world. Never again would I take the simple act of jogging for granted. Now I saw it as a privilege, and I revelled in it. Still ahead lay a long slog towards full fitness, starting to kick a ball again, gingerly at first then steadily increasing the power until I could give it a proper whack. Then came the stamina work and the first tackles, playing mostly at inside-forward in practice games to make sure I was kept busy all the time, eventually moving on to a proper game for the Spurs 'A' team at Biggleswade.

At first I was hesitant, understandably over-cautious, and I admit to feeling worried. I felt very much on the fringe of the action, not properly involved at all, and there was fleeting anxiety that football might never be quite the same for me again. But then instinct must have taken over. Without thinking, I won possession, nipped past a couple of markers and something clicked in my head, the old confidence came flooding back. There followed a few more matches at lower levels and then, by early December, I was judged ready for my First Division comeback.

At this stage, I must make it clear that no blame whatsoever attaches to Peter Baker for my broken leg. Our coming together was a rotten mishap, the kind of thing that happens all the time in football. We were two committed professionals, both doing our jobs to the best of our ability, both our minds wholly on going for the ball, and there wasn't the merest trace of malice involved. Certainly he was a strong tackler and I've never met a winger who relished tangling with him, but he was scrupulously fair, absolutely not the type to go over the top in any challenge, and he was mortified by the outcome of our crash. As for the damage to Peter, I'm delighted to say that, while he was severely shaken up by the impact and had to miss a couple of games at the start of the season, he was back in regular action by the end of the month and remained a fixture at right-back for the next six years, during which he became one of my best friends.

I must mention, too, a persuasive theory among some shrewd contemporary observers of the White Hart Lane scene that might surprise a lot of people, namely that when Peter snapped my tibia he was unwittingly doing me an immense favour. Remember that I had appeared to be jaded during my first months at the club, and many thought that my performances in the World Cup had indicated that, after a long period of non-stop activity, what I really needed was a good rest. Now Peter,

My chum Peter Baker, who never meant to break my leg but might have done me a favour in the long term.

God bless him, didn't intend to give me one, but that was the very outcome of our accident at Cheshunt. Of course, it was a hideous thing to happen, but it did have its up-side – it gave me an enforced lay-off in which I was able to recharge my batteries, allow my engine to build up to full power again, something which I desperately needed although I hadn't appreciated it at the time. There's never a good moment to break your leg, but this injury gave me the chance to sit down, reflect on all the crowded events that had been going on in my life, take stock and ready myself for an exciting future.

During my absence from action, there had been some significant occurrences in the world of football. For a start, I was no longer the most expensive British footballer on these islands. That mantle had passed to the England international inside-forward Albert Quixall, signed for £45,000 in September by Manchester United from Sheffield Wednesday as Matt Busby strove to rebuild his devastated club in the aftermath of the Munich air disaster in the previous February. Though I had never worried about my own fee – now looking comparatively slender, a mere £35,000! – I suppose it did create a certain pressure of expectation among supporters, and it was referred to constantly in the press. So that was a monkey off my back, albeit one which I believe I wore lightly.

Far more importantly, there had been a change in the management at White Hart Lane, where Jimmy Anderson had been replaced as boss by his former assistant, Bill Nicholson, who was destined to become the most influential figure in my entire career.

Jimmy had been at the club for half a century in a wide range of roles, from boot boy to youth coach, then later he became a talent scout who had brought some terrific players to Tottenham, including members of the current squad such as the full-backs Peter Baker and Ron Henry, wing-half Tony Marchi and left winger Terry Dyson.

He succeeded Arthur Rowe as manager in 1955 when the architect of Spurs' push-and-run glory at the start of the decade, which had brought the Second and First Division championships to White Hart Lane in successive seasons, suffered a nervous breakdown.

Jimmy was in charge for three complete campaigns, and lifted the side from the wrong half of the table in his first term to finish second in 1956/57 and third in 1957/58. With the eloquent Irish wing-half Danny Blanchflower and that most magical of ball manipulators, the inside-forward Tommy Harmer, orchestrating in midfield and with big Bobby Smith banging in the goals, the future looked extremely encouraging.

But with the team suffering a chronically disappointing start to 1958/59, with five defeats and only three wins in the first 11 games, Jimmy's own health was suffering and in October he stepped down in favour of Bill.

The new number one was Tottenham to the very core of his being, having been an influential defensive wing-half in Rowe's sumptuously entertaining side, then coaching at White Hart Lane for four years. Nobody could have been better qualified for the job and nobody could have made a more auspicious start.

Still being laid low with my broken leg, I was in the stand to witness Bill's debut as manager against Everton, who had also started the campaign disastrously with six straight defeats, but had stabilised under the temporary guidance of Gordon Watson and had revived to win four of their last five games.

What unfolded before my startled gaze was utterly extraordinary. Spurs won 10–4 with Smithy scoring four times, Alfie Stokes bagging two and a goal apiece from George Robb, Terry Medwin, Tommy Harmer and John Ryden. I had to feel sorry for Jimmy Harris, the Everton inside-right, who scored a hat-trick and still saw his side annihilated. At that time there was a popular American cop series on television called *Highway Patrol*, in which Broderick Crawford played the leading character, who would phone into the precinct at the end of each episode, signing off with the words "Ten Four and Out." Hence one newspaper headline the following day was "Highway Patrol Spurs 10, Everton 4 and out!"

It was an exceptional performance by a rampant side in which little Tommy Harmer had been spellbinding, creating mayhem with his artistry on the ball. Danny Blanchflower had also put in a dazzling display, but he was always a realist, declaring with typically piercing humour at the end of Bill Nick's first 90 minutes at the helm: "It can only get worse from here!"

And for a while, so it did. Under the new boss, Tottenham won their next game, 4–3 at Leicester, but then came only one victory in the next 11 outings, a debilitating sequence which I joined in early December when we faced Preston North End at the Lane. I slotted in on the left wing and we lost 2–1, a dispiriting experience in itself, made all the more disappointing for me because Tom Finney was missing from their team through injury.

'The Preston Plumber' was a truly magnificent footballer and I had been looking forward to seeing him in action again at first hand, a privilege that was postponed until the last day of the season, when our teams drew 2–2 in the Deepdale return. Bill Shankly famously described Finney as the best player who ever lived, and Shanks wasn't the worst judge in the world. Tom is often compared to his brilliant contemporary, Stanley Matthews, but I've always thought that was daft because they were such hugely different types of performers.

Whereas Tom could play anywhere along the front line, or even graft in the midfield, Stan was the ultimate specialist outside-right. There was never the slightest question about what number he was going to wear on his back. He sported the number seven so often that it must have been imprinted on his skin. But Tom did everything – scored goals, made goals, won the ball and protected it. He was so, so strong, capable of riding the most horrendous of tackles – it was practically impossible to shake him off the ball. Yet for all that power, and the ability to look after himself at need, he was an impeccable gentleman, one of the nicest people in the game.

It's fair to say that, even at the veteran stage and on the brink of retirement, Finney would have been a golden asset to Tottenham, or to any other side that season, but, of course, he would never have turned out for anyone but his beloved Preston.

As it was, we laboured on towards the end of an anti-climactic campaign in which we limped to 18th position in the First Division, only half a dozen points better off than Aston Villa in the second relegation slot, and suffered a humbling exit from the FA Cup at the hands of Third Division Norwich City. That came as a demoralising blow after we had done pretty well in disposing of the seemingly far more formidable West Ham in the third round, beating them 2–0 at White Hart Lane.

My form had been patchy as I strove to readjust to life in the First Division after my long injury lay-off, and I had been particularly off-colour in our two defeats by the Hammers on Christmas Day and Boxing Day. I have to admit that John Bond, their right-back, had bottled me up pretty effectively on both occasions, but now I felt I had his measure, and in all modesty I can say I gave him a tough time in our FA Cup encounter, which I managed to embellish with our first goal.

Next we played host to third-tier Newport County and disposed of them 4–1, though I was delighted from a family point of view to note that my brother, Bryn, put in a terrific performance for the Welshmen.

After that, a home tie with Norwich did not seem insurmountable, but if any hint of complacency had crept into our thinking – despite the ultra-professional approach of Bill Nick, who stamped ruthlessly on such an attitude any time he noticed it – then we were to be punished for it emphatically.

Utterly unfazed by facing mighty Tottenham in front of more than 67,000 expectant fans at White Hart Lane, the valiant Canaries addressed their task with courage, determination and not a little flair, and they thoroughly deserved to be leading through a goal by Terry Allcock as the final whistle drew worryingly near. I was desperate to turn the tide, we all were, and in the last of the 90 minutes I finally escaped my marker, the right-back Bryan Thurlow, who had policed me relentlessly all afternoon. Dave Dunmore delivered a cross, the ball bounced and sat up invitingly, and I cracked it on the volley with my left foot. Ron Ashman, the defender who would one day manage Norwich, desperately tried to keep it out with his hand, but it flashed just inside a post to give us the draw our overall display barely merited.

The relief was overwhelming. I hoped fervently that the goal would give me the momentum I needed to step up my level of performance on a consistent basis to justify the record fee Spurs had paid for me. More importantly, it gave us the chance to salvage a lacklustre League season with a run at the most famous knockout competition in the world, one that was arguably revered more than any other in those innocent, far-off days before financial considerations came to dominate our game so completely.

Sadly, that heaven-sent opportunity for salvation was spurned. Four days later at Carrow Road, we were overturned by the prolific centre-forward Terry Bly, who scored the only goal of the game in front of one of the most rabidly partisan crowds I have ever experienced. I ended up the villain of the piece with those marvellous home supporters, who barracked me for a (relatively!) innocuous challenge on Thurlow. It was no fun being jeered, but I can't deny that the Canaries deserved their flight of fantasy on that chilly East Anglian evening. Archie Macaulay's enterprising underdogs made it all the way to the semi-finals, having also beaten Manchester United on the way, and they missed out on a trip to Wembley only after a tight replay defeat by Luton Town.

For Tottenham, the underwhelming results continued for the remainder of the season, but for me the Norwich clashes marked a crucial turning point. At last I felt I was making a sustained meaningful contribution to the team effort and I was able to push on from there, retaining my place until the end of term with some much brighter displays.

It was blatantly obvious, though, that for all the gifted individuals at Bill Nick's disposal, the side lacked drive and dynamism at key moments. It needed a character who would utterly refuse to yield in any circumstances, a force of footballing nature. That shortfall was to be addressed by the White Hart Lane boss in the spring when he beat a host of other keen suitors to sign the inspirational Dave Mackay from Hearts. In that one move, Bill Nick proved he was a managerial genius, as Dave went on to serve the club heroically for the best part of a decade.

Before then, there had been a periodic lack of focus within the group of players which was nothing to do with Bill, merely the way people were. For instance, there was a smashing guy, Alfie Stokes, an inside-forward who could score goals for fun and was cracking company, always extremely entertaining, but you did have to wonder, at times, about the strength of his ambition and his professional intent.

Blond, full of life and I suppose you might say disarmingly charming, Alfie was a bit of a lad who liked the ladies and who loved a flutter on the dogs and the horses. He was always borrowing money to finance his bets. On a Friday we'd all be in the dressing room and he'd write down on slips of paper the names of the lads who had lent him a quid or two. Then he'd put them in a hat, and whoever's name was pulled out first got paid while the others had to wait. If you complained about this repayment method, Alf would say: "If you keep on moaning your name won't even go in the hat!" Often he was asked the question: "When are you getting married, Alfie?" His stock reply came to be: "I'd better settle up before I settle down!"

On the pitch, he could be much more businesslike. One night at the Lane he put five goals past the Birmingham and England keeper Gil Merrick, and he had hit the target 42 times in only 69 Spurs appearances when Bill Nick decided to sell him to Fulham for a mere £10,000 in the summer of 1959. Still only 26, he should have been approaching his prime, but obviously the manager was unimpressed by his commitment, which might have been a wise decision, given the way his career subsequently petered out rather lamely at Craven Cottage, Cambridge City, Watford and Nuneaton Borough before he made his living as a chauffeur. The amiable Alfie left the Lane having lived life to the full but surely nursing a regret or two about all that unrealised potential.

Bill wasn't against his players having a good time – with the likes of Mackay and John White, of whom much more later, I had some uproarious fun down the years – but he did require total dedication to the cause, something which no amount of raw talent could override.

CHAPTER NINE

The warrior and the scholar

If there was one defining moment when Bill Nick's Spurs made the quantum leap from enchanting but inconsistent crowd-pleasers to dazzling entertainers who also happened to be fiercely committed winners, it was when Dave Mackay put pen to paper on his move to White Hart Lane from the crack Edinburgh side Hearts.

In Scotland, Dave had played a mammoth part as the Jam Tarts had won the full set of domestic trophies, the League Cup in 1955 and 1959, the Scottish Cup in 1956 and, best of the lot, the League championship in 1958, while also making a major impact in the international arena after a tentative start against Spain in which he ran up against a gentleman named Alfredo Di Stefano at the peak of his powers.

It was hardly surprising that a whole bunch of leading English clubs were keen to sign this phenomenally dynamic wing-half, and Bill was desperate to nip in ahead of them. However, when he put it to the Hearts boss, Tommy Walker, he was so firmly rebuffed that, for a time, he switched his attention to my old chum Mel Charles, who was on the point of leaving Swansea. Mel, though, had set his sights firmly on the Arsenal, so Bill went back to Tommy and this time came to agreement on a £32,000 deal.

All this happened in March 1959 and it gave me a tremendous personal boost. I had experienced my share of difficulties since arriving at White Hart Lane a year or so earlier, but although I didn't feel I had quite recaptured my top form, it did seem to me that I was moving firmly in the right direction. I was delighted with the quality of most of the players around me, believing

Typical Mackay! Larger than life as ever, Dave demonstrates his phenomenal athleticism by taking to the air at Tottenham's picturesque Cheshunt training ground. I'm on the left taking evasive action, while Ron Henry (centre) and Jimmy Greaves appear slightly less surprised.

that in time I could gel effectively with Danny Blanchflower and company, which would bring the best out of me. What we did lack, though, or so it seemed to me, was a certain spark, a communal spirit which would lift us even when we were up against the odds. We needed a man who would just refuse to lie down and accept defeat, a character who would be the beating heart of our team and would inspire the lads around him to give more in terms of passionate effort than they ever knew they possessed – and Bill had found him in Dave Mackay.

I had played with Dave in the Army and knew the difference he could make. I have never known anyone with such an appetite for the fray, so eager to be on the ball, so transfixed by the notion of winning. Don't worry, if there was anyone in his side who appeared to be flagging, Dave would let them know at the top of his voice in no uncertain terms, and he was no respecter of reputations. Everyone had to be at it 100 per cent of the time or he wanted to know the reason why.

I can't help but dwell on Dave's fearsome desire and iron determination because it defined him as a man, but what is not always recognised is that he was a technically superb footballer, too. There was pretty well nothing he couldn't do with the ball at his feet, and he was ready to demonstrate that prowess in training sessions from his earliest days at the club. For instance, he would stand 10–15 yards from a wall and volley the ball against it continuously without letting it touch the ground. If you doubt the difficulty of that particular manoeuvre, then please, just try it!

Then he could hammer the ball skywards, so high that you thought it might never come back down, and then kill it stone dead on his instep. That was a trick he would perform occasionally when running out for a match. It told the opposition: "I can play a bit." And it demanded of them: "Do you think you can cope with that?" As for ball juggling, Dave could do it in his sleep, he was deft enough to be a circus performer. Not that he restricted himself to the ball, he could do amazing things with a coin, too, flipping it from his instep to his neck, on to his forehead, then his knee and back to his instep before closing the act with an outrageous flick into his top pocket. It was dazzling stuff.

Mackay relished being a showman, but he was no Flash Harry who thought he was a cut above anybody else. As a bloke he was outgoing and

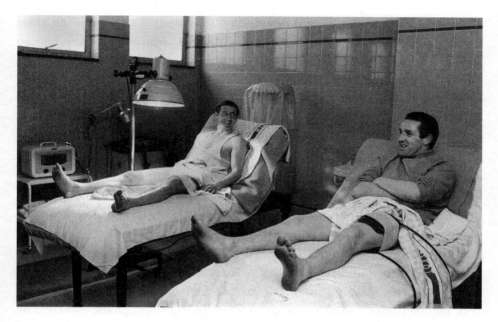

Confined to the treatment room but still managing a laugh, Dave Mackay (right) is probably telling me some unspeakable Scottish joke. The trouble was, half the time I couldn't understand a word he was saying!

popular, always in the centre of what was going on, up for every bit of fun imaginable. He liked a drink, like so many of us, and enjoyed every aspect of his life to the very hilt, but it never affected his football. There were one or two occasions when I could hardly believe what he was taking on board while still managing to stand up straight, but he was one of those who could soak it up and just carry on. If he had a heavy session then he would sweat it out in training the next day – certainly I never once saw his performance level drop as a result of his socialising.

To sum up Dave Mackay, he was the complete player, a team-changer, a man who made the difference. He did it with Hearts, he did it at Tottenham, later he did it for Derby County, and then he did it for various clubs as a successful manager. I have no hesitation in declaring that Dave was the best and most influential player I have ever lined up alongside. Given that I've taken the field with some of the greats, such as John Charles and Ivor

Allchurch, I think that's quite a statement, although I must add the rider that we never saw the best of Duncan Edwards, who would have had so much to come if he hadn't been cut down long before his prime.

But Mackay was the man you'd want with you if you had to go to war. You couldn't imagine anyone you'd rather have beside you in the trenches. He would back you up in any circumstances, you could rely on him utterly, you could bet your life on him. He was a fantastic man.

At the time of Dave's arrival we were far from clear of the relegation trapdoor, though nobody at White Hart Lane truly entertained the notion that we would drop into the Second Division. Still, we needed a few points to be safe and Dave helped us gather them in, despite missing five of our last nine games with a troublesome injury.

Towards the end of the season, Bill Nicholson dropped a bit of a bombshell. He marched into the dressing room and announced: "We're going on tour, lads." This was exciting news, and we had visions of some glamorous trip, maybe to the United States or to a few European capitals. But then he told us where we were headed and our jaws dropped. "We're off to Russia," he said, and we could not believe our ears. Remember that the Cold War was at its height, with British folk imagining all sorts of horrors going on inside the Soviet Union, and it was not exactly our destination of choice. When we got there, everything appeared very drab, just as we had expected, and most of the people on the streets of Moscow looked miserable. Lenin and Stalin were lying in state in the Mausoleum in Red Square, the KGB was everywhere and our movements were extremely restricted. We were told to be careful, not to do anything daft and to walk around in groups of at least three, so nobody would become isolated.

But whoever decided we should spend late spring and early summer in the USSR had pulled a master-stroke because the football was brilliant and the experience blended us together as a team in exactly the way that we needed. We won our first two matches, 1–0 against Torpedo Moscow with Terry Medwin getting the winner, and 2–0 over Dynamo Kiev, with inside-forward Johnny Brooks supplying both goals. We lost our last one, 3–1 to a Soviet Select XI in Leningrad, with Johnny on target again, but even in that game it was apparent that Bill was making real progress. All three contests were fiercely competitive, taken very seriously without any hint of the holiday atmosphere that sometimes used to pervade summer tours, and they set us up beautifully for the following season.

Though he was never one to wear his emotions on his sleeve or make rash predictions of future success, our manager was clearly pleased with the progress we were making, and he demonstrated his capacity for innovative thinking with a brainwave which came to him while we were spending an evening at the Bolshoi Ballet. The dancers were so incredibly supple, and Bill wanted to know how they could achieve such exceptional athleticism. On discovering that they used weight training and controlled their diets sensibly,

Smart as paint in our club blazers, the Tottenham party is ready to depart for Russia in the spring of 1959, a trip which helped hugely in moulding a team which would go on to extraordinary achievements. Back row, left to right: Dave Mackay, Johnny Brooks, Peter Baker, Ron Henry, Terry Medwin, Eddie Clayton. Middle: Bobby Smith, Johnny Hollowbread, Ron Reynolds, Maurice Norman, Mel Hopkins, Dave Dunmore, Jim Iley. Front: Tommy Harmer, manager Bill Nicholson, director Sidney Wale, vice-chairman Fred Wale, Danny Blanchflower, director Douglas Deacock, trainer Cecil Poynton and me.

he adopted those practices, bringing in a specialist trainer, Dave Watson, and that made a huge difference to our fitness levels and endurance capacity.

So overall, the expedition behind the Iron Curtain was an unqualified success, though I did encounter one unexpected personal difficulty. I found myself rooming with Dave Mackay and most of the time I couldn't understand a word he said! Goodness knows what he was nattering on about. His broad Edinburgh brogue left me so completely in the dark that I went to Bill Nicholson and asked for an interpreter. "A Russian one?" he enquired. "No, a Scottish one!" I replied. "I don't have a clue what Mackay is talking about!"

Also I had the theory that Dave was the untidiest man in the universe. I've always been a neat sort of person who folds clothes away carefully and likes a bit of order in his surroundings, but when I was sharing with Mackay the room was an absolute dump, with bits of kit and his everyday clobber all over the place. When I got to know him better I realised that this was an incurable condition – his car was always stacked with rubbish, it was such a mess that sometimes he had trouble climbing in, and passengers had no chance. But nobody was seriously complaining about Dave Mackay – not then, not now, not ever.

From the day he made his debut for Spurs, in a much-needed 3–1 win against Manchester City at White Hart Lane, I always felt I was lucky to be playing directly in front of such a titan, with Dave lining up at left-half and me starting on the left touchline.

Meanwhile I could see another member of the team positively glowing at his link-up with the Scottish newcomer. I'm talking about our right-half and skipper Danny Blanchflower, who offered such a huge contrast in playing style, but the two men complemented each other so perfectly in the middle of the pitch.

Where Dave was a warrior, you might call Danny a footballing scholar. Deeply intelligent and astute, endlessly eloquent and argumentative, the articulate Ulsterman played the game as impressively as he spoke about it. He didn't catch the eye in the manner of the barnstorming Mackay, but rather he was a subtle operator, making creative runs, delivering perceptive passes, dictating the tempo of a match, continuously assessing the needs of the team.

Tommy Harmer and his mop of black curls dominates this shot, with Dave Mackay (left), myself and Danny Blanchflower all finding plenty to smile about. That's Les Allen peering over Tommy's shoulder.

Bill Nicholson was the main man at White Hart Lane, nobody should ever be in the slightest doubt on that score, but once the game started, Danny, who had all the initiative and self-belief in the world, became a kind of manager on the pitch. He was very strong-minded and decisive, and if the game wasn't going right, he was ready to make changes on the hoof without running to the touch-line to ask permission. Usually those changes worked, occasionally they didn't, but although we had some immensely strong characters in the side – the likes of Mackay and Bobby Smith spring to mind – we all had the utmost respect for Danny's judgement and experience, and so did Bill. Once in a blue moon the two men might disagree, and there might be a few harsh words spoken, but overall they were on the same wavelength, understood each other perfectly,

Our skipper Danny Blanchflower, a brilliant leader even though we didn't always know what he was talking about!

knowing they were pulling in the same direction, always for the benefit of Tottenham Hotspur.

Everybody at White Hart Lane looked up to Danny, but as a bloke he was never quite like the rest of the lads, he held himself just a little bit apart. The truth was that he was on a different mental plane to most footballers. I'm not saying that many people in the game are thick – that's absolutely not the case – but Danny was a real intellectual who had a way with words, both spoken and written. For example, he wrote his own newspaper column and he would have laughed at the idea of a journalistic ghost.

Then there was the time when he was both manager and captain of Northern Ireland, and also a presenter for the BBC, that he staged an interview with himself, employing all his lilting Irish charm. It was a lovely bit of television that not many people could have carried off, but it was all grist to the Blanchflower mill. Suave, debonair and cultured, with a devastatingly piercing wit, he was the full package.

He was very popular at the club and there were plenty of insiders who thought he might have been the next manager after Bill Nick. Certainly I thought he'd be a successful boss at some point, and he did have a go with both Chelsea and Northern Ireland, but it never quite worked out for him. I suppose his chance at White Hart Lane slipped away because Bill remained in post until the mid-1970s, by which time Danny had moved on, taking his own path as a terrific writer.

The contrast between the two men is a fascinating one. I guess that for all his command of language, a lot of what Danny had to say might have passed over the heads of his players. On the other hand, Bill always made himself crystal clear in very simple terms. You knew exactly where you stood with Bill, there was never any room for doubt. Sometimes Danny would express himself in outrageous, whimsical terms, such as: "The best way to bring the crowds back is to let them in for nothing and charge them to go out!" He could be right off the wall and would have represented a radical change of pace from Bill.

I must admit that sometimes at team meetings we didn't have a clue what the skipper was talking about. Bill would make his points briefly and succinctly before asking if anyone else had anything to add. That would be the cue for Danny to pipe up, invariably declaring: "I'd like a quick word." As if! Then he would be off on flights of descriptive language that often left his listeners bemused. You could actually see some of the lads glazing over. Then eventually he would announce: "I'm just going to finish on this", which usually was the signal for at least another 15 minutes. Bobby Smith and Terry Dyson, who were often straining at the leash to get to the dog track, would be rolling their eyes as the Irishman's words washed over them.

When I was playing on the right wing, as I did throughout most of our League and FA Cup double-winning campaign of 1960/61, I was in close contact with Danny on the field as he was operating directly behind me at right-half. In most situations I'd be happy to receive the ball from him and just run with it. That was my game and it was part of our team pattern. But clearly there were occasions when such simplicity irked Danny, and it provoked his light-hearted but exasperated rant to me about the roundness of the ball, which I mentioned earlier. When he topped his outburst by demanding that, as the ball was round, why didn't I f****** pass it now and again, I thought it was hilarious. Certainly I wasn't offended, and it never changed the way I played. That was just his way of getting over his point. Frequently Danny would have similar exchanges with other members of the team, but that didn't alter the way we all felt about him. He was genuinely loved by all the players for the man he was, an absolute one-off.

To be teammates of two such midfield maestros as Dave Mackay and Danny Blanchflower would have been a luxury for any player, but soon enough, when a slim, deceptively waif-like young Scot named John White arrived to complete an exquisitely balanced trinity, we would be in footballing heaven.

CHAPTER TEN

Putting bums on seats

There was an unshakeable belief among everyone connected with Tottenham Hotspur that the shockingly disappointing 1958/59 campaign would turn out to be a minor blip in the march towards glory. When Jimmy Anderson had presided over second- and third-place finishes in the previous two seasons, expectations among supporters of an imminent championship charge had been massaged. Thus when Bill Nicholson's first term ended with an unseemly scramble to avoid relegation, there was dismay on the terraces and in the stands.

However, there were mitigating circumstances which had contributed to the setback, and grounds for immense optimism that the future was bright. Bill Nicholson was a new manager who needed a little time to take stock of the job, and to assemble a team capable of winning trophies. Clearly there were players whom Anderson had believed in who were surplus to Bill's requirements and they had to be moved on while, as a direct consequence, top-quality new recruits were needed and had to be bedded in.

The arrival of Dave Mackay in the spring of 1959 and his integration on the subsequent tour of Russia was one colossal indication of positive change, and another arrived in the summer in the tall, slender shape of goalkeeper Bill Brown. Since the war, and on through the 1950s, Spurs had been magnificently served between their posts by the England international Ted Ditchburn, a dominant figure who represented rock-like stability on the pitch and was a forthright influence off it. He had been a hero of Arthur Rowe's wonderful push-and-run champions, and was the last of their number to bow to the inevitable ravages of age, but when the towering Kentish custodian reached his late thirties, a comparable replacement had proved difficult to find.

There were times when Ron Reynolds displaced the ageing Ditchburn on merit, and the younger Johnny Hollowbread had his admirers, but in all honesty neither of them were in the very front rank. So, just as he had when recruiting the swashbuckling Mackay, our manager turned his attention north of the border, where it alighted on the fellow guarding the net for Dundee and, with increasing regularity, for Scotland.

Bill Brown turned out to be a superb signing, and a bargain at only £16,500. Perhaps he wasn't the best in the world at coming off his line to catch crosses – he was nowhere near as physical as, say, Manchester United's Harry Gregg or Bert Trautmann of Manchester City – but as a shot-stopper he was sensational, incredibly athletic. Bill was an excellent kicker of the ball, too, and a marvellous all-round sportsman, a golfer who played off a handicap of one. In fact, there had been a period of his youth when, so impressive was he on the greens and the fairways, that he had to make a choice between football and golf as a career. He never quite got down to scratch, but you would never have played Bill for money, that was certain.

Of paramount importance, too, he was an intelligent, courteous character and a model professional who worked tirelessly to improve every aspect of his game, just the sort of reliable fellow Bill Nick needed as a last line of defence. In particular, his levels of concentration were astonishing, which was crucial in a team which spent so much time on the attack that the rearguard could go long periods of time without the ball coming near them. He was also very composed, completely unflappable no matter how intense the pressure might become, radiating the sort of confidence that every defence needs. It might seem old-fashioned to some, but I've always maintained that every top team needs a strong spine – keeper, centre-half and centre-forward – and with our giant stopper Maurice Norman already in place, and big Bobby Smith charging around in attack like a bull in a china shop, we now had completed the set.

And there was an added bonus, at least for me, in Bill becoming our new goalkeeper. At long last I had met a Scot whom I could understand when he spoke to me. After the recent arrival of Dave Mackay, another unintelligible teammate from the wilds of Caledonia would have driven me to distraction. Mind you, Dave might have mentioned that he couldn't tell what this Swansea Jack was muttering about most of the time, so you might say we were even on that score.

All our spirits were sky-high as we launched into the 1959/60 League campaign, and we made an ideal start with a blazing 5–1 victory over Newcastle United on their own Tyneside turf. I was particularly elated as we strolled off at St James's Park as I had contributed a hat-trick, my first as a Spur, but although I enjoyed the praise that came my way, I have to say that the real man of the match was Dave Mackay, who made his presence felt in all areas of the pitch.

My three goals were particularly pleasing as they were so varied in type. The first was a pretty fierce shot following a typical inch-perfect pass from Blanchflower, the second was a header from a corner, and the third involved a bit of trickery, which brings a glow of satisfaction to any winger when it comes off. Some crisp interplay between myself and Mackay left me through on Newcastle keeper Ronnie Simpson, though with little apparent likelihood of scoring because I was at such a narrow angle to the posts. But my confidence was high and I sensed that he expected me to chip the ball inside, where Bobby Smith was lurking. So as he shifted his weight outwards to cover the cross, I dummied with my left foot, then threaded the ball through the narrow gap between Simpson and his near upright. It was a terrific feeling to see that one nestle in the old onion bag and I shall never forget how the Geordie fans, who know and love their football, stayed after the final whistle to clap us on our way. I think they realised that we were something special in the making and, putting their customary partisan outlook temporarily to one side, they wanted to show that they recognised our quality.

Also enjoying himself that day was Johnny Brooks, who lined up alongside me at inside-left and scored two goals. If ever a man deserved the tag of 'enigma', often employed by football writers to describe players endowed with vast talent but who somehow contrive not to make the most of it, that fellow was Johnny. He was blessed with every skill imaginable, being capable of scheming goals for others as well as delivering them himself, and when he

It looks like I've come out on top in this aerial battle with classy England international full-back Don Howe during a typically muddy midwinter encounter with West Bromwich Albion.

John White, not a household name on arrival, but soon to emerge as one of the finest midfield generals British football has ever known.

picked up his three England caps in 1956 it seemed certain that a long-term international future was beckoning.

But despite approaching what should have been his prime years at White Hart Lane with every chance of being a cornerstone of the promising new team being built by Jimmy Anderson, then Bill Nicholson, Johnny was woefully inconsistent. To be honest, he wasn't the bravest physically, and in the end he lacked just that bit of heart, or devil, call it what you will, to be a long-term fixture at the top level. For instance, he hated going to Bolton, where we would be confronted by a fearsome defence in which the full-backs, Roy Hartle and Tommy Banks, and the centre-half, John Higgins, were especially intimidating. It always seemed to be raining, there was always a brass band playing – it was like another country – and, my goodness, it was always tough.

Recently my son, Steve, got hold of Tommy Banks' book and sent it for him to autograph for me because he had been a direct opponent of mine about whom I had told so many stories down the years. Tommy sent it back with the hilarious inscription: 'To Cliff – I'll get you next time!'

He was an amazing character who would give you a hard, hard time during the game, then have a laugh with you afterwards. I shall always remember him, too, as a passionate union man who was active in the successful movement in the early 1960s to abolish the maximum wage for footballers and also get rid of the medieval retain-and-transfer system, which tied a player to a club for life, even at the end of his contract, if the employer didn't want to let him go. Tommy worked manually until he was well into his seventies, carrying hods of bricks on building sites, and he looked none the worse for it. To this day, whenever I hear a brass band play, I think of Burnden Park, lashing rain, cinder track, Messrs Banks and Hartle... it all comes flooding back so vividly – and I shudder!

As for Johnny Brooks, for all his ample ability, he never struck me as Bill Nick's type of player, and so it proved, as in December 1959 he was allowed to move to Chelsea in exchange for Les Allen. Without being unkind, I think it's fair to say that Spurs got the better of that deal, with the doughty, hard-working Les going on to be part of the side that lifted the League and FA Cup double while Johnny, after helping the Pensioners to stave off relegation that term, saw out his professional playing days in the lower divisions with Brentford and Crystal Palace.

As our own 1959/60 season progressed through a fruitful autumn, I saw more and more reason to become excited by our potential. We went unbeaten for our first dozen games, with highlights including three more 5–1 wins – it seemed to be our favourite scoreline that season – starting with the thrashing of Manchester United at Old Trafford. I hit the target a couple of times as we beat Preston – featuring the great Tom Finney in his last term before retirement – by the same scoreline, then Bobby Smith hammered four goals past reigning champions Wolverhampton Wanderers, with me chipping in with the fifth.

It was a pleasure in these weeks to be part of a team which I felt to be very definitely on the rise. We were at the right end of the division, the defence was reassuringly sound, the goals were going in at the other end and, perhaps most encouraging of all, there was so much midfield creativity in the sharply contrasting shapes of Danny Blanchflower and little Tommy Harmer.

Watching the captain now, it seemed inconceivable that Bill Nicholson had left him out of the side for a few games during the previous January and February in favour of the forceful youngster Billy Dodge. It turned out to be a canny move by the manager, who wanted to emphasise to Danny the need for more defensive responsibility. Because of the vast reservoir of respect between the two men, Bill Nick's approach paid off, and when Danny returned he was a more complete player than ever, giving at least an occasional thought to what was going on at the back while not compromising the captivating nature of his attacking play.

Tall and deceptively languid in appearance as he made his elegant way around the pitch, Blanchflower offered a vivid contrast in style to the sorcerer Tommy Harmer. The spindly, you might even say scrawny little Eastender, who sported such a mop of black, curly hair that sometimes he looked top-heavy, was perhaps the most audacious artist, the most beguiling manipulator of a football it has ever been my pleasure to witness. The only way to get the best out of Tommy was to give him a pass and let him work his magic. For instance, often you could slip the ball to him at a short corner and move infield, then watch him wriggle his way along the byline, constantly shaping to deliver it back to you while going past defender after defender.

He wasn't a graceful mover, rather he got round the pitch with jerky little steps which could seem awkward – that is until the ball arrived at his feet. Then he was Harmer the Charmer, an impudent maestro with a delicious passing repertoire, the like of which I have never seen equalled. Every manner of delivery was his to command – he could swerve the ball either way, drive it, dispatch it with backspin, you name it and Tommy could make a football do it.

But for all this astounding dexterity, he was no circus act, nor was he out for personal aggrandisement at the expense of everything else. Rather our skinny little wizard was an instinctive improviser whose subtly intricate wiles were employed faithfully in the team's cause. He was brilliant at switching the direction of play with a sudden, penetrating through-pass which could unhinge the most clam-like of defences. Some teammates found him unpredictable and difficult to read, but if we didn't know what he was going to do, then what hope did the opposition have?

Clearly Tommy was an exceptionally gifted performer, but it might be argued that he was born too late. His exceptional skills would surely have made him a superstar, a national treasure, in earlier eras when inside-forwards had more time and space in which to operate. As it was he was never awarded even a single England cap – the nearest he got was an outing in one 'B' international – and never helped to win a major club honour.

Yet during the early part of 1959/60, he might have thought his luck was going to change, even after Bill Nicholson went back to Scotland yet again to recruit another extraordinary talent, the 22-year-old playmaker John White, whom he signed from Falkirk for £20,000 that October. In time the newcomer would supplant Tommy as Danny Blanchflower's principal co-schemer in the middle of the park, and emerge – in my humble opinion – as one of the most outstanding footballers of his generation and a key influence on Tottenham's glory days in the early 1960s. But back in that transformational autumn of the manager's first full season at the helm, Bill did his utmost to accommodate all his major talents, often playing John on the right wing in tandem with 'Tom Thumb', as Harmer was often dubbed by newspapermen.

Looking back, I contend that the signing of White was a major turning point in the comprehensive renaissance of Tottenham Hotspur, so it's a little perverse that his debut, against Sheffield Wednesday at Hillsborough, marked our first defeat of the season. Despite that, John, who lined up with a number ten on his back as a replacement for the less subtle, more direct Dave Dunmore, was on the scoresheet as we went down 2–1 to one of the best teams in the country, who would give us more trouble than most during the glory years that lay ahead.

Though it would take much more time for the full value of John White to become apparent, it was quickly obvious that he offered a different dimension to Tommy, Danny, Dave or anyone else in the club. Bill Nick, who had done an awful lot of homework on John before bringing him down south from Brockville, knew all about his skill on the ball and his knack of grabbing important goals, but he was also attracted by his phenomenal athleticism. He might have been slender and pale, even frail in appearance, but that was very deceptive. Bill found out that John had been an Army cross-country champion during his National Service and could get around the field far more quickly than, say, Tommy, who the fans loved to see making the ball talk but who could sometimes slow down the momentum of a flowing move.

Opposing defenders just couldn't match White's stamina, couldn't keep up with his non-stop movement, which made him a constant option to receive a pass. If ever any Spurs player found himself under pressure when he was in possession, then it was a pound to a penny that John would be on the scene in a trice to help him out. To paraphrase a modern chant which I shan't repeat in its entirety because it's not exactly family-friendly, 'White was here, he was there, he was every f****** where!' Anyone who has played the game will understand what an invaluable asset that is for any team. For us it meant that our attacking impetus could be maintained far more fluidly than in the past and it gave each of us the freedom to try manoeuvres which might be considered risky in other circumstances, but were far safer with John in the side because he would always be there to bail you out of trouble. Even better, when you gave him the ball he could use it brilliantly, so often freeing one of the wingers to get behind our markers or sending in a striker for a shot on goal. White was by no means a household name when he arrived from Falkirk, but I don't think there was a player in Britain who would have been better suited to the fluent team that Bill was building than John White, which is a colossal tribute to the acumen of a manager who had been in the White Hart Lane hot seat for a mere 12 months.

As the season wore on we emerged as genuine championship contenders, topping the table a week before Christmas after completing our League double over Newcastle with a 4–0 thrashing at White Hart Lane, and I was happier with my own form than at any time in my life. I was so pleased to be paying back something towards my fee after all the difficulties I had experienced, a major factor being that I was enjoying my first full campaign without injuries since my transfer. I was really buzzing, believing that I was living up to my potential at last. Importantly I relished the training so I was in fine physical condition and, now in my middle twenties, I felt I was entering my prime. I was starting each match on the left wing, but Bill had given me freedom to roam, and I took full advantage of that licence, cutting inside for a shot whenever I sniffed the opportunity, and also switching flanks frequently with Terry Medwin, who wore the number-seven shirt more often than anyone else that term.

Statistically it was my best ever season as I managed 25 goals in the League and FA Cup – let's call it a quarter of a century, because it sounds more, doesn't it? – with only centre-forward Bobby Smith, who hammered in 30, a relatively modest total for him, exceeding my tally. A lot of my strikes were made at the far post, and for that I have to give a huge amount of credit to Bill Nick, who noticed so much about every aspect of the game that escaped most people. He saw that I was quick and pretty strong for my size, with a knack of nipping in front of markers. He said to me: "When you're beyond the far post and the play is on the other side, just stand back a bit, you can see your defender, you can track the flight of the ball, you have the whole picture. So come at it just a little bit later than the full-back might expect, cut across him at the last moment just as he's concentrating hard, and you can catch him off balance. So often you'll pinch the ball and you'll score lots of goals." And that's what happened. I went for deliveries from Terry on the right wing, but also from John White and others in deep positions. John could put it on the spot for me perfectly. He knew that if he floated it into my general area then I'd be reading it, popping up, and probably getting on the end of it.

Of course, I also picked up plenty of bruises and cuts through this ploy because the lads I was trying to beat didn't just stand aside and say "After you, Cliff." Could you imagine Tommy Banks or Roy Hartle doing that? People said it took a lot of courage on my behalf, but to me soaking up a few knocks had always been part of the game. In all honesty, when I was lurking with intent, expecting a cross from White or Medwin, Blanchflower or Terry Dyson, the last thing on my mind was getting injured. At this point I was completely single-minded. My only objective was hitting the back of the net and if I took a smack or two along the way, then so what? If I'd stopped to worry about that, then I'd never have scored a goal. I'd have been a spare part, no use to anyone, and I'm certain I wouldn't have enjoyed the lengthy career that I did.

As we moved into the New Year, I don't think there was a side in the country to top us for entertainment value. Wolves, who had lifted the crown for the past two seasons, Sheffield Wednesday and Burnley looked to be shaping up as our main rivals, and while we didn't take them lightly they didn't frighten us in the least. Thus we were in superlatively confident mood as we kicked off our tilt at the FA Cup at Newport, close to my old stamping ground in South Wales. Les Allen continued his excellent start as a Spur, scoring twice as we won 4–0 at Somerton Park to set up a fourth-round tie with Crewe Alexandra at Gresty Road, where life suddenly became a lot more taxing.

The side from the basement division performed well above expectations, holding Spurs to 1–1 until about a quarter of an hour from time, when I scored to seemingly seal our passage to the next round. But then Mervyn Jones, no relation, cracked in a late equaliser before almost winning the game at the death, only to be thwarted by a sensational save from Bill Brown at full stretch.

It's a wonderful life!

Thus chastised, with pride well and truly dented, we were determined to put the record straight in the White Hart Lane replay, and did so to the tune of 13–2. Were we praised for running up a cricket score against a team of fellow professionals, albeit lads who made their living at a lower level? Not in every quarter. One popular view was that we had been too harsh, that we had been lacking in sportsmanship to dismiss our valiant opponents so ruthlessly, but I believe this was a naïve reaction verging on the idiotic.

What were we supposed to do? Go easy on Crewe by playing a nice polite game? I believe that would have been unforgivably patronising to decent opposition for whom we had genuine respect. Also it would have been dishonest because more than 64,000 fans had paid their hard-earned cash to see us do our very best, and that's just what we did. Sub-consciously, perhaps, we did ease up a bit in the second half because we'd been ten up at the interval, but we never knowingly took our foot off the pedal. Indeed, Dave Mackay was chided by the referee for tackling too hard when we'd scored seven, and he displayed utter devastation when he missed a great chance to score when we'd already knocked in a dozen. I'm not ashamed to say that I tried my hardest throughout, netting three times in the process, including once from the penalty spot, while Les Allen bagged five and Bobby Smith four. The truth is we would have scored 20 if we could have done, and I make no apology for that.

Inevitably in the circumstances, there was a deal of gloating from neutrals when we came unstuck in the fifth round at home to Blackburn Rovers. We lost 3–1 and I took little consolation from the fact that I scored one of the finest goals of my career, going past three defenders at top speed before chipping the ball over keeper Harry Leyland. It was just a shame that such a satisfying effort could not turn around a losing cause. Seven days later, though, I extracted some measure of revenge, hitting the target in a 4–1 win over Rovers at their own Ewood Park, which left us a point clear of the pack in the race for the First Division title.

We were pegged back by a 2–0 reverse at Burnley in what the newspapers called a four-pointer, but immediately got back on track by beating Harry Catterick's fiercely competitive Sheffield Wednesday 4–1 at the Lane, a triumph to which I was delighted to contribute my third hat-trick of the season.

Come the end of March we were sitting pretty on the First Division pinnacle, but there were signs that we were losing our rhythm. Bill Nick always insisted that we thought only about the next game, rather than dwelling on the possibilities of what we might achieve, but maybe some tension was creeping in as a lot of people were making us championship favourites. Suddenly points were being haemorrhaged where previously they had been calmly gathered in. We drew 1–1 at home to Fulham, then lost 2–1 at Bolton, which set us off on a calamitous sequence which saw us beaten four times in our last eight games, a run which cost us the title.

It was particularly frustrating that Wolves, Burnley and Wednesday were all faltering, too, and if we could have managed to maintain anything like our best form around the crucial Easter period then we would have been wearing that elusive crown. As it was, heading towards the holiday weekend, when six points would be up for grabs in the space of four days, we drew 1–1 with bottom-of-the-table Luton at White Hart Lane, then lost 2–1 to Everton at Goodison Park.

Still, though, there were five games left and the situation at the summit remained very fluid, so when we recorded a 3–1 Good Friday victory over Chelsea at Stamford Bridge, with Bobby Smith knocking in a hat-trick against his old club, it looked like we might have turned the corner. But just 24 hours later – such fixture congestion simply wouldn't be allowed today – we lost at home to another struggling side, Manchester City, on an Easter Saturday afternoon that will always be imprinted painfully on my memory.

On the blower while receiving a spot of familial advice from my cousin Ken Jones, one of the outstanding journalists of his generation and a more-than-useful footballer in his time.

Looking at our respective League positions, we might have been considered as bankers to win, but City weren't clear of the drop and they had some exceptional players in their team, not least the dazzling young Scottish striker Denis Law, whom they had just broken the British transfer record to sign from Huddersfield for £53,000, and the shrewd, vastly experienced wing-half and midfield general Ken Barnes. But their top star at that time was their goalkeeper, the giant German ex-paratrooper Bert Trautmann, and it was he, along with referee Gilbert Pullin, who made the decisive contribution.

Shortly before the interval, with the game still goalless, we were awarded a penalty for handball and I stepped up to take it. Big Bert seemed to fill the goal but I was confident from the spot, having already put away four of the 12-yarders earlier in the season. I dummied to shoot to his left, then side-footed firmly for a point just inside his right post. It wasn't as accurate as I would have liked, but certainly I had found the net with worse efforts, and in the split second that I hit it I expected to score. But Bert had other ideas, plunging athletically across his line and somehow managing to parry the ball. He couldn't hang on to it though and my eyes lit up as I charged forward to whack the ball past him, making me the most relieved man in the stadium – but only for a few delirious seconds.

The whistle blew and Mr Pullin was pointing, but to the dressing room rather than the centre spot. It turned out he had extended the first half long enough for the kick to be taken, but it had ended the moment Trautmann had made the save. Confusion reigned, with neither the players nor the crowd knowing what had happened until we buttonholed the official in the tunnel. His decision seemed harsh to me. How on earth could he have been that precise with his timing? Surely it would have been fairer to allow the phase of play to be completed. But then, I would say that, wouldn't I, and it was no use complaining. Of course, Sod's Law had it that City would grab the only goal of the second period – it was put away by the Northern Ireland international Billy McAdams – and we lost vital ground in the championship race. Afterwards I went to Bill Nick and told him I didn't want to take any more penalties, half expecting him to argue me round. His response? "Good decision, son!"

Looking at the incident dispassionately, which it's impossible to do in the heat of the moment, the fellow who comes out of it best is clearly Bert

Trautmann, surely one of the finest keepers who ever stood in front of a net. But of even greater relevance when placing Bert into context is the phenomenal strength of his character. When I played for the Football League against the Italian League, he was our captain and I was struck by his immense presence, his sheer charisma. His life story, and the hardships he had to overcome on the way to becoming a Manchester City legend, remove him firmly from the category of mere sporting hero. As a German soldier in the Second World War he had survived bloody battles and debilitating deprivations. Then, after becoming a prisoner of war, he settled in England and chose to make his living in the public eye, which opened him up to a barrage of xenophobic vitriol from those who could not put aside the bitterness of the recent conflict. He deserves so much respect, not only for coping with life in this country and rising above all the abuse, but for emerging from it all as such a beloved figure. Bert became a hero to many, including my friend Bob Wilson, himself a tremendous custodian with Arsenal. Bob always talks of Bert as an overwhelmingly generous person who never stopped giving of himself, and as a brave and brilliant keeper, surely one of the best of all time.

Mind, it was of scant consolation on that Easter Saturday to dwell on the Trautmann qualities, and we didn't, instead turning our attention to the return encounter with Chelsea at the Lane on Easter Monday, a game which we needed to win to stand any realistic chance of taking the title. Bill shuffled his pack, leaving out Terry Medwin and Tommy Harmer, bringing in Terry Dyson and taking the radical step of throwing the buccaneering Mackay into attack from midfield. But it was all to no avail as we somehow contrived to lose 1–0, the vital strike coming from a young goal machine by the name of Jimmy Greaves, whose immense importance to my career, and to my later life, will unfold in the pages to come.

Now Spurs were off the top for the first time since before Christmas, with Wolves leading the way by three points and Burnley lurking ominously, level with us but with two games in hand. It hurt to accept it, but now we were rank outsiders for the big prize, a situation which lifted the tension and enabled us to return to our best when it was, almost certainly, too late.

As it transpired, our penultimate match was against Wolves at Molineux, where victory for Stan Cullis' men would put them in a tremendously strong position to seal a title hat-trick, which had not been done since Arsenal managed it in the 1930s. In fact, it was an even bigger deal for the Black Countrymen because they were also through to the FA Cup final, and were the bookies' favourites to become the first club in the twentieth century to lift the League and FA Cup double. It was a feat that quite a few teams had got close to down the years, but something always seemed to happen to prevent it. For instance, in 1957 Manchester United won the title and were regarded as near-certainties to beat Aston Villa in the FA Cup final. But then their goalkeeper, Ray Wood, was seriously injured only a few minutes into the action and, in those days before the use of substitutes, that proved too severe a handicap even for the likes of Duncan Edwards, Bobby Charlton and company.

So winning that very special double was an elusive dream, a target that seemed somehow jinxed, and it fell to Spurs – ironically in view of what happened a year later – to prevent Wolves from reaching it. Against a very strong side with a formidable defence marshalled by Bill Slater, and with terrific forwards such as Peter Broadbent, Jimmy Murray and Norman Deeley, we gave one of our best displays of the season to win 3–1, with a goal apiece from myself, Bobby Smith and Dave Mackay, who was still being deployed at inside-left. All that remained for us was to win our last match, 4–1 at home to Blackpool, and we finished third, only two points behind the champions, Burnley, and with a better goal average, the ridiculously complicated predecessor to goal difference for separating teams on the same number of points.

Wolves so nearly made it, finishing their programme on the last Saturday of the campaign a point ahead of the Clarets, who had one more game to play. But in that last contest, at Manchester City on the Monday, Harry Potts' men triumphed 2–1 to take the title, a staggering accomplishment for a club based in a town of only 80,000 people, about the same size as Bath.

Obviously we looked back at so many games where we could have picked up the couple of points which would have made us champions, but I realise that any club can say that in any season, and in the end I could only congratulate Burnley on a job fabulously well done on comparatively slender resources. I had great admiration for them, not least because they played lovely football and were quite similar to Tottenham in many ways. Indeed, so many of the players matched up. You could equate their cerebral wing-half and captain Jimmy Adamson with our Danny Blanchflower, their subtle midfield general Jimmy McIlroy with our John White, their brave and irrepressible centre-forward Ray Pointer with our Bobby Smith, and, with all due modesty, their goal-scoring winger John Connelly with myself. There was one massive difference, though. They didn't have an equivalent to our inspirational driving force, Dave Mackay – but then again, nor did anybody else.

So, when all was done and dusted at the close of 1959/60, and all the baubles had been handed out, we could feel a little bit aggrieved because we had won nothing, but we knew, deep down, that we had arrived at the top table. Beneath that feeling of sharp disappointment was one of burgeoning confidence and determination not to miss out on the next opportunity. Everything we needed for success had been brought together by Bill Nicholson, and he was making sure it all fell into place. He had made us click, he had given us belief, and not a man among us doubted that we would be in serious contention for the top prizes in 1960/61. There was a full range of skills spread throughout the team, we had pace and power in the right places, the management and coaching was of the highest order and the support was fantastic. It felt to us that White Hart Lane was rocking every time we walked out to play, with ear-splitting noise pouring down from the terraces and stands.

It often happens that a team profits from a near miss, and I think that was the case with us. If you've got everything right, then memories of the bad times can only make you stronger.

I shall never forget the words of Danny Blanchflower in the Molineux dressing room before we ran out to face Wolves after the title had all but slipped away. "We might not be champions," he told us, "but let's go out and show them we are the best side in the country." With every respect to our opponents, and to Burnley, I believe our skipper spoke the truth. I don't want to sound big-headed, even at a distance of more than half a century, but we were the team people wanted to see, we were beautiful to watch, we put bums on seats. And now our time had come.

CHAPTER ELEVEN

The main man

It takes great footballers to win the game's premier prizes, of course it does, and I would be the first to acknowledge that Tottenham Hotspur's Glory Glory Days of the early 1960s flowed from the excellence of their multi-talented and perfectly complementary midfield triumvirate of Danny Blanchflower, Dave Mackay and John White. They were the core, the beating heart of the team, inspiring everyone around them with their creativity and dynamism and we all bounced off them. But they in turn, if only they were here today, would join with me in admitting that the main man behind the serial success which came to White Hart Lane during our time together at the club was the manager, Bill Nicholson. He was the man without whom nothing would have happened, and he ran the operation from boot room to boardroom.

Essentially Bill was a quiet, modest, self-contained individual who lived up to his popular image of a dour Yorkshireman, but there was far, far more to him than that. His background was as a Spurs stalwart in Arthur Rowe's revered push-and-run side of the early 1950s. After featuring briefly as a left-back before the war, he then put in a stint at centre-half before it was realised that his ideal niche was as a defensive right-half. I never had the pleasure of seeing him play, but I'm told he was as robust as any situation required, he worked his socks off and he was endlessly efficient and reliable, all of which is easy to believe because he retained all those admirable but unshowy characteristics as our boss in later years. Bill wasn't a scintillating performer, he wasn't blessed with dazzling gifts, but he was a key

Bill Nicholson where so many people will remember him, slaving away in his office, often until late at night as he attended to every last tiny detail of any matter that might affect his beloved team.

component of Arthur Rowe's engine room, breaking up attacks to win the ball, then moving it on simply but effectively, making sure that attacks kept flowing, the sort of functional workhorse that is gold-dust to any trophy-seeking team.

People whose judgement I trusted implicitly have told me that he was extremely unlucky to collect only one England cap, though he celebrated that in untypically dramatic fashion, scoring from long distance with his first kick in international football, against Portugal at Goodison Park in 1951. From all that I learned about him at first hand when he was in charge of me, he would not have let that go to his head. Rather he would have knuckled down and worked like a Trojan for the rest of the 90 minutes, and it's that utter dedication to duty that ran through his entire being like the name of Blackpool was stamped through a stick of the old-fashioned pink seaside rock.

Bill didn't delegate anything like as much as most managers. Though he had his ebullient and often cheerfully profane former Tottenham teammate Eddie Baily, a quicksilver inside-forward in the Rowe side, to take a major role in training, and a nice man named Harry Evans – whose daughter, Sandra, married John White – as another assistant who took some of the administrative load, Bill concerned himself with every aspect of the club. And I do mean *every* aspect. Sometimes you would see him on a Tuesday afternoon closeted in deep discussion with the fellow who looked after the fabric of the ground, and we used to joke that he would make sure he was on hand if a light bulb needed changing in one of the dressing rooms.

The question was often asked: how could one man do so much for so many? Well, he was so wrapped up in the life of the club, its wellbeing and its chances of success, that he wanted to leave nothing, not the seemingly most insignificant issue, to chance. There were echoes of his approach in the Liverpool method, which underpinned the garnering of such a colossal weight of silverware for a quarter of a century from the mid-1960s onwards. The Anfield motto was, basically, that if you looked after the little details season after season, then the big ones would look after themselves. Through all those long years of European Cups, League titles and the rest, the so-called mystery of the Merseyside Reds' continued success exercised the game's finest minds. They racked their brains in vain as they sought some illusory formula that would explain Liverpool's unflagging supremacy, but in reality it was all very, very straightforward. Bill Shankly, Bob Paisley and company were not witch doctors dispensing magical incantations which kept the trophies rolling in. Rather they adhered to a down-to-earth creed and they always retained their essential humility. The simplest matters received minute attention. Liverpool in those days never allowed the small things to go wrong, and that all added up to the big things going right. Take one straw on its own, and it's easy to snap it. But put a hundred together and they are unbreakable. Meanwhile, everybody at the club kept their feet on the ground. That was the Liverpool ethos and it worked, and I would say that Bill Nick adopted a similar approach at White Hart Lane.

He gave himself body and soul to the Tottenham cause, often working ridiculously long hours. He used to live near the ground and people passing his office late in the evening would see his light still burning as he continued with his ceaseless graft. Was that a healthy approach for any balanced human being, especially a family man, which Bill certainly was? I can only refer to his well-documented dismay at the wedding of one of his daughters, when it was borne in upon him that he had never watched her grow up because of his preoccupation with football. I'm not saying he was right or wrong, I would never dream of sitting in judgement on such a man. I can only record my own

The great Bill Nicholson with the fruit of his exceptional labour, the European Cup Winners' Cup, in 1963. Ever the perfectionist, our manager enjoyed our superb display in the final against Atletico Madrid far more than our less expressive performance in our previous cup victory, over Leicester two years earlier.

impressions and reflect in wonderment, while admitting that I could never have emulated such astonishing single-mindedness.

How was such a resolute, iron-willed character to deal with on a man-to-man basis? Well, the last thing you ever wanted to hear from trainer Cecil Poynton was that Bill wanted to see you in his office. If that summons arrived, then you knew you were in trouble. I'm happy to say that never happened to me, but it did to a few of the boys and Bill always sorted them out. He was as tough as he needed to be, making sure that nobody got away with anything. Crucially, he never had favourites, which would have caused resentment and a breaking down of trust. He treated everyone the same, without fear or favour, and he rejoiced in universal respect as a result. The message to any newcomer to White Hart Lane was: "You mess with Bill Nicholson at your peril." Anyone who ignored that rule paid the price.

Bill took us on tour to South Africa in June 1963, and after a game in Durban I met up with two fellow Welshmen, Stanley Baker and Ivor Emmanuel. They were on location starring in the film *Zulu*, a brilliant piece of cinema which won a number of awards. They were real boyos, and could they drink! They asked me if I would like to go with them to the place where they were shooting the film, so I went to see Bill to ask his permission. He took one look at my compatriots and said: "No chance, if you go with those two I might never see you again." I wouldn't have crossed our manager, so sadly I passed the message on to Stan and Ivor and they muttered something along the lines of "Miserable bastard – but anyway, Cliff, what are you having to drink?" Those were the days.

A far more serious aspect of that tour was the way it brought home to all of us the essential wrongness of the apartheid policy which then prevailed in South Africa. Nelson Mendela was in captivity and there were signs around the place declaring 'No blacks allowed.' Now, I'm not very political, but I knew this was not right. However, we were on a football tour so we just got on with it. We went into a couple of townships to play against their teams and we were well received. These games, and mixing with the footballers afterwards, emphasised to us the awful situation and we learned the phrase 'M'bia Africa', meaning 'Africa for everyone.' Amen to that.

Returning to Bill Nicholson, although he was a hard man at need, I must stress that he was far more than a mere disciplinarian. He understood football deeply, perhaps thinking about it more profoundly because he had not been a brilliant player himself. To the stars the game comes easily, instinctively, and it's no coincidence that not many such richly talented performers go on to be outstanding coaches.

Undoubtedly he was influenced in a major way by Rowe, his own mentor. Certainly Arthur's trademark push-and-run style came into our own approach, but I think we added to it, gave it an extra dimension, by injecting a bit more pace, and that was at the insistence of Bill. He was thirsty for knowledge, always looking for improvements and refinements, such as the strides we took in our fitness due to weight training and a more controlled diet as inspired by that visit to the Bolshoi Ballet. That was an example of Bill being ahead of his time, and of how he was always, always thinking.

I know I'm biased – I can't deny it and wouldn't even want to – but for me the name of Nicholson should be allotted a place of honour in the very front rank of all the football managers there have ever been. It irritates me sometimes when the great bosses are being talked about and we hear of Matt Busby, Bill Shankly, Bob Paisley, Joe Mercer, Alex Ferguson and the rest, and Bill Nick doesn't even get a mention. I think that's wrong, a serious omission.

It was obvious when he got the Spurs job in the autumn of 1958 that football was in his bones, and he proved that by so quickly building the team to the gilded peak of 1960/61, then going beyond domestic boundaries to conquer Europe two years later. There were agonising frustrations after that, and circumstances beyond the realm of football that came into play, but already he had done enough to secure his own indelible niche in the folklore of the game way beyond the confines of north London.

He was the first in modern times to preside over the winning of the League and FA Cup double, the first to lift a European trophy and, as in any field, it's the trailblazer, the pioneer, who is the most important in historical terms – like Edmund Hillary being the first to scale Everest and Roger Bannister beating everyone to shatter the four-minute-mile barrier.

Of course, he didn't achieve all that without being ruthless when he had to be, but that didn't preclude him from being a decent human being. For instance, he always felt an acute responsibility to the fans, invariably describing them to us as the people who paid our wages, which they were in those far-off days before so much cash flooded into the game from the coffers of television companies. Bill held sternly to the principle that most supporters worked hard all week and deserved to be entertained by us on a Saturday. He saw it as a sacred duty to do just that, and if we fell short he told us about it in no uncertain terms.

None of which is to suggest that he didn't have a sense of humour, albeit of the exceedingly dry variety. True, he wasn't going to be cracking many jokes in the dressing room, and he didn't possess the easy way with words of, say, Bill Shankly, that master of the devastating one-liner. But he did have his moments. There was one time when I thought I had played well, and had the temerity to suggest to the boss that I deserved a pat on the back. His response was priceless: "Yes, you might get a pat on the back, but just remember, it's only two feet away from a kick up the ass!"

***

Prophetically enough, the manager seemed in a good mood, although still remorselessly professional, as we commenced our summer training in preparation for the 1960/61 campaign. We always did our legwork in the morning, while looking forward to spending time with the ball in the afternoon, which made sense because it gave us something enjoyable to anticipate. During the first week back from holiday we would be building up our stamina on the local roads, which always made me spare a thought for athletes who did the marathon in two and a half hours or less, a truly mind-blowing thought. Not that we ever attempted marathons, of course, even when we were fully fit. Our usual course was two or three miles, which was tailored to the needs of a footballer and later augmented by sprints over short distances. We had to last 90 minutes, not go for Olympic gold over 26 miles, and our preparation had to reflect that requirement. There were about 40 players, all training together when we started back, and we must have been quite a sight puffing through the tranquil community of Cheshunt. It was enough to frighten the local residents, though inevitably there were always a few locals shouting at us that we were lazy sods, telling us to lift our feet and get the work done, but nothing more than good-natured banter.

For the first three days we would only walk, admittedly pretty quickly, and Bill Nick usually accompanied us. When we started running our companion would be Eddie Baily, and when he was around no one would dream of shirking. If they did his language wouldn't just turn the air blue, it would turn it sky-blue-pink. It's fair to say that Eddie possessed a luridly imaginative turn of phrase and he wasn't shy at using it!

I wasn't bad at the running, but I was always behind Danny Blanchflower. Some people might not have suspected it because of our captain's studious, rather deliberate game, his movement around the pitch tending to be stately rather than obviously energetic, rather like an ocean-going schooner in full sail, but he was a magnificent athlete. That was very deceptive to opponents, as was the endless durability of the slim, almost wraith-like John White, who had been a top cross-country competitor in his Army days. In vivid contrast, Bobby Smith didn't cope very well with pounding the tarmac. He was a big, heavily built lad, it wasn't what he did best and he didn't like it. But he did it, and with good grace, like the rest of us buying into Bill's mantra that footballers played the way they trained. The manager dinned into us that if we trained with effort and concentration then we would play that way. But if we trained lackadaisically, without focus, then that, too, would be reflected in our matchday performances.

That summer, it's fair to say in the light of what followed over the next nine months, we must have got something right.

CHAPTER TWELVE

The history boys

For me, the most momentous season in the history of Tottenham Hotspur began in agony and, ironically enough, it was inflicted by an old teammate of mine. After our storming finish to the previous campaign, the excitement in the Spurs camp was equalled only by the burgeoning self-belief. Our confidence had not been dented by a frankly disappointing display in the public trial match in which our reserves had bounced back from 4–1 down to hold us to a 4–4 draw, and while we did not treat the challenge of Everton, our opening-day visitors to White Hart Lane, lightly, we were at full strength and more than ready to rumble.

Though I had spent most of the previous term on the left flank, Bill had switched me to the right to start 1960/61, which meant my old pal from Swansea, Terry Medwin, losing his place, while Terry Dyson came in on the left. Basically Bill Nick had what he considered to be three first-team wingers and I was fortunate in that he considered me the first choice. Fitness permitting, I always played, while he juggled around with the two Terries depending on the current needs of the team. If Medwin was flying then I'd line up on the left, but if Dyson was the man in form then I'd be wearing the number-seven shirt. I guess the situation can't have been easy for the pair of them, both lovely lads, but I never detected the slightest hint of ill feeling – we all wanted what was best for Spurs, and we all agreed that Bill was the man who knew best.

Against Everton in the first half, we played some attractive attacking football, but our moves tended to peter out when we got near goal. That was frustrating, and it was 0–0 at the break. Still, I was enjoying the game. As ever, Bill had given me a pretty free role, with license to switch wings from time to time, which we knew from experience could be a way of throwing even a tight, well-organised defence off balance. I'd had a few runs on which I'd managed to go past a couple of defenders, and early in the second period I set off again. After nipping beyond the Scottish wing-half Jimmy Gabriel, I was confronted by his superbly accomplished but ruggedly uncompromising countryman, the full-back Alex Parker.

Now, I had played alongside Alex in the Army and we had got on well, but that friendship counted for nothing on this occasion. I had managed to leave him for dead a couple of times earlier in the game, and clearly he had made up his mind that it wasn't going to happen again. To put it bluntly, he did me big time! I slipped the ball inside to John White and made to dart outside Alex, looking to find space for one of John's inch-perfect return passes which would have set me free for a run on goal. But just as I reached the Everton man, he turned his shoulder and hit me sideways with a tackle like a runaway bulldozer. In the instant I went down I thought I was in the worst sort of trouble. I thought I had broken my ankle. It flashed across my mind that it was the Peter Baker incident all over again, with the difference that Parker had hit me deliberately. I said to him afterwards: "Alex, I thought we were mates." He came back with a grim smile and the eye-opening rejoinder: "Nay laddie, not today."

I don't know how I'd have felt about that if I had suffered another fracture, but it turned out that I had had a miraculous escape. I was badly bruised, with horribly wrenched ligaments, which left me extremely sore and out of action for half a dozen games, but it was only a painful punctuation in my season, not the end of it.

In those daft days before the use of substitutes was permitted, I didn't even leave the pitch, but limped on to the final whistle as a passenger, hoping that I might be of nuisance value to my team. As it turned out, I had nothing to do with the two late goals which gave us victory. Bobby Smith was fouled in the box, but even as he yelled for a penalty Les Allen put the ball in the net, then Smithy stooped to his knees to head home a typically exquisite chip from John White. A winning start, then, but I was disgruntled to find myself on the treatment table so early in the season. Not that I ever feared

A bowler-hatted Bill Nicholson looking as happy as I've ever seen him, clutching a bottle of bubbly in the White Hart Lane dressing room in September 1960. We had just beaten Aston Villa 6–2 to set up a new League record of ten straight victories at the start of a season. Standing, left to right: Bobby Smith, Terry Dyson, myself, John White, Bill Brown, Maurice Norman, Ron Henry and vice-chairman Fred Wale. Sitting are Dave Mackay, Danny Blanchflower and Peter Baker, with Les Allen crouching at the front.

for my place. Though Terry Medwin, who stepped up to replace me, could be relied upon to do a terrific job, I had come off a tremendous season, I was confident in my ability and I felt completely established in the side.

Mind, I can't put my hand on my heart and say that I was missed particularly in those six games which I had to watch from the sidelines. All of them were won, starting with a 3–1 defeat of Blackpool at Bloomfield Road to which Terry D contributed two goals and Terry M chipped in with the other.

Big Bobby Smith netted eight times in three games spread over a week, a devastating run which included the 4–1 drubbing of Manchester United at White Hart Lane, and during that sequence he became the highest scorer in the club's history, beating the record of 138 strikes set by George Hunt in the 1930s. Given that Bob was still only 27 and right in the middle of his fearsome pomp that was an incredibly encouraging statistic for all who marched beneath the banner of the Spurs cockerel.

I had set my sights on being fit again for the first north London derby of the campaign, at Highbury in September, but my ankle wasn't quite ready and, yet again, the boys managed brilliantly without me, beating Arsenal 3–2 to rack up our seventh successive victory, the best-ever start by any First Division club. I couldn't have complained if Bill Nick had opted not to change a winning team, but he decided to bring me back for the midweek visit of Bolton, hardly the side you would choose to convalesce against, what with 'Nurse' Banks and 'Nurse' Hartle on your case. Happily, both my ankle and our 100 per cent record emerged unscathed from the encounter, which we won 3–2 with two more goals from Bobby and a Blanchflower penalty. The skipper now had my spot-kick job for keeps, doing the business calmly and expertly for virtually the rest of his career, before Jimmy Greaves took over a few years down the line – and he wasn't too shabby from 12 yards, either!

As the autumn wore on, we proved unstoppable, chalking up 11 straight wins with a 4–0 tanning of Wolves at Molineux which prompted their hugely demanding manager, Stan Cullis, to describe us as the greatest team he'd ever seen, and moved one reporter to trumpet: "Send for Real Madrid, Barcelona, Juventus, the lot. Let's get a team here capable of giving some idea of how good these super Spurs really are."

In the short term, Manchester City brought the debate down to earth by holding us to a 1–1 draw at the Lane in our 12th game. But that did nothing to burst our bubble. We were loving our football and each other's company, everybody trusted everybody else, and over it all Bill Nicholson presided so wisely, with such impeccable judgement. It was wonderful to know that, all over the country, gates were being closed on full houses. We were the entertainers, the people everybody wanted to see, and that felt very, very good.

Our reaction to dropping that point against City was a dominant performance to win 4–0 at Nottingham Forest, an effort to which I contributed a couple of goals. Then we showed another side to our collective character at Newcastle, where we fell behind three times before Bobby Smith popped up with the winner only four minutes from the final whistle.

Inevitably enough, round about now came fanciful whispers that we were invincible, that we were good enough to go through the whole season without being beaten, and that we could win the fabled double of League championship and FA Cup. At that stage nobody at White Hart Lane had raised that possibility. Bill Nick was a great one for keeping everybody's feet on the ground, and his word was law. Throughout that whole astonishing season, the manager didn't change one iota from his normal approach. He didn't get more expansive and he didn't make predictions, he just fulfilled the time-honoured cliché of taking each game as it came.

Certainly that was the plan as we arrived at Hillsborough to face Sheffield Wednesday on 12 November, our record reading: played 16, won 15, drawn one, lost none. That was phenomenal, but it shouldn't be forgotten that Wednesday weren't exactly suffering a bad run, either, their record standing at: played 15, won ten, drawn four, lost one. They were second in the League table and, by my reckoning, they were the hardest of all our opponents to beat that season. Managed by the immensely shrewd and tough Harry Catterick, who would go on to guide Everton to several major trophies in the years ahead, they were stacked with excellent footballers and not given to throwing in the towel when the going became difficult.

Their man I recall most vividly was the little red-haired wing-half Tony Kay. He was a yard-dog, a ratter, almost impossible to shake off and horrible to play against. He went on to earn an England call-up and Catterick took him to Goodison Park, but he was guilty of pushing the self-destruct button when he accepted a bribe to influence the result of a match, being banned for life as a result. Though it didn't come out until his career was really taking off with the Merseysiders, the incident happened while he was at Wednesday, and it also brought down his Hillsborough teammate, the England centre-half Peter Swan, who was another who faced us as we ran out for that crucial clash on that late autumn afternoon in Sheffield.

Also in their ranks was that terrific goal-scoring inside-forward Johnny Fantham, a decidedly underrated performer, and they boasted a formidably rugged, physically challenging defence, in which Swan and full-back Don Megson stand out in my memory. Then there was the England goalkeeper, Ron Springett, who had proved himself one of the best net-minders in the land, though he never liked playing against Spurs because he knew his international teammate, Bobby Smith, would be charging at him at every possible opportunity. It was a characteristic of Bobby's game, and a legitimate one as he saw it, that he tested out the opposing keeper early in every match, just to see how he coped with the physical stuff. Ron was very agile, and he was brave, too, but he wasn't the biggest and it must have been daunting to see Big Bob bearing down at him at full pelt, like Attila the Hun after a bad day at the office.

However, this turned out to be the Yorkshiremen's day. For once John White was outshone by another creative inside-forward, his fellow Scot

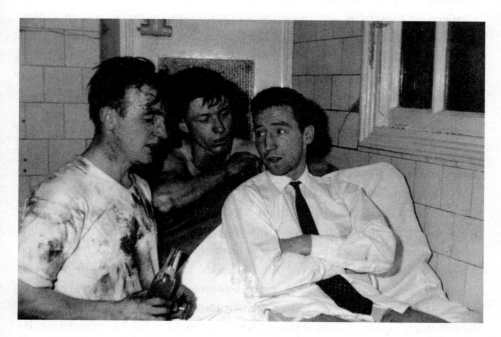

Sympathy from Terry Dyson (left) and John White after I suffered a nasty knee injury which cost me several games midway through 1960/61, including our FA Cup third-round clash with Charlton Athletic.

Bobby Craig, and when winger Billy Griffin put Wednesday in front after 40 minutes it was no more than they deserved. Our giant centre-half Maurice Norman equalised almost immediately with a trademark towering header, but Fantham poached the winner in the second half and we were invincible no more. Still, we weren't too badly off, remaining five points clear of Catterick's men, although we had played one game more.

Some of my teammates have ventured the opinion that the defeat was actually welcome in that it released us from the pressure of maintaining an unbeaten record. There were reports of hilarity and an almost celebratory sing-song on the bus afterwards, but personally I felt no pressure through remaining undefeated for so long and I'd say any singing was no more than the usual expression of our irrepressible high spirits, which never flagged. Week in and week out, we were just enjoying ourselves so much, playing such good stuff on a regular basis that we didn't worry about failure. We just relished getting out on to that grass and performing.

Indeed, if there was any pressure around the championship race at that time, then I reckon it was felt by Wednesday rather than us. They had not lost until their 13th game, at Wolverhampton, and after sending us on our way pointless they had still tasted defeat only once. But then, out of a clear blue sky, they lost their next three and won only one in a sequence of seven, thus handing us back any initiative we might have forfeited.

That was an invitation we didn't spurn. A 6–0 home victory over Birmingham City marked the start of an eight-match unbeaten First Division run, which did not end until we went down 2–0 at Old Trafford midway through January.

When we ran out to face Birmingham it was as though we had to make a statement, to show that the setback against Wednesday was not going to throw us out of our stride, and within little more than a quarter of an hour we were three up. That was a truly joyous sequence of play which expressed all the freedom, flair and power that had come to characterise our play, and all three goals – by John White, Terry Dyson and myself – were absolutely leathered into the Blues' net. Just a word here for the young man between Birmingham's posts, Colin Withers, who was making his League debut. He was in no way to blame for the hammering handed out to his side – indeed, he could be proud of a series of acrobatic saves and courageous plunges at

It might be a contrived image, but it's an engaging one of the League and FA Cup double-winners at White Hart Lane. Left to right: Bill Brown, Peter Baker, Ron Henry, Danny Blanchflower, Maurice Norman, Dave Mackay, myself, John White, Bobby Smith, Les Allen and Terry Dyson.

the feet of our forwards which limited the final score to six. Had Colin not been on his mettle the final scoreline could have been embarrassing, but he showed the quality that shone throughout a terrific career which was to peak with City's local rivals, Aston Villa, later in the decade.

We carried our scintillating form into the next match and a half, which took in a 3–1 win over West Bromwich Albion at the Hawthorns and then the first 45 minutes of what turned out to be a nerve-janglingly dramatic encounter with the reigning champions, Burnley, on a cloying, energy-sapping quagmire at White Hart Lane. Harry Potts' team had slipped to fifth place in the table, 11 points behind us and with a whole range of mountains to climb if they were going to get back into the title reckoning, but were they bothered? Not a bit, if the opening exchanges of a remarkable game were anything to go by.

They came at us like tigers, playing beautiful, precise football, pinning us back and raining shots on Bill Brown's goal. But they didn't break through and around midway through the half we thought we had broken their hearts with a devastating spell of three goals in as many minutes, the first through a diving header by Maurice Norman, then I managed to tuck away a couple of chances from inside the box. Thus when Dave Mackay bowed cheekily to the crowd after scoring the fourth after 36 minutes, the outcome seemed to be a formality.

But Burnley hadn't been first over the line in 1959/60 without displaying rare fighting spirit to go with their undoubted all-round quality and within two minutes John Connelly had pulled a goal back.

Still, as we trooped into the dressing room at the interval 4–1 to the good, alarm bells were not exactly ringing and we remained supremely confident. Straight after the restart I might have completed my hat-trick, only to be foiled by a fabulous save by their Scottish keeper Adam Blacklaw, and the Clarets seemed to take heart from that moment of brilliant defiance. They continued to play their football, skating over the mud, until a couple of mis-kicks on the slippery surface, first by Ron Henry and then by Big Maurice, enabled Jimmy Robson and Ray Pointer to make it 4–3.

Now, from seemingly coasting to a comfortable victory, we had a neck-or-nothing battle on our hands and, to be fair to us, we didn't lie down. Instead we poured forward and practically laid siege to the Burnley goal, only to be undone by a classic breakaway. My opposite number Connelly, who could run like a cheetah, sprinted out of defence and exchanged passes with Robson before charging on to whack the ball past Bill Brown for a stunning equaliser. After that we huffed and puffed, and Les Allen hit their post with a shot, but if I'm totally honest, they deserved their point for such an epic fightback.

Nearly all the 58,000-plus supporters who had abandoned their firesides to brave the miserable elements had been desperate for Spurs to win, but they honoured Burnley's courage and skill as all 22 players were applauded off at the end. That might be seen as an uplifting occurrence, and so it was in a way, but I can assure you that all was not sweetness and light when we returned to the dressing room. Bill Nicholson was not a man to rant and rave as a rule, but he did not hide his feelings at our profligacy in letting a four-goal advantage over one of our main rivals slip away. He was as close to incandescent as I ever saw him, and his post-match comment to waiting journalists, though characteristically brief and understated, was dripping with meaning. "We scored all eight goals and we only drew," he growled. Enough said.

If we needed a well-judged boot up the backside for dropping that point, it certainly worked. Now we were at the halfway stage of the campaign, which we marked with one of those 1–0 wins which any champion team needs to record. This was our first of the season and it came at Deepdale, where Preston were sorely missing their recently retired talisman, Tom Finney, and were destined for relegation. It wasn't one of our best displays, but we were efficient and hard-working, and that was enough. That said, we did have one outstanding performer that day – John White, who contributed the only goal. He was everywhere, making himself available, prompting, filling in, passing like a dream.

John maintained this form in the four consecutive victories which followed – including victories over West Ham on Christmas Eve and Boxing Day which gave us the merriest of yuletides, apart from the twisted knee I suffered in the second game which kept me out for three weeks – and the Scot's combination in the middle of the park with Blanchflower and Mackay was sumptuous to watch. In modern times I have been reminded of the dazzling, one-touch football served up on a regular basis by our influential trio whenever I have seen the famous three at Barcelona, Iniesta, Xavi and Messi. Mind, I'd say the ball went forward a bit quicker with us than it did with Pep Guardiola's team, but it would be hard to find fault with such masterful footballers. Still, the English Premier League is a vastly different proposition to the Spanish competition, and it will be fascinating to see how Pep fares in our country with Manchester City.

Back in January 1961, fortified by a ten-point lead over second-placed Wolves – which seemed like an enormous chasm at the time, when only two points were awarded for a win – we turned our attention to the FA Cup, starting with a seemingly undemanding home tie against Charlton Athletic of the Second Division. As it turned out, the Addicks put up a storming show, losing only by the odd goal in five and putting Spurs under severe pressure for much of the second half.

My knee problem had sidelined me for that game, and I continued to hold a watching brief when we travelled north to Old Trafford later that month.

Manchester United were still recovering from the tragic accident at Munich, but they were on tremendous form on this occasion, and their hero – neither for the first nor the last time – was my much-admired adversary, the Irish goalkeeper Harry Gregg. United were already a goal up through Nobby Stiles when Harry was forced to leave the pitch with a shoulder injury shortly before half-time, with centre-forward Alex Dawson taking over between the posts. But if we thought we'd seen the last of the fiery Ulsterman, who had the deserved reputation of being too brave for his own good at times, then we had another think coming.

Back out he marched for the second half with his shoulder heavily strapped and took up position at centre-forward. Most people in his situation would have

I count my blessings whenever I recall the marvellous men I played alongside for Spurs, none more so than Danny Blanchflower (centre) and John White (left), here with me at an awards ceremony at the Café Royal in the wake of our League and FA Cup double.

been happy to offer nuisance value, perhaps attempting to distract opponents while making little concrete contribution, but Harry wasn't cut out for such a passive role. So I shouldn't have been surprised, but couldn't help my jaw dropping along with everybody else's, when he back-heeled the ball cheekily to set up the goal for Mark Pearson that sealed United's 2–0 victory. What a character and what a warrior! They don't make 'em like Harry Gregg any more.

I had been champing at the bit for a return to action, fearing that I would miss the north London derby, but I was back in time to face Arsenal at the Lane. We beat them 4–2, thanks in massive measure to the BMW factor – that's Blanchflower, Mackay and White – with all three at their superlative best.

Meanwhile our draw for the fourth round of the FA Cup featured a perverse element of serendipity, pairing us once more with Crewe, who had shipped 13 goals against us a year earlier. Could the football fates possibly be conspiring to serve up the ultimate giant-killing act, thus giving the Alex the most unlikely revenge? It was a romantic notion in keeping with the traditions of the world's oldest professional competition, but we needn't have worried as we eased past Jimmy McGuigan's courageous side, winning 5–1 this time.

As we were still romping away at the head of the First Division table, our knockout progress sparked inevitable press speculation about the elusive League and FA Cup double, and while Bill Nick refused to countenance any discussion on the subject, never uttering a syllable that would throw pressure on to his players, his lieutenant, Danny Blanchflower, was increasingly convinced we could do it. Sensibly, he didn't make a public song and dance about it, and the rest of us just got on with our jobs.

Thus far we had sailed along pretty merrily, with barely a serious injury to hinder our progress – I was the only regular first-teamer to be absent for any appreciable length of time – and we had not lost at home all season.

That proud record came to an end in February when Leicester City came calling. Their boss, Matt Gillies, had assembled a hugely efficient side, supremely well organised and endlessly hard-working, and they were willing to scrap it out with anyone. Somehow we never really got going in the game, twice equalising but never managing to impose ourselves as we had in most matches that term, and their captain, Jimmy Walsh, poached what proved to be the winner about 25 minutes from the end.

One of the newspapers had a giggle by proclaiming "Spurs lose again!", then that night a Tottenham story broke that dominated many front pages, never mind the back. One of the most popular television programmes of the time was *This Is Your Life*, in which the Irish host, Eamonn Andrews, would chat to a famous person in between bringing on to the stage a succession of friends, family members and various celebrities relevant to the subject of the show. Having decided to honour Danny, the BBC had flown in folk from Ireland and even the United States, as well as from all over England. It really was a massive deal.

So, with the players smarting from defeat but looking forward to an entertaining evening, including an appearance as the show was recorded, all that remained was for Eamonn to surprise our skipper with the words: "Danny Blanchflower, This Is Your Life!" The only problem was, Danny was having none of it. He said something like "Oh no, it's not" or words to that effect and quickly departed from the Television Centre. Imagine the confusion that reigned. People had been rounded up from all over at great expense, there was an expectant studio audience and now the intended star of the show had walked out! The producer went on stage and announced that for the first time in the history of the programme, somebody had refused to co-operate. Most people would have been hugely flattered by the attention but Danny was always a law unto himself, an incredibly strong-minded character who went his own way.

Of course, any such examination of anyone's life was bound to involve a certain amount of intrusion, although the programme was invariably positive towards its subject. But Danny was always jealous of his privacy, certain aspects of his life might be described as colourful, and we could only assume that he didn't want it raked over in public. Not that he ever explained himself, that wasn't his way, but it did cause much hilarity among his teammates. Bill Nicholson, though, was less amused. "Typical Blanchflower" was how he put it.

But for all the commotion it caused, the incident had no discernible effect on his football, which continued to be inspirational. However, after disposing of Aston Villa and Sunderland, after a replay, to reach the last four of the FA Cup, the Tottenham stutter which had begun with the loss at Old Trafford continued worryingly. There was a spell in February and

March encompassing seven League games, of which three were lost, at home to Leicester and Newcastle and away to Cardiff, and two were drawn, at home to Wolves and at Fulham, with only narrow victories against Aston Villa and Manchester City to keep the championship pot boiling.

Of those disappointments, perhaps the sharpest for me was the 3–2 reverse at Ninian Park. It was a game that meant so much to me, firstly because it was the only game of the campaign to be played in Wales, and secondly because Cardiff were a team I was always desperate to beat, due to their keen local rivalry with my old club, Swansea.

The game had been put back until the evening because of the rugby international at the Arms Park in which Wales had beaten Ireland 9–0. So with the pubs full to capacity with celebrating Welshmen, and thousands of Irishmen drowning their sorrows, the city was really hopping by the time we kicked off. As for the scene after the final whistle, with the Bluebirds having shot the Tottenham cockerel out of the sky, no mere words of mine could do it justice.

It wasn't that we performed badly, rather that our hosts, who were in the bottom half of the table, truly excelled themselves. We started brightly with an early goal by Terry Dyson, only to be pegged back almost immediately by the left winger Derek Hogg. Still, when Les Allen had fired us back in front before the interval, I was confident that we'd be heading back to the capital with two points. But that hopeful notion was shattered comprehensively in a devastating 60-second spell early in the second period. First the Cardiff outside-right Brian Walsh, who had broken through with Arsenal but failed to carve himself a long-term niche at Highbury, cut in from his touchline to level the scores with a cracking shot, just the sort of goal I loved to score, and then my Welsh international teammate Derek Tapscott, another former Gunner, nipped in to put City in front.

Cue total bedlam as the old stadium, packed to the rafters with 47,000 supporters, easily Cardiff's biggest gate of the season, rocked for the next 40 minutes and we did our damnedest to find an equaliser. We couldn't do it, and in the end I could only congratulate our conquerors, who had defended heroically, on a job extremely well done.

It was a painful blow, but we remained the bookies' tip to lift the League title and, more magical still, to become the first team in the 20th century

– since Aston Villa in 1897, in fact – to capture the League and FA Cup double. Standing resolutely in our way were our old rivals, Burnley, whom we faced, ironically enough, at Villa Park. A glance at the record books will tell you that we beat them 3–0, which suggests a comfortable afternoon in the Midlands, but as so often is the case, the bare statistics are monstrously misleading.

The memory of the Clarets' courageous comeback from 4–0 down to claim a point back in December was still vivid in our minds, as was the thought that they would want revenge against a side who were still on course to succeed them as champions. To make no bones about it, Burnley played the better football on the day and could feel they deserved to win, but we got the breaks, and the goals.

After they had dominated for half an hour, and we had relied heavily on the strength of our defence and the cool leadership of Blanchflower, their skipper Jimmy Adamson made a rare slip which allowed Bobby Smith to open the scoring. The luck continued to run against them as a seemingly good goal by Jimmy Robson was disallowed for a supposed foul, a confident penalty shout was rejected and a succession of shots were blocked on the goal-line. Then, as so often happens when a team is constantly frustrated, they were hit on the break by the excellent Bobby Smith, who confirmed his emergence from a period of indifferent form by doubling our lead with a sweet volley. Still Burnley tried to push on, but we were able to soak up the pressure and I rendered the final tally even harsher by adding our third near the end. I'm the first to admit that it wasn't one of our best displays, but I do believe that luck levels itself out over the course of a season, and we were only too happy that fortune favoured us that day.

After running rampant and playing beautifully for so long, I guess it was inevitable that Spurs should experience a slight falter at some point, which gave a few pessimists the chance to point out that we had slipped in similar fashion when well placed in the previous title race. Were we afraid that history might repeat itself, and that we might let the prize slide away at the death? Honestly, no, that never entered our minds for one moment. It just never occurred to us. Without being swollen-headed, we knew we were an exceptional team, that we could beat anybody, and that if we suffered a disappointing spell then we would come out of it. It's funny how form can evaporate at times without any apparent reason, but if the genuine class is there then it always comes back.

I suppose one factor was that everybody was out to shoot Spurs down because we had become the number-one attraction. But we just had to live with that and when we did turn the corner, as we knew we would, then we were straight back into our successful stride. Obviously Bill Nick did have a word with us about the need to keep up our work-rate as well as our spirits. Our method demanded constant effort to support the man on the ball, and it was essential to our rhythm that the flowing movement was maintained. As ever, we took the boss's words of wisdom on board, but there was never the slightest sense of panic or dismay, and that despite the fact that Sheffield Wednesday, who just kept on winning, were only three points behind us with eight games to play as Easter loomed.

To our utmost relief, a decisive upturn in our League fortunes arrived over the holiday period and I was overjoyed to make a significant contribution – about time, too, because I hadn't been on the scoresheet in a First Division game since the 4–4 against Burnley way back in early December. Our Good Friday opponents were Chelsea at White Hart Lane and I'd be lying if I didn't admit there were a few nerves beforehand, owing to our recent struggles. Tension mounted among more than 65,000 fans as the first half ended goalless, although we weren't over-anxious as we had totally dominated proceedings throughout the first 45 minutes.

Eventually, early in the second period, our luck changed as one of the Chelsea defenders played a stray pass into my path and all I had to do was shepherd the ball into the empty net. Soon I added a second goal on the way to one of the most one-sided 4–2 wins I can ever recall, the visitors' two late hits giving a misleading gloss to the scoreline from their point of view.

Now the mood in our camp had been transformed, the confident (but never over-confident) swagger of autumn came flooding back and, only 24 hours later, our soon-to-be demoted visitors, Preston, felt the full force of our attacking power as we swept them aside 5–0. This time my input was a hat-trick which included two goals that have lingered in my memory. For the first – the team's 100th of the season, no less – I had to sidestep several fierce challenges before shooting in from somewhere near the penalty spot, and for the second I was able to execute a perfect overhead kick, the sort which looks fabulous when it comes off but could just as easily finish up in Row Z.

After that there was just time to attend the wedding of centre-half Maurice Norman in the pretty little church in the Hertfordshire village of Northaw before heading off to Stamford Bridge for the Easter Monday return with Chelsea. This time Jimmy Greaves and company put up much stiffer resistance and we had to come from behind to win 3–2 thanks to a brave header late in the game from – who else on this of all weekends? – Big Maurice.

Back in gear, back in form, back in control, we resisted a valiant fightback at Birmingham, where we surged into a three-goal lead in half an hour before conceding twice, to win 3–2, and that gave us the ideal opportunity to lift the championship in style by beating our principal challengers, Sheffield Wednesday, in front of our own supporters.

More than 61,000 of them crammed into the Lane that night, some of them having queued outside the ground since early morning. Journalists had arrived from all over the world, so many of them that with the *Daily Mirror's* place in the press box having gone to its chief football reporter Bill Holden, my cousin Ken, Holden's colleague on the red-top and himself a marvellous writer, could not be squeezed in. Luckily I was able to help, telling Ken that if he turned up in good time I could find him a spot on the track alongside the touchline. Needless to say, he was there long before kick-off, and was close enough to the action to exchange a few breathless words with Dave Mackay when our Scottish wing-half was taking a throw-in.

It was never going to be an easy game, nor a pretty one, and so it proved. Harry Catterick's Wednesday, five points behind us with four games to play, were a granite-hard and well-balanced side with bags of ability and limitless reserves of character. They had not been beaten in 19 League games – practically half a season – and this was their last stand. They simply had to win to keep alive their hopes of becoming champions. At the very least they had no intention now of rolling over on their bellies for the southern title favourites. And nor did they, sending butterflies fluttering around the Lane's packed stands and terraces by taking the lead after half an hour when their mountainous left-back Don Megson drilled a free-kick into our defensive wall, then

Bobby Smith (second left) steers the ball past his England colleague, goal-keeper Ron Springett, to set Spurs on their way to clinching the title against their closest rivals, Sheffield Wednesday, at White Hart Lane in April 1961. We won 2–1, with Les Allen contributing the winner.

rammed the rebound unstoppably past Bill Brown. We might even have gone two down around the 40-minute mark when their big centre-forward Keith Ellis nodded firmly against the frame of our goal. But even though we were based in the south we were anything but softies, and in the twinkling of an eye we stood the game on its head.

On 42 minutes – according to newspaper reports, I wasn't actually carrying a stopwatch! – little Terry Dyson somehow climbed above the hulking Megson to nod a long clearance from Peter Baker down to Bobby Smith, and in that moment our bustling number nine did a fair imitation of Pele in the 1958 World Cup final. First he flicked the ball over one of his England teammates, centre-half Peter Swan, then ran round behind him before thrashing the ball past another, keeper Ron Springett, to bring the scores level.

Next, as joyous Spurs supporters were still bouncing up and down in unrestrained glee, Danny Blanchflower floated a free-kick towards the Wednesday box, Maurice Norman headed it down to Les Allen and our oft-underrated inside-left grabbed the most important goal of his life with a superlative shoulder-high volley from some 15 yards.

I was limping badly at the time, the result of a vigorous tackle that was entirely in keeping with the game as a whole and which required two stitches during the interval, but the pain dissolved as I joined in the riotous cavorting celebrations of my teammates. The injury would keep me out of Wales' World Cup qualifier against Spain at Ninian Park two days later, and I would miss Spurs' next two games, at Burnley and at home to Nottingham Forest, but that was never going to bother me on such an occasion.

Though there were still 45 minutes to play, there never seemed the remotest possibility that we would slacken our grip on the prize – after all, we only needed a draw – and, indeed, there had been no more goals when the referee blew the final whistle to make it official: Tottenham Hotspur were champions of England.

Not surprisingly in an era when crowd control was nowhere near as rigorous as it is today, the pitch was invaded by about 5,000 fans while many thousands more remained in the stadium to join in the incessant chant which roared into the night sky: "We want Danny, we want Danny." Our skipper wasn't an explosive, spectacular type of performer, but our supporters knew their football and they understood his vast influence, the way he controlled the pace and rhythm of our game, slowing it down and speeding it up at need, so often delivering the crucial pass, all the while motivating and inspiring the rest of us. Though I will never tire of pointing out that Bill Nick was the main man in our great enterprise, certainly Danny was the equivalent of a manager on the pitch, and now he attracted universal admiration in our hour of triumph.

Having reached the sanctuary of the dressing room with some difficulty, and with the champagne uncorked and ready for consumption, there might have been one or two among us in favour of remaining indoors, but there was absolutely no denying that passionate public. So after listening to about ten minutes of deafening entreaty, we bowed to the inevitable and trooped to the directors' box behind the man of the moment, our white shirts smeared with mud and many of us clutching bath towels, which were tossed into the multitude.

As for Bill Nicholson, he remained, as ever, the perfectionist. We had three

Soapy, steamy, ecstatic, Spurs celebrate in the communal bath at White Hart Lane after being crowned League champions in the spring of 1961. Left to right: Les Allen, myself (with soap in my eyes, by the look of it), John White, Dave Mackay, Peter Baker, Terry Dyson, Bill Brown, Ron Henry and Bobby Smith. Missing from the muddy water, or perhaps even below the surface, are Maurice Norman and skipper Danny Blanchflower.

games to play and needed only three points to beat Arsenal's record total of 66 for a First Division season. Now the trophy was in the bag, Bill wanted desperately to pass that mark, but he was to be disappointed. Perhaps inevitably after the climax of such a momentous campaign, the intensity of our performance dropped a tad, and we lost 4–2 at Burnley. A 1–0 win over Forest equalled the Gunners' record, so we needed only a draw in our last game, at home to West Bromwich Albion, to pass it. There was no silverware at stake any more, yet in excess of 52,000 people turned up to watch us make history. Though they would have enjoyed the general air of celebration, they didn't shell out their hard-earned entrance money just to see us presented with the trophy and our medals by League president Joe Richards. They wanted to see us take something off the Arsenal, but we couldn't quite achieve that for them, slipping to a 2–1 defeat. But that wasn't quite the end of our season...

He came from nowhere, like an eagle

Harry Gregg remembers . . .

Cliff Jones... aaah, now he was a footballer, a real flying machine, exceptionally quick and one of the best I've ever seen in his position – but you did have to keep your eyes open when you were facing the little bugger!

You see, Spurs had Dave Mackay, who was a long-throw expert. Now Jonesy wasn't big and he would hide himself among your defenders when Dave launched the ball, but you forgot about him at your peril. Suddenly he would come from nowhere, like an eagle, and the ball would be in your net before you had time to do anything about it. Cliff was so courageous. It's one thing to be brave on the ground, where it's a case of two men in boots facing off, but it's quite another in the air, where you can quite easily get your head taken off if you get it wrong. Cliffy didn't worry about that, he came at you anyway, and his timing was just magnificent.

Bill Nicholson's Spurs were a truly great side and I feel lucky to have known such men. I had nothing but respect for them. It was a fine time to be playing the game, when it was all about ability and manliness. Cliffy was a great example of that, while another I would tip my hat to was Bobby Smith, the hardest and strongest centre-forward I ever came up against. He feared nobody and he met you head on, there were no back doors for him. He was also a wonderful all-round footballer, I'd say one of the most underrated in the history of the game.

As for that day at Old Trafford when I dislocated my shoulder against Spurs, I remember it perfectly. I was in the medical room, on the floor.

Our physio took his shoes off and tried to push the shoulder back in, but he couldn't manage it so he went looking for help. There was a grounds-man there and I asked him to lend a hand, but in the end I was attempting a complicated manoeuvre with a coathook myself, trying to put my jersey back on.

Eventually I was strapped up and ran out on to the pitch to play on as emergency centre-forward. Maurice Norman, a lovely man and the fellow who would now be marking me, thought I was mad. "H, what on earth are you doing?" he asked me.

Later Danny Blanchflower, my captain in the Northern Ireland team, spoke about being tackled by a man with one arm. Danny always loved Manchester United because of their adventurous football in the years before the Munich air crash, through he would say we had one or two hooligans – and that day he reckoned I was the biggest hooligan of the lot!

It was always a pleasure to play against Cliffy, though, going right back to the days when we faced each other in games between Swansea and Doncaster. But I will take issue with him on one point. I just can't think what he was talking about, saying that I used to charge around my box like a man possessed. I always saw myself as such a quiet and charming individual...

CHAPTER THIRTEEN

Rainbow's end

The fiercely coveted League and FA Cup double had become so elusive that by the start of the decade it had assumed almost mythical proportions. For teams which got close, something always went wrong. There was talk of a jinx and it became fashionable to declare that the winning of both trophies in the same season was impossible in the modern game.

But in the first week of May 1961, with the League title already tucked firmly under our belts, Tottenham Hotspur were not buying into that. Danny Blanchflower had been telling us for weeks that we could do the double, and while Bill Nicholson was, by nature, far less prone to expansive statements, we all knew he was quietly confident, too.

And why not? It would have been false modesty to pretend that we weren't the best side in the country, and while we didn't underestimate our doughty opponents, Leicester City, for a split second – after all, they had beaten us at White Hart Lane in February, though we had taken the points at Filbert Street back in September – it was a fact that they had finished in sixth place in the table, no fewer than 21 points behind us. That was the equivalent of ten wins and a draw in those days, when only two points were awarded for a victory, so in terms of recent achievement there was plainly no comparison. Of course, the FA Cup could make nonsense of such calculations, as it had proved all too often in the past when favourites had been overturned. That was part of its timeless appeal, but it also added to the challenge. And we were always up for a challenge.

In the week before the game, our quest for the double seemed to have become a national obsession, and the demand for tickets – seemingly from half the population of Wales, loads of them not even casual acquaintances – was unrelenting. I was unable to meet most of the requests because I come from such a large family and wanted as many of the Jones clan as possible to see me in action at Wembley on what I hoped would be the best day of my career.

Bill Nick, as level-headed as ever, ensured that outside distractions were kept to a minimum as we contemplated the task ahead, which suddenly seemed just a wee bit less forbidding when Leicester dropped the midweek bombshell that their tough and talented spearhead, my Wales teammate Ken Leek, who had scored in every round of the competition so far, was to be replaced by the inexperienced Scottish rookie Hugh McIlmoyle. It was a development that shocked the football world as Ken was recognised as the Foxes' most likely match-winner. You might say it was the equivalent of Spurs axing our own leading scorer, Bobby Smith. Certainly it was a huge call by Matt Gillies, who maintained that it was for purely football reasons, but few people accepted that explanation at face value. I never found out the answer to the mystery, though I was well aware that Ken could be a bit of a lad, perhaps something of a handful to manage. If anything untoward had gone on, Gillies, by refusing to bend just because it was the FA Cup final, had demonstrated similarly strong principles to those of Bill Nicholson, who would always do the right thing no matter what the circumstances.

Most Leicester supporters were dismayed by Leek's omission, but the decision had made at least one man hugely happy and relieved. Ken was a very awkward customer to mark and our big stopper, Maurice Norman, hated playing against him. Now Maurice was a magnificent centre-half, one of the finest I've seen, but if anything occurred before a game to introduce an element of negativity to his mind, he was not always at his best. When our number five heard the news, a huge smile appeared on his face and that feel-good factor remained with him throughout the build-up, helping no end by removing any hint of tension. It wasn't that he was underrating young McIlmoyle, a skilful, thoughtful operator who played pretty well at Wembley and went on to enjoy a worthy career, but he didn't come close to upsetting Maurice in the way that Leek might have done.

It's a wonderful life!

After we arrived beneath the famous Twin Towers for a stroll on the stadium's lush turf, John White and I found ourselves in the goalmouth near the entrance to the long tunnel which led to the dressing rooms. On fetching up seven or eight yards from the posts John, my best mate in the team and an engaging character who loved a laugh, turned to me with a wide grin and announced: "If I get the ball right here tomorrow I shall move forward – like this – and swing my right leg – like this – and, hey presto, the ball will be in the back of that net. Nothing to it!" That sounded like a tremendous scenario to me but I was a tad sceptical, telling him: "More than likely you'll hit it out of the ground." As it turned out, one of us was right and one of us was wrong, as we shall see.

That evening we all relaxed at a showing of the splendid Gregory Peck film *The Guns Of Navarone* at a cinema in Leicester Square, which set us up for a much-needed good night's sleep. The next morning we enjoyed a session on our hotel's putting green followed by a steak lunch before watching a television film of how Leicester and ourselves had reached Wembley. Undoubtedly the central figure in the Leicester footage was Ken Leek, which appeared to amuse Maurice Norman no end.

It was a grey, blustery afternoon at Wembley with rain in the offing, which might have contributed to my slight disappointment with the atmosphere. Though the fans of both clubs were in full voice, the Spurs contingent desperate to acclaim a momentous piece of football history, the Leicester brigade hoping to hail their club's first top-level honour, the sizeable balance of the 100,000 crowd appeared to be treating it more as a social event than a dramatic sporting showdown.

It seemed to me that we started the game in correspondingly muted fashion, as if we needed time to settle, until an incident after about eight minutes proved that I was a more reliable prophet than my pal White. Dave Mackay set up Terry Dyson for a cross which found John on precisely the same spot of turf where we had been standing the previous afternoon when he told me how he was going to burst the net. It was a terrific opportunity and it seemed uncanny in view of our jokey exchange but, sadly for us, it was my prediction which came true as he blazed the ball high over the crossbar and on to the running track behind the goal.

As if buoyed by that early escape Leicester, who were refusing to be

Just for a moment or two, I was in football paradise. I had scored the opening goal in the FA Cup final, or so I thought. But the referee decreed otherwise and, though I remain convinced to this day that he was wrong, and that I was not offside, all I could do was get on with the game.

overawed, moved forward with purpose, with the likes of wing-half Frank McLintock and winger Howard Riley troubling us, and there were a couple of half-chances which McIlmoyle was unable to convert. I was trying to play my usual running game, but after a quarter of an hour I was halted in my tracks when their skipper, the inside-forward Jimmy Walsh, accidentally planted a boot in my chest. Our trainer, Cecil Poynton, revived me with his 'magic' sponge – it's amazing how a splash of cold water under your shirt can get you moving again – shortly before the incident which, for uncommitted onlookers, ruined the game as a spectacle.

The Leicester right-back Len Chalmers was disputing possession with Bobby Smith, when Les Allen arrived on the scene with a typically vigorous but completely fair challenge. Chalmers went down in a twisted heap, writhing in extreme pain, and it was clear that his meaningful part in the game was over. Les was always a bit of a cruncher in the tackle, but I'm convinced that he never meant to hurt the lad, he was just after the ball. In fact, although we went on to win, it ruined what should have been the happiest afternoon in his life. After the collision Les wasn't himself, couldn't seem to settle, knowing the damage he had unwittingly caused.

In those primitive days before the use of substitutes, injured players rarely left the pitch and Chalmers was no exception, limping out to the left wing, where he remained a pathetic passenger for the duration. It was the seventh time in nine seasons that the FA Cup final, then the grand showpiece of the English game, had been radically unbalanced by the so-called Wembley hoodoo. Some folk spoke fancifully of a curse, but I think there was a simple explanation to do with players being used to hard, bare pitches at the end of

Gordon Banks flies through the air to no avail as Terry Dyson's firm header puts Spurs two up against Leicester at Wembley. I'm running in just in case there might be a rebound and an easy tap-in, but no such luck!

the season, then coming to a Wembley surface covered with thick grass. It was so easy to catch your studs in it. They would hold and as you twisted your leg to make your next movement, it put massive strain on your knee and ankle.

It was a crying shame for the game to be skewed when it seemed so perfectly balanced, although it's often more difficult to play against ten men than 11 because the afflicted side shifts to ultra-defensive mode while somehow finding a way to lift themselves for the fight. That's what happened with Leicester, who were always impeccably organised by Matt Gillies anyway, and now reshuffled effectively to deal with the situation. Spurs could do nothing except play on as normal, knowing that the double was still at stake, but for a long time we found it very hard to break through.

I thought I had managed it after 38 minutes, having temporarily switched wings with Terry Dyson. He delivered a low cross from the right, I dashed forward to meet it at the far post and sidefooted it first time into the net beyond keeper Gordon Banks. I turned to celebrate, arms in the air and joy in my heart, only to be confronted by the linesman waving his flag for offside. It was a truly terrible moment. To score a goal in the FA Cup final is every boy's dream, and for a fleeting instant I thought it had come true for me. But it wasn't to be and I felt absolutely gutted because I was convinced, and still am to this day, that the goal should have stood. I believe I'd timed my run past the full-back perfectly and film of the incident bears me out. So does Terry, who made the pass and had the perfect angle from which to judge where the Leicester defenders were standing.

I was supremely unhappy about the decision, and soon afterwards, as I was trotting past the linesman, I asked him why he had disallowed my effort. He just told me to shut up, which didn't do much for my frame of mind. Still, there was no way I would have made a real protest. I know that officiating is horrendously difficult, something that Bill Nicholson always emphasised to us. He said never to start moaning and whinging to him about referees because a lot of us didn't know the rules anyway! His favourite line was: "OK, the ref is only human and will make the occasional mistake, but I can pretty well guarantee that he will never make as many as you." It was a tremendous sporting attitude, and one that typified the man. You'd be unlikely to hear that from a top manager today, but Bill was very protective of the purity of the game and keeping it in the proper perspective.

Pushing that near thing to the back of my mind, I could only get on with the game, believing that it would come right in the end. We nearly broke through early in the second half when Dyson somehow contrived to head over the bar from right beneath it following a nod-back from Smith, but soon the irrepressible little Yorkshireman was to make up for that inaccuracy with two decisive contributions.

About halfway through the second period, he speared a beautiful pass to Bobby, who had found space just to the right of the penalty spot. The Big Fella controlled it with one deft touch, swivelled like a ballet dancer and cracked it powerfully past Banks, who was launching himself across his line without a hope in the world of reaching the hurtling ball. People always make the point about Bob's toughness, but he was also blessed with a surprisingly delicate touch and he showed it here.

After that there was only going to be one winner, as finally we settled down to play with something approaching our customary freedom. Terry sealed it for us a quarter of an hour from the end, flying through the air to find the net with a powerful header, Smithy having returned the earlier favour by providing the assist. Later in the dressing room Dyson was looking for praise from his manager for his double-sealing effort, but really he should have known better. Bill, ever the stickler and the ultra-demanding perfectionist, even in the wake of one of the most remarkable achievements in English football history, came back with: "Yes, but what about the one you missed?"

The rest of the game passed by in a flash, and Spurs had scaled what had been deemed for so long to be an insurmountable pinnacle. I was part of the team that had won the League and FA Cup double, creating priceless memories that would live with me forever. That there was another side to the afternoon, though, was brought home to me by the uneasy expression on the face of Les Allen. For all the joy that poured forth around him, it was clear that he was still haunted by the accident to poor Len Chalmers. He wanted to express his regrets in person to the Leicester full-back, who had wagged an admonishing finger at him in the heat of the moment on the pitch. I went with him into the City dressing room for moral support, but although we spoke to the stricken Chalmers, he barely seemed to notice us, still being dazed and disappointed in the wake of his traumatic experience. Happily, though, there

"We'll be running round Wembley with the Cup" sang the Spurs fans before kick-off, and they weren't wrong. Celebrating here, left to right: Ron Henry, Bill Brown, Peter Baker, Les Allen (half hidden), Danny Blanchflower, myself, Maurice Norman, Terry Dyson and Bobby Smith.

was a heart-warming sequel. Les still wasn't himself as we celebrated that evening at the Savoy Hotel until a telegram arrived for him, which read: "Forget about it. Congratulations. Len Chalmers."

But still there was one member of the Spurs party who wasn't completely euphoric about the day's events and, perversely enough, it was the fellow who had been the inspiration for it all, our brilliant boss Bill Nicholson. By any reckoning, it hadn't been a wildly entertaining game. In all honesty it must have been an enormous letdown for neutrals who had been expecting a dazzling display by what was being called the team of the century. At the time, Bill found that overwhelmingly disappointing. He had wanted not only to win, but also to demonstrate to the wider world just what a wonderful side Tottenham Hotspur had become. I would agree that we could have played better, perhaps the immensity of the occasion had got the better of us, but that wasn't worrying the players one tiny bit as we cavorted around the Savoy.

It comforts me to reflect, though, that as Bill looked back in later years, he had reached a more comfortable interpretation of what he had done. He came to see our double in its unique historical context and to take pleasure in it. It's the very least that he deserved.

On top of the bus – and the world! Hailing the double, and showing off our two precious baubles, are, left to right: assistant manager Harry Evans, Peter Baker with the FA Cup, a fan got up as a clown, myself with a flowery cockerel, trainer Cecil Poynton, Danny Blanchflower, Dave Mackay, Maurice Norman, Bill Brown, Terry Dyson and Ron Henry with the League championship trophy. Smashing!

CHAPTER FOURTEEN

The best of mates

If a man can trust his workmates to do their jobs no matter what, to mix flair, industry and dedication in equal measure, to stand brave and resolute alongside him at every turn, to laugh with him often and cry with him when the occasion demands, then he is lucky, indeed. And that was me as a member of the glorious Tottenham Hotspur team that became the first in the twentieth century to lift the League and FA Cup double.

The band of disparate characters guided so shrewdly by Bill Nicholson, one of the greatest football men who ever lived, formed a mutual bond – every man jack of us, one with another – that only death could break. It's overwhelmingly sad to me that, at the time of writing, so many of the squad have passed on. Their names will remain immortal but Danny Blanchflower, Dave Mackay, John White, Bill Brown, Peter Baker, Ron Henry, Mel Hopkins and Bobby Smith have all gone. I'm one of the lucky ones, 81 years old and still able, give or take the odd creaking joint, to hop around the golf course, help my wife Joan with the shopping and play with the grandchildren and great-grandchildren. But often, when the toys have been put away and, for a while, peace reigns in the Jones household, then I think of my old comrades, remembering them and honouring them, both as magnificent players and wonderful friends.

Some of them I have already mentioned in detail in earlier chapters – Bill Nick himself, Danny, Dave, Bill Brown, and my best pal and roommate John White, to whom I will return later to recall some of the uproariously merry times we shared as well as the unutterably tragic circumstances of his premature demise. Those names will crop up again, too, as I run through the rest of a line-up that is carved indelibly into White Hart Lane folklore, frozen in time to be remembered as long as there is a football club on the Tottenham High Road.

I'm going to start with one of the most underrated performers in Britain, maybe the whole of Europe, throughout his Spurs career, our beefy, barn-storming centre-forward Bobby Smith. A down-to-earth, forthright York-shireman, he played the game in line with his persona, which was straight from the shoulder.

Bobby was one of the toughest customers I ever encountered in football, a man accustomed to handing out punishment to defenders, keepers, anybody who stood in his pathway to the goal. But he could take the knocks, too, never moaning about being kicked up in the air by ruthless centre-halves, always picking himself up, dusting himself down and returning to the fray with renewed determination. But although his formidable physical presence must have made him seem like a ravening monster to his oppo-nents, both in the air and on the deck, far too often he was pigeonholed as a mere bruiser. In fact, Bobby was superbly skilful at need, capable of caressing the ball with the subtlest of touches, such as his exquisitely deli-cate chip in England's 4–2 victory over Spain in a friendly at Wembley in October 1960. At the end of the game, no less a personage than the peer-less Alfredo Di Stefano approached our man and congratulated him on a staggering piece of skill of which he himself would have been proud. Luckily there was a photographer on hand to capture the moment and Bob treasured that snap for many years. For him the tribute from the great Alfredo was the ultimate accolade, and he was right.

Of course, the popular image of the Smith method was not entirely mis-leading. He was very much in the mould of Nat Lofthouse and Trevor Ford, arguably the two most intimidating powerhouses since the war. Would-be markers would bounce off him like powder-puffs from a bulldozer and he was not above playing on their fear of his physical prowess. He relished the dispensing of lurid threats, and the effect of his menace on opponents who must often have been quaking inside when confronted by such a bullishly powerful specimen. He was devilishly difficult to dislodge from possession,

The League and FA Cup double was not won by 11 players, but by a terrific squad – and here they all are. Back row, left to right: Ron Henry, Maurice Norman, Johnny Hollowbread, Bill Brown, Mel Hopkins and Ken Barton. Middle: Peter Baker, Tony Marchi, trainer Cecil Poynton, Danny Blanchflower, manager Bill Nicholson, Dave Mackay and John Smith. Front: myself, Terry Medwin, John White, Bobby Smith, Les Allen, Frank Saul, Eddie Clayton and Terry Dyson.

but also he could lay the ball off beautifully, bringing others into play, and was capable of sudden flashes of artistry, perhaps turning on a two-bob bit – his feet were too big for the traditional sixpence! – to fire in an unexpected shot. For all these reasons he was a dream to play alongside.

Bobby scored in each of his first five internationals, finished with a tally of 13 goals in his 15 appearances for his country, and for my money he deserved to collect plenty more caps. Meanwhile for Spurs he was a goal machine, hitting the target 30 times or more in four successive seasons, starting with 1957/58, my first at the club. I always thought of him as one of our main players and I was sorry when he left. Sadly, part of the reason for his departure to join Brighton in the spring of 1964 was because he had a problem with gambling. It got to the stage where people were turning up at the club to collect money that he owed, and that became too much for Bill Nicholson. It was a difficult decision for the manager because Bobby had served him so well, but there was no way the boss was going to allow that sort of activity to be going on around the club.

Also, Bobby had struggled with injuries towards the end of his time at White Hart Lane, and now he had reached his thirties he was finding it harder to shake them off. Being of a naturally heavy build, he tended to be over-weight when he came back from his summer holidays, often needing a sweat-suit under his kit when the pre-season got under way. He didn't enjoy that, but he was conscientious and always worked very hard, though that sort of thing doesn't get easier as you grow older.

As a bloke Bobby was popular, great fun, always at the centre of the banter and friendly arguments that are the lifeblood of any football dressing room, though I seem to recall that many of his conversations tended to be about his need for cash, no doubt as a result of his love of betting. Perhaps the phrase 'loveable rogue' sums Bob up the best, though fundamentally he was a very decent lad and our families became very close when we were neighbours in Palmers Green, north London, for a few years.

Rather less noticeable on a football pitch than Bobby, but no less lethal on his day, was his strike partner and fellow ex-Chelsea man Les Allen. He was a sharp mover and a tremendous finisher with a smart football brain, and he deserved far more of the glory than ever went his way.

Acquired by Bill Nick in exchange for the far more stylish and flamboyant but, in the final reckoning, much less effective Johnny Brooks, Les was a born worker. He was always ready to drop deep or roam wide to forage for the ball, often providing a link between defence and attack and frequently Bobby and myself profited from his selfless labour in terms of scoring opportunities. Historically Les tends to be underrated, even to the extent that lots of people believe, wrongly, that Jimmy Greaves was Smithy's partner in the team that won the double. In fact, Jimmy arrived halfway through the following season and Les scored 27 goals in his 49 appearances during that hallowed 1960/61 campaign, a colossal contribution by any measure. Off the pitch he could be a bit dour, a bit of a moaner, but nothing serious. One of the secrets of our success was an unshakeable team spirit, and he was part of that. Nobody should doubt the scale of his contribution to the Tottenham cause, and it didn't end when he left to join Queen's Park Rangers in the summer of 1965. Les is the father of Clive Allen, who followed in his dad's prolific bootsteps, particularly in 1986/87, when he shattered Jimmy Greaves' Spurs record for goals in a single season by finding the net a phenomenal 49 times. Clearly Les taught him plenty during all those kickabouts in the family garden.

During the double term both our strikers were extremely consistent, with Les not missing a match and Bobby absent only for six, but had there been a problem we had admirable cover in the form of Frank Saul, who was only 17 and immensely promising. A Canvey Island boy and a smashing character, Frank contributed three goals in his half-dozen outings as Bobby's deputy and looked to be nailed on for a long-term future at White Hart Lane. Hard-working, skilful and versatile enough to switch to either wing at need, he did well in the years ahead without quite being consistent enough to make himself indispensable and eventually he moved to Southampton as part of the deal which took Martin Chivers to Tottenham.

At the other end of the pitch, Spurs were particularly well served during the double season with a collection of the staunchest defenders any club has ever been lucky enough to employ. We were particularly well served at full-back, where we had the first-choice pairing of Peter Baker and Ron Henry backed up by the excellent Mel Hopkins, who could consider himself unlucky not to be in the team on a regular basis.

Right-back Peter Baker was coolness personified, totally reliable, the sort of footballer you could bet your mortgage on if you were that way inclined. Actually, he had to be, because he played directly behind the endlessly adventurous Danny Blanchflower. Our captain was supremely creative but he was an inveterate wanderer to all areas of the pitch and we wouldn't have had him any other way. But his excursions did leave gaping gaps in defence at times, so we needed someone intelligent, decisive and strong to plug the holes. Bill Nick found him in Peter.

Often Baker was faced with a couple of opposition attackers bearing down on him, enough to induce panic in many a defender. At this point the fans would be screaming at him to make a neck-or-nothing tackle, but that wasn't Peter's way. He was a master of subtle positional play and he would refuse to dive in and sell himself, knowing that, against the top-quality wingers he confronted on a regular basis that would often prove disastrous. Instead, when he was outnumbered, his method was to jockey opponents into less dangerous areas, holding them up until reinforcements arrived.

Of course, he was a tough nut and could tackle like a runaway plough – as I found out to my cost, accidentally but painfully, at Cheshunt in my first summer as a Spur – and he was a perceptive if unflashy user of the ball, invariably preferring to find Blanchflower, Mackay or White rather than attempt something needlessly risky.

Certainly he was a superlative athlete and a fantastic sportsman, the most comprehensively talented all-rounder I ever encountered apart from Alf Sherwood, the old Welsh international full-back. Peter played cricket for Middlesex Seconds, performed at Wimbledon as a promising young tennis hopeful, boasted a golf handicap of four, being capable of giving even Bill Brown a decent game. As for snooker, always a popular pastime with professional footballers, the sensible advice was never to take him on, because you'd be sure to lose your money. Blessed with blond good looks, with a ready smile and plenty of self-confidence, he might have had a chance as a film star, but we were glad to have him at White Hart Lane with the number two on his back.

Left-back Ron Henry was similar to Peter in many respects, while differing vividly in others. Like his partner, Ron was rock solid, incredibly industrious and near-metronomically consistent in his high level of performance. Strong and watchful, he provided a tremendously sound defensive base down our left flank and was particularly excellent at covering if Peter or centre-half Maurice Norman came under pressure. Ron was not to be underestimated going forward, either, possessing an immensely sweet left foot from which I received some lovely passes when I was operating in front of him.

However, you could say Ron was lucky to be in the team at all, as he inherited the number-three shirt from Mel Hopkins when my Welsh international teammate suffered a horrendous facial injury in a collision with the Scotland centre-forward Ian St John in the autumn of 1959, just as Bill Nicholson was making enormous strides in knitting his Tottenham team together. But still Ron had to make the most of his opportunity, and he did. He was a revelation, looking the part straight away and never taking a backward step.

Yet for all that, I would still contend that Mel Hopkins was the better full-back. When asked to make a judgement between two opponents, I always ask myself a simple question: which of the pair would I have preferred to play against? The truth is that I would always rather have faced Ron than Mel, though that is certainly not to denigrate the Englishman, whom I valued both as a footballer and a friend.

Though Baker and Henry are so often considered together, almost as a single, ultra-efficient entity, in fact they were radically different as personalities. Where Peter was notably outgoing, Ron was inclined to be dour in comparison. He liked to have a whinge from time to time, and he was known for looking after his money very closely, a trait which I'm sure served him admirably in his successful business as a market gardener. But still he was a good bloke who was well-liked around the club, with people recognising that we can't all be the same.

As for Mel, what happened to him at Hampden Park was horrific. I never saw anything like it on a football pitch, either before or after. I'm sure it was an accident, but when the back of St John's head made contact with Mel's face the impact was sickening. Our man went down like a sack of potatoes and as he lay flat out on the ground, I could see from a few yards away that he was very badly hurt. But when I ran over to him it was far worse than I'd imagined. There was blood all over the place and his nose was spread right across his face. At the time he was a regular in the Spurs team, having created a tremendous back-line combination with Peter Baker and Maurice Norman, missing only one match all season. But now it was clear he was out of the picture for the foreseeable future, and with Ron stepping in so decisively, it proved a calamitous turning point in Mel's career.

What made it worse for his mates was that Mel was a really smashing lad who dealt with his misfortune so bravely and professionally. Not once did he moan or whinge about his rotten luck, he just got on with his football when eventually he recovered, doing his level best to win back his place from Ron but never quite succeeding. He filled in effectively for both Peter and Ron at various times, and did have a little run in the side during 1963/64. But never did he get back in on a regular basis and in the autumn of 1964 he followed Bobby Smith to Brighton, where he proved a tower of strength in helping the Seagulls lift the Fourth Division championship in the following spring.

That was to his immense credit, but that such a classy performer should be struck down when he was on the threshold of his prime was a crying shame. Mel was such a terrific full-back, and I shall never forget his magnificent display against the great Garrincha in the World Cup quarter-final of 1958. So often that day he showed the brilliant Brazilian down the touchline, then shot out a long, spidery left leg to rob him of the ball. Mel deserved a long and successful career at the game's top tables, but life teaches us, often brutally, that good people don't always get what they deserve.

The final member of Tottenham's double-winning rearguard, and the most physically prominent, was our very own BFG, the Big Friendly Giant who went by the name of Maurice Norman. As befitted his size – well above 6ft and appearing even taller because of that mound of thick crinkly hair – Maurice presented a formidably steely barrier to opposing attackers, but away from the action he was such an amiable, kind-hearted soul, a former farm labourer who was never happier than when he was working in the fields of his beloved Norfolk countryside. He was given the nickname of 'Swede', and he accepted it with typical good humour.

Having arrived at White Hart Lane from Norwich as a full-back, Maurice was always quicker and more mobile than he might have appeared, his huge stride gobbling up the ground like some galloping giraffe. Yet still he much preferred facing centre-forwards who would give him an old-fashioned physical battle, rather than the nippy, clever type who would drop deep, pull him out of position and pose an entirely different set of problems, the likes of Arsenal's Joe Baker, Alex Young of Everton or West Ham's Johnny 'Budgie' Byrne.

Bill Nick liked to utilise Maurice close to the full-backs, sometimes even behind them, which allowed wing-halves Dave Mackay and Danny Blanch-flower to surge forward, knowing there was plenty of cover behind them. Our big stopper, though rightly renowned for his aerial command, was no mug with the ball at his feet, either, and just occasionally he would confound opponents with his deft skills on an attacking sortie. Usually, though, he made his excursions into enemy territory when we had won a corner or a free-kick in a threatening position, and he grabbed some crucial goals in that way, four in the double season alone. Also, if Maurice was roaming free in the opposition box, it distracted the men who were meant to be marking Bobby, Les and myself, creating confusion which often we were able to exploit.

Maurice replaced Sheffield Wednesday's Peter Swan in the England side, collecting 23 caps and playing in the 1962 World Cup finals in Chile, and having entered his thirties had reverted to a full-back role when he suffered a compound fracture of his leg in 1965. It was a grisly affair, with the bone poking out through the skin, and though he slaved like a Trojan to make a comeback, he was never going to return to the top level after such a terrible mishap.

We were lucky to have Maurice as long as we did, though, and the same can be said about Tony Marchi, frequently dubbed the best reserve in English football. That was a tag which was wholly accurate but it must have been infuriating to a former Tottenham captain who had enjoyed a successful spell in Italy, his father's homeland, then returned to the Lane in the summer of 1959. Tall and elegant, his immense power equalled by his assured skill on the ball, wing-half Tony was the perfect deputy for both Danny Blanchflower and Dave Mackay, and such was his quality that the two stars were rarely missed when they were out of the team. Probably Bill Nick brought him back as a long-term replacement for the much older Irishman, but Danny didn't see it that way and his ultimate longevity sabotaged the Marchi prospects. Most players of his impressive calibre would not have been content to remain at White Hart Lane in the circumstances, but he was Tottenham through and through, loved the club to bits, and accordingly made what must have been a difficult decision. At least he can rest assured that he never let anyone down and that he was a key part of the Spurs family, a security blanket of the highest order.

The final regular member of the double-winners was small in stature but gigantic of heart. I'm talking about Terry Dyson, the infectiously effervescent

5ft 3in Yorkshireman who chipped in with 17 League and FA Cup goals in 1960/61, a mammoth contribution which rendered him impossible to omit, thus consigning the bigger, more stylish Welshman, Terry Medwin, to the sidelines for the bulk of that unforgettable campaign.

The tiny Terry was utterly irrepressible, both on the pitch and off it, where invariably he was at the centre of all the social activities, be it a trip to a greyhound stadium – often with Bobby Smith, a case of Little and Large if ever there were – or to the Tottenham Royal after a game on a Saturday where, being a single boy, he would cast his eyes over the young ladies and dance the night away.

Terry hailed from a horse-racing family, where his old man had been a successful professional jockey. There was even a time when he might have followed his dad into the saddle, but he turned to football and, without being extravagantly talented, he made a real go of it. The wee man always battled for his place as if his life depended on it, and when he did get into the side he threw absolutely everything into staying there.

But to dwell purely on his phenomenal enthusiasm to the exclusion of all other attributes is to do Dyson a grave disservice. He had an educated left foot, he was a tremendous crosser, he had an eye for goal, he would work till he dropped, and no loose ball ever appeared in his vicinity without him fighting for it with every shred of his being.

Terry shared in Tottenham's most rarefied triumphs of the Glory Glory Days, being absent for only a couple of games during the entire double term, then seizing the star role as Spurs became the first British side to lift a European trophy two years later. Another of his claims to fame is that he remains the only Tottenham man to score a hat-trick in a north London derby.

As the boss put it once: "If I had to nominate a player who had the attitude I wanted, it was Terry. He needed no motivation." Dead right. Judged purely as a morale-booster in the dressing room, the chirpy chappie with the sandy-blond hair was a blessing from heaven for any manager, but Bill Nick would never have picked him merely for making his teammates smile. He was a fine footballer in his own right and his part in our ground-breaking achievement must never be forgotten.

Not that there is much chance of that happening while the voluble Dyson is around, because he keeps reminding us! When we had both retired as players we worked together for a time as PE instructors at the Highbury Grove School in Islington, where we were surrounded by Arsenal fans to whom he delighted in recalling our victories against the old enemy – especially that hat-trick.

During our time together at White Hart Lane, our fates were bound up with one another as we were two of three wingers, along with Terry Medwin, nominally vying for two places in the team. I was the lucky one who was always picked when fit, meaning that one or other of the Terries missed out, which must have been particularly galling for such a classy all-rounder as Medwin, my long-standing chum from our Swansea days. But I'm happy to say that although he was never first choice during 1960/61, he did make 14 appearances in the League, exactly the number needed to qualify for a title medal, representing a third of the 42 games. It's different today, with extra gongs sometimes dispensed to men who enjoyed far fewer outings than that, but such rules were rigorously applied back in the day.

For myself during that landmark season, I couldn't have been more delighted with the way my fortune was panning out. At last I felt I was realising every scrap of my potential. I like to think I got people up off their seats when I received the ball and set off on a run. I loved to entertain and relished the fact that a buzz of expectancy seemed to ripple round the ground whenever I took possession. My first instinct was always to go directly for goal rather than head for the corner flag to get in a cross. If I'm honest, I don't think I was ever particularly brilliant at crossing, there were plenty better than me at launching the ball into the box. Bill Nick understood this and always wanted me to be on the business end, either shooting, which I adored doing, or getting in a header. I was a team player in the sense that I was always ready to work my socks off, but essentially I was an individualist within a team framework. I was quick and nimble enough to dart past defenders on either side, and Bill knew that was the best way to use me. I always preferred cutting in from the left on to my right foot, and when I lined up on the right I was more likely to bring width to our attack by hugging the touchline.

During my football career I came across all manner of full-backs, including many who liked to manoeuvre me into blind alleys, but more frequently those looking to discourage me by giving me a clout. One or two of them really got my goat by making their hit cleverly, without the referee realising what was going on.

One of the very top performers who springs to mind – and he certainly wasn't among those who went in for any sort of subterfuge – is George Cohen, who starred for Fulham and England. Quick, fit and strong, he was a crucially important member of Sir Alf Ramsey's great England team which won the World Cup against West Germany at Wembley in 1966. When I moved to Fulham in 1968, George and I became close friends, and even now it's terrific to meet up with him and his lovely wife, Daphne, at various functions.

Another out-and-out thoroughbred was Jimmy Armfield of Blackpool, who gave the Seasiders magnificent service over many seasons. In recognition of all Jim did for them, the club named a stand at Bloomfield Road after him, which says it all.

Talking of high-class operators, there was also Don Howe, who enjoyed his peak years with West Bromwich Albion and was a stylish, attacking full-back who always liked to play constructively. Strangely enough, when he became coach at Arsenal, he became very defensively minded, making the Gunners a very difficult team to play against.

Burnley's Alex Elder was another marvellous flank defender. We had many tussles against each other and I always had to be at my very best to get any advantage over him. That also applies to his Turf Moor teammate and full-back partner John Angus, who I came up against repeatedly when our two teams were the best in the land. I was always on the lookout for him, and when I escaped his clutches I'd always let him know at the end of the game, telling him: "You didn't get me this time, did you?" Invariably he'd respond along the lines of: "There's always next time, Cliff!" There was no malice, and plenty of mutual respect, but I have to admit our clashes could be painful. And talking of supremely effective pairs, it's difficult to imagine many more respected then Roy Hartle and Tommy Banks of Bolton Wanderers, great lads I've mentioned earlier and whose proud boast was that any winger who ventured to Burnden Park would be nursing a case of 'gravel rash' on their way home.

I didn't bump into Paul Reaney until mid-decade because he was a few years younger and his club, Leeds United, were in the Second Division when we won the double, but certainly he was an opponent who often gave me trouble. That was something I had in common with George Best, no less, who like me found Reaney to be a real terror – quick, strong and two-footed, though always impeccably fair, never going over the top.

I was never too bothered by a full-back just because he was quick, as I always had pace to burn myself. Truth to tell, while realising that any top opponent was going to have his moments, I did fancy myself against most of them. You need that sort of self-belief to succeed at the highest level – you wouldn't get far without it. It's nothing to do with being big-headed or arrogant, you just have to carry total confidence on to the pitch. You have to know that if you're as quick as you can be over those first few vital yards then you will put any marker at a serious disadvantage. After all, you can *know* which way you're going to go and you can dart away, while if it's common knowledge that you're two-footed, he hasn't a clue which way you're headed.

Another crucially important part of the game which not every winger excelled at, but which I always tried to embrace, was chasing back to help out the defence. To me, it was an integral part of my job, a responsibility not to be shirked, especially when I was playing on the right – such as during the double year – with Danny Blanchflower wandering off in all directions. Bill Nick expected every winger to do his bit defensively, always emphasising the importance of tracking back when the ball was on the opposite side of the pitch, the point being to stop opponents from changing the play with a long crossfield pass.

I was once chatting to Harry Johnston, who was the centre-half and captain of Blackpool when the Seasiders won the FA Cup in 1953, and he asked me: "Would you believe me if I said we have this winger who doesn't score goals, doesn't head a ball and will not in any circumstance run back to give the defence a hand – and yet he's the greatest winger you've ever seen?" Of course, he was talking about Stanley Matthews, who was recognised universally as the finest player on earth during the middle years of the last century, his name a byword for brilliance. Stan saw his role as beating his markers and laying on scoring opportunities for his fellow forwards, and in his time he did that better than anyone else. Traditionally wingers were in that mould, but times change and even before the Matthews career had drawn to an end there were flankmen ready to run themselves into the ground, off the ball, in the team's cause. There was John Berry in Matt Busby's sensational Manchester United team that was decimated at Munich, then there was John Connelly at Burnley and United, Arsenal's Geordie Armstrong, Mike Summerbee of Manchester City, Liverpool's Ian Callaghan and the incomparable George Best. They were all superb on the ball when they got the chance, but they all put in a shift as a matter of course, and that became the norm.

For all that, what makes a winger truly special will always be boosting the attack by running with the ball, scoring goals, thrilling the fans. In short, entertaining. I have to admit that I got a tremendous kick out of being an entertainer, having the ability to excite people, put smiles on their faces, getting them to cheer. Not that I ever wanted to put myself on any sort of pedestal. I like to think that the fans identified with me as being an ordinary bloke like them, just a lad from Sandfields in Swansea who happened to be okay at kicking a ball and was lucky enough to do it for his living. Encouraging a connection between the players and supporters was very important to Bill Nicholson, a key plank of his football ethos. Often we'd be in the same pub as the fans after the game, having a drink and a laugh with the folk who had just paid their hard-earned cash to watch us. That was good for all concerned – the players, the supporters and the club as part of the community.

Going into The Bell and Hare on the Tottenham High Road in the evening after a match became a Spurs ritual. Certainly Mackay was always there, and Smith, although Bobby was never a big drinker. Perhaps Norman, Henry and Brown were not always there, but sometimes they would be and they were all part of the team spirit. Nobody was outside that. After a couple of drinks most of us would adjourn elsewhere for a meal with our wives or girlfriends, while Dyson, the only single fella in the team during 1960/61, would end up at the Tottenham Royal, strutting his stuff on the dancefloor and pulling a girl if he was lucky. They were simple days but, looking back on them, they were so, so glorious.

CHAPTER FIFTEEN

Raw in tooth and claw

How do you follow the fulfilment of a seemingly impossible dream? Well, if you emulate the example of Spurs in 1961/62, then you tilt at an even crazier windmill. In our case it was not merely the double we were after, but the utterly mind-blowing *treble*, adding the European Cup to our League title and FA Cup ambitions.

In the end, we came agonisingly close, finishing just behind surprise package Ipswich Town and our old foes, Burnley, in the championship race, beating the Clarets at Wembley to retain our domestic knockout supremacy, and reaching the semi-final of the glamorous continental competition, then bowing out to the eventual winners, Benfica, in bitterly controversial fashion, only by a hair's breadth and after a titanic battle.

Our status as the top team in the land was reflected aptly by the identity of our opponents in the Charity Shield, the season's tradition curtain-raiser. As champions we should have been facing the FA Cup winners, but as we'd gathered in that trophy as well, the FA wheeled out their own Select XI, which was nothing more than a thin disguise for the current England side. Not that we were thrown out of our stride – we won 3–2 at White Hart Lane, to set us up perfectly for the start of our title defence at Blackpool a week later.

That went well, too, with goals from Bobby Smith and myself giving us a 2–1 victory over Jimmy Armfield, Gordon West and company which, considering Bill Nicholson was fielding basically the same side that had swept all before us in 1960/61, augured favourably for our latest silverware quest. However, there were a few of us carrying niggling injuries, somehow our

Spurs were already the best team in England – then they signed the greatest goalscorer I've ever seen. Playing alongside Jimmy Greaves was a pleasure, especially as he turned out to be such a tremendous bloke.

impetus slipped and by Christmas we had lost seven League games – not championship form at all.

So it was a more than timely boost that December when Bill signed Jimmy Greaves, the finest British goalscorer of his or any other generation, from AC Milan for £99,999, the odd fee agreed so as not to saddle him with a £100,000 transfer tag. There was so much excitement among the fans about the arrival of Jim, who had not settled in Italy following his previous move from Chelsea. Lane regulars were positively drooling about what the greatest team could achieve when augmented by the greatest marksman, who would surely fill his boots on the chances created for him by Messrs Blanchflower, White and Mackay.

Although I had played against him a few times, I didn't know Jim personally at that point, but he fitted in superbly, both football-wise and socially. Off the pitch he was chirpy, full of fun, a great mixer who was very easy to get on with, while out on the grass he was downright fabulous. Joe Mercer once called him a 'blinking little genius' and he wasn't wrong. He could grab goals out of nothing, having a God-given instinct for turning up in the right spot at the right time. Then, when he was in position, he was so cool and composed, so often just passing the ball into the net, almost gently. Sometimes, though, I don't think he gets the full credit for his range of skills, because he could ghost past markers as neatly as anyone I've seen, leaving them floundering helplessly behind him or, as often was the case, sat on their bums in the mud.

In view of what they'd achieved, I guess it was hard lines on Les Allen or Bobby Smith, having to make way for Jim. But although we'd won the double with a fantastic blend, it would be daft to say that the addition of Greaves didn't improve it. Les lost out more frequently than Bobby, and I must admit that I always liked the mixture of the big man and the small man, of which Smith and Greaves was the ideal example.

Jim could hardly have made a more emphatic impact in his first game as a Spur, helping himself to a spectacular hat-trick in the return fixture with Blackpool, which we won 5–2, an effort which kept up his record of scoring on debut for virtually every team at every level he had ever played.

Shortly before Greaves' arrival, clearly worried by our inconsistent form, Bill Nick had tinkered with our front line, shifting me to the left wing in place of Terry Dyson and bringing Terry Medwin in on the right, or sometimes drafting in a deeper-lying player, Tony Marchi or Eddie Clayton. This seemed tough on Dyson, who had done so much towards the double, but he was a resilient character and, as we shall see, he would come again with a vengeance.

Happily for me Bill always continued to pick me when I was fit, which was nearly all the time, and I managed to keep my goal tally ticking along, for example with a hat-trick in a 5–2 home win over Chelsea in our last game of the calendar year. Sadly that elusive consistency remained beyond us in the second half of the League campaign, and by the end of March it was Burnley and, astonishingly, Ipswich who were slugging it out for the top prize.

It was a colossal achievement by the former Tottenham full-back Alf Ramsey to have the East Anglian outfit in title contention in their first season after winning promotion as champions of the Second Division. At the start of the season most pundits predicted that a team consisting mainly of bargain buys and cast-offs from other clubs would struggle to stay afloat among the elite, but so canny was Alf – as he would go on to prove on the grandest stage of all by guiding England to World Cup glory in 1966 – that he saw off all comers, eventually pipping Harry Potts' Clarets by three points, with us a point further adrift in third place.

What cost us the League was losing to Ipswich both away and home, 3–2 at Portman Road in October, when my brace of goals availed us of nothing, and then 3–1 at White Hart Lane in mid-March. How could that happen against our star-studded line-up? Well, Alf was incredibly shrewd, and he had worked out how to counter the tactics of Bill Nick, who had played just in front of him at right-half in Arthur Rowe's push-and-run winners of the early 1950s. The Ipswich boss deployed two deep-lying wingers, Roy Stephenson on the right and Jimmy Leadbetter, who looked much older than he was and, it might be said without a shred of malice, bore a passing resemblance to Albert Steptoe, on the left. That meant the opposing full-backs would go looking for the flankmen to mark, which created plenty of space in wide areas for their two prolific front-runners, Ray Crawford and Ted Phillips, to exploit. Those two boys were both lethal finishers and prodigiously hard workers, a winning combination which took many a team by surprise.

Having thought long and deep, though, Bill had the last laugh on his old mate, adopting a different approach for the Charity Shield clash in front of Ipswich's supporters in August 1962. He ordered our full-backs, Peter Baker and Ron Henry, to move inside to pick up Crawford and Phillips, while our wing-halves, Danny Blanchflower and Dave Mackay, pushed up on Stephenson and Leadbetter, leaving our centre-half, Maurice Norman, free to sweep. This time, instead of them surprising us it was the other way round. Bill's ploy worked a treat and we thrashed them 5–1, after which other teams saw through their tactics and they only just escaped relegation, a fate that did overtake them – after Alf had departed – in 1963/64.

That was so typically astute of Bill, a brilliant response to Alf's innovation, and although he was never one to crow, it must have felt so satisfying to come out on top in what amounted to their own personal bout of tactical chess. Our manager hated to lose anyway, but to see the 1961/62 title slip away to his old teammate must have been particularly painful, a situation which just had to be redressed.

Bill was much happier with our 1962 FA Cup campaign, although it kicked off on an uncertain note, with a 3–3 draw at St Andrew's, the home of Birmingham City, who were toiling towards the wrong end of the First Division table. We won the replay 4–2, then went past Plymouth Argyle, West Bromwich Albion and Aston Villa without too much trouble before beating Manchester United, who were showing distinct signs of improvement as Matt Busby rebuilt in the wake of the Munich disaster, 3–1 on a Hillsborough quagmire.

That took us to Wembley where we were matched against Burnley, still a very fine team and likely to provide our stiffest test. Some argued that because nine of our number had winner's medals at home from the previous year – the two exceptions were Jimmy Greaves and Terry Medwin – we would

I'm at the head of the queue as John White pours the tea at Cheshunt. I just hope he was impressed by that snazzy scarf!

be under less pressure, but I don't think that made a scrap of difference once the game got under way. Beforehand Jimmy had joked about opening his account in the fourth minute, but in the event he did so with 60 seconds to spare, courtesy of a little luck and a wee bit of inspired improvisation. He overran the ball in the box, but even in the act of stumbling he got away a gentle, hit-it-and-hope shot which wrong-footed several defenders, then crept over 15 yards of lush turf before coming to rest snugly in the rigging behind Clarets keeper Adam Blacklaw.

After that we got on top for a while, but Burnley were a spirited bunch and they fought back for Jimmy Robson to poach a deserved equaliser early in the second half. That might have been a turning point but perhaps we caught them at a vulnerable moment psychologically, when maybe they were still celebrating in their heads, and we were back in front within a minute. John White was the creator, finding Bobby Smith about 15 yards out, setting up the centre-forward for a deliciously slick swivel and powerful shot, almost a carbon copy of his goal against Leicester a year earlier. Danny Blanchflower, calmness personified, sealed the win with a beautiful penalty kick, sending Blacklaw the wrong way ten minutes from time, and pretty soon we were climbing those 39 steps to receive our winner's medals.

On the day we couldn't have been happier, although a wider overview of the domestic season left us with the unavoidable feeling that we should have been toasting a second successive double. That said, certainly with the benefit of more than half a century's perspective, perhaps we should be sparing a thought for our beaten opponents, who had finished runners-up in both competitions and, had Dame Fortune smiled on them just a tiny bit more generously, might have been hailing a double of their own.

As for the third leg of our possible treble, we felt we had covered ourselves with credit and done enough to suggest that, not too far down the line, the White Hart Lane trophy cabinet might have to be rearranged to accommodate the European Cup.

Yet our start in the biggest of all club competitions had been anything but auspicious. We had been drawn against the Polish club Gornik Zabrze, located in the drab, dismally grey coalmining town of Katowice where the local population looked worryingly under-nourished. Bill Nicholson had been

Burnley have been beaten in the 1962 FA Cup final and the lads are ready to party amid the mess of the Wembley dressing room. Jimmy Greaves takes charge of the uncorking, John White looks a mite apprehensive, Bobby Smith can hardly wait, while I'm offering Jim my unstinting support.

on a fact-finding mission, noting the downtrodden nature of the place and seeing the pitch – which was admittedly immaculate – being manicured by women on their hands and knees using scissors to cut the grass. In the town there were wartime bombsites everywhere, the shops were few and far between, and people plodded around heavily and dispiritedly. But if the surroundings were grimly downbeat, the opposition was anything but. Gornik turned out to be a very accomplished team and in that first leg our inexperience let us down badly. The Poles roared into us from the start, backed by an almost savagely partisan, deafeningly vociferous 70,000 crowd and, to put it bluntly, we fell apart.

Despite having had Gornik watched, Bill didn't expect anything more taxing than an average First Division game, but we didn't have a clue about how to approach a two-legged tie. So we tried to attack from the first whistle and they just picked us off. We were three down at the break, conceded another goal early in the second half and then the fans went berserk when Dave Mackay put one of their lads on the deck with a ferocious tackle. After that things got very physical, with some wild challenges going in from both sides, but late in the game we managed to salvage something from the proceedings with a couple of goals – my header and Terry Dyson's sharp drive, both set up by the marauding Dave – which kept the tie alive at 4–2. Afterwards we were panned in the Polish press, who denounced us as barbarians, but I have to say they did exaggerate! Needless to say, Bill was not happy, either with our work-rate or the appliance of our quality, telling us we had not shown ourselves in our true light and that we had to do much better in the re-match – and so we did.

I shall always treasure memories of our 8–1 triumph over Gornik at White Hart Lane because they take me back to a charmed, magical night when that Spurs team played better than at any other time when we were all together. Following the debacle in the first leg, Bill had shrewdly picked the same team, knowing we would all be desperate to make amends and he wasn't wrong. For all his genuine devotion to fair play, our manager wasn't above a few mind games, and he had ordered the biggest, most menacing members of our groundstaff to line the tunnel from the dressing room, with the idea of intimidating the Gornik players as they walked beside us up to the pitch.

As we strode into the open air, the atmosphere was absolutely incredible, the most fervent I've ever experienced. The din from our fans was at fever pitch, you couldn't hear yourself think, let alone speak. As the Poles gazed around them, I could see the apprehension in their eyes. They looked like nothing more than defenceless rabbits caught in the headlights of a runaway tank. The noise just cascaded down from the stands and terraces, with the waving, swaying fans seeming to be right on top of the players, in vivid contrast to their home surroundings, where a running track separated the crowd from the pitch. Psychologically I reckon they were a goal down before a ball was kicked, and soon their worst nightmare began to unfold.

We looked slick and confident in our all-white kit, and from the first whistle we moved with a power and smoothness which made the outcome feel inevitable to us and, I'm sure, to Gornik as well. With the strains of 'Glory, Glory

Hallelujah' threatening to lift the roofs off every building inside the Lane, and in the streets around the ground for that matter, we set to work from the first whistle with a staggering intensity. Almost immediately Danny Blanchfower dispatched the ball into the box and Les Allen smacked it against the crossbar. That proved to be a narrow escape for the fearful visitors but the merest sighter for the rampant hosts as we quickly took control.

The skipper opened our account for the evening from the penalty spot after nine minutes, and it fell to me to level the tie not long afterwards with a decent nod from a Dyson lob. Now I was flying, we all were, and I completed a quick-fire hat-trick – a perfect one, head, left foot, right foot – with only a solitary reply from the Poles, actually a wonderful volley from their influential captain, Ernest Pohl. Bobby Smith made it 5–1 before the interval, after which he struck again, with further hits by Dyson and White to round off our scintillating performance. We annihilated Gornik and had we accepted all the scoring chances that came our way we could have reached double figures, and not low double figures at that.

I don't believe any team from any era could have lived with us that night. Our moves flowed like liquid gold, everything we tried came off. I don't want to sound boastful, but we really did play like gods. I used to love playing under lights because somehow the air always seemed that little bit fresher and sharper, you seemed to run faster and harder, some indefinable magic would be present, making anything seem possible. That display sent out an uncompromising message to everybody left in the competition. It boiled down to this – don't mess with the boys at White Hart Lane! Our first continental venture had given us an appetite for success and now we were downright ravenous. At this point, only Manchester United, Wolves and Burnley had trod the European Cup trail before us, and only United had enjoyed much success, reaching a couple of semi-finals. Now we were consumed with ambition to outstrip them, and burning with belief that we could do it at our first attempt.

That season we were fortunate enough to be drawn away from home for the first leg every time and that was a considerable advantage, as it always helps to be on your own turf for the decisive encounter. In the last 16 we faced the formidable Dutch club, Feyenoord, their side packed with flair players but not short of muscle, either. In all honesty – the very least always demanded by our manager – we gave a below-par, error-strewn display and we were so lucky to leave Rotterdam with a 3–1 victory under our belts. Bill summed it up admirably when he said we muddled through, and that we did so was down to the expertise and composure of young Frank Saul, who had temporarily displaced Bobby Smith and who scored twice. My only clear memories of an eminently forgettable evening was setting up Frank's second goal – who said I never passed? – and sighing with relief when the final whistle went shortly after they hit our crossbar twice in quick succession.

However, I do carry with me a vivid image from the second leg in north London, an unforgiving, attritional encounter which finished 1–1, enough to see us through to the quarter-finals on a 4–2 aggregate. Early in the game, with both goals already scored, Dave Mackay, playing at inside-left with Tony Marchi handed the Scot's customary number-six shirt, was involved in a sickening mid-air collision with the powerful Dutch defender Hans Kraay. Dave went down as if he'd been shot, lying flat on the deck, and any time he didn't rise to his feet after a clash then you knew it must be something serious. Trainer Cecil Poynton ran on, looking worried, and as they gently rolled Mackay over there was blood pouring from his ear. I was petrified for him then, I thought he must have fractured his skull at the very least.

He was stretchered off and for the next 20 minutes a shadow hung over the proceedings, as everyone in our camp was anxious on Dave's behalf. Then suddenly this huge roar went up and I glanced across to the touchline to see Mackay, standing there in blood-spattered shorts, demanding to be brought back on. The referee duly waved him back into the action and he went all the way to 90 minutes, undaunted by what must have been quite a headache. At the end he collapsed in the dressing room and was carted off to hospital, where it was discovered that he *had* fractured his skull. He was forced to miss several matches after that, unwillingly of course, but that's a story which says everything about the ultimate football warrior. These days, of course, he'd never get away with it. You're off if there's even the slightest hint of concussion, and rightly so, but in our time football really was raw in tooth and claw.

Totally irrepressible, Dave was back for the quarter-final confrontation with Dukla Prague in the snowy Czechoslovakian capital, where the blood-red pitch markings seemed appropriate for another, shall we say, briskly physical encounter in which I was cautioned for reacting with what I can honestly say was uncharacteristic fury to an appalling tackle. Bill was getting ever more canny with his European tactics and he opted for caution in this away leg, drafting in Tony Marchi as an extra centre-half alongside Maurice Norman, which worked in that we limited a very capable team to a 1–0 victory. It was in complete contrast to the gung-ho manner in which we had approached the trip to Poland at the outset of the campaign, and we did attract some criticism over perceived negativity, but you do live and learn. The strategy paid off handsomely as we felt free to produce some of our best attacking football in the return at the Lane, in which the teams had to contend with another hard, frosty surface, and which we won 4–1 courtesy of two goals each from Smith and Mackay.

And so to what was then the greatest test in the modern history of Tottenham Hotspur, the mighty Benfica of Portugal in the semi-finals. A year earlier Bela Guttmann's wonderful team had become only the second to win the European Cup, Real Madrid having monopolised the trophy for the first five seasons of its existence, and since then the men from Lisbon had been enhanced immeasurably by the addition of a lithe, sumptuously talented youngster from Mozambique, a certain Eusebio. Since lighting up Europe that term, he had been hailed as the European answer to Pele, with his explosive power, exquisite control and insatiable appetite for goals, and while the peerless Brazilian remained essentially in a class of his own, this lad wasn't half bad.

Not that Benfica were a one-man team. They also boasted Mario Coluna, so dynamic and constructive in midfield; centre-forward and captain Jose Aguas, a high-quality performer who led by example; a dazzling pair of wingers in Jose Augusto and Antonio Simoes; and that immovable object, Germano, at centre-half. Not that we were in the slightest bit overawed. We had just come off the back of the domestic double, since when we had added Jimmy Greaves to the team and now felt we were a match for anyone. We were confident, in fact, that this would be the first of many tilts at the European Cup with Bill's super side, and it remains supremely frustrating in retrospect that we could never quite pin down that second League title which would have given us another chance. Back then, of course, you had to be

Flat out in the White Hart Lane mud, I've just dispatched a diving header past Aston Villa keeper Geoff Sidebottom during our 2–0 FA Cup quarter-final victory in March 1962. Our big centre-forward Bobby Smith seems quite pleased, while Villa wing-half Vic Crowe is helpless to intervene.

champions to enter the competition – none of this modern top-four business, which does make rather a mockery of the original intention of a competition reserved exclusively for the best team in every country.

Ahead of the first leg in Lisbon, the general feeling was that whoever came out on top would go on to take the trophy, the other semi being between Real Madrid and Standard Liege. Clearly the Spanish aristocrats were still a potent force, with Alfredo Di Stefano, Ferenc Puskas and Francisco Gento all remaining in harness, but they were ageing as a group and understandably in decline, while the Belgian champs, though competent and well respected, did not fill us with dread.

Thus our spirits were sky-high as we arrived in Lisbon, though it didn't take John White and myself long to get right up the nose of poor Bill Nicholson, diverting his attention temporarily from laying plans to bring Guttmann's Glorious Eagles down to earth, occupying him instead with the daft antics of Tottenham's two overgrown schoolboys.

John and I roomed together, we shared a crazy sense of humour and, especially on away trips, we had tremendous fun. Generally speaking, I'm sure that Bill saw our pranks as being good for team spirit, but on this occasion we pushed him too far and he got fed up. When we arrived at the hotel in Estoril, near Lisbon, we'd already been larking about a bit, and now we noticed there were lots of historical bits and bobs around the place, including a couple of ceremonial swords on the wall. We'd already had a few drinks, so inevitably one of us – and I can't remember which one – suggested taking down the blades for a fencing match. The next thing you know, John and I are surging up and down the stairs like Errol Flynn in a

Hollywood blockbuster, and although we didn't cause any physical damage, it didn't go down too well with the hotel management. They called Bill who, it is fair to say, was not amused. He told us in colourful terms that we were in Portugal on serious business and it was time we stopped acting like a couple of dopey six-year-olds. There'd been previous escapades involving John and myself, but this time he felt we'd gone overboard, so much so that he stopped us rooming together for the rest of the trip. He knew, deep down, that there was no harm in us, that our messing around was never going to hurt anybody, but this time we'd caught him on the raw.

It was all forgotten by the time we ran out in front of a capacity 70,000 crowd at the impressive Estadio da Luz, where I think we can claim to have played some incisive attacking football without enjoying one iota of luck, while making a few costly defensive errors.

The tempestuous nature of away crowds in Europe was something we were getting used to – and, to be fair, our own fans at White Hart Lane were not exactly shrinking violets – but even by recent standards the Lisbon audience was raucous. That was when we walked out before the game and the decibels grew more extreme after the Portuguese skipper, the wily and energetic Jose Aguas, put them in front after only five minutes. Some 60 seconds later we thought we might have quietened the screaming hordes when Jimmy Greaves nipped beyond his markers to put the ball in the net with typical efficiency, only for the effort to be disallowed for offside. It must have been an agonisingly marginal decision and soon it was rendered all the more telling when Jose Augusto doubled Benfica's lead a quarter of an hour later.

We didn't cave in, though, and created a couple of decent scoring chances of our own before the interval, but Jimmy and I were both off-target and it took Bobby Smith to reduce the arrears early in the second half. That might have been the turning point, as it seemed we were coming to terms with their combination of attacking brilliance and stern tackling, and even after Augusto made it 3–1 we didn't feel out of it. But we received another hammer-blow near the end when Jimmy played the ball *back* for Bobby Smith to find the net again, only to be devastated by another contentious offside flag. The rules state that you can't be offside if the last ball is played back, but the linesman made his judgement and Bill Nicholson, as ever, wasn't blaming the officials for his team's travail, declaring that we hadn't played well enough and had made stupid mistakes.

The players couldn't argue with that, but our confidence remained high that when the European Cup holders rocked up at White Hart Lane, we could take them down. That notion took a fearful blow after 15 minutes when Aguas made it 4–1 on aggregate, and soon afterwards we suffered what felt like a cruel injustice when Jimmy darted past two defenders and beat keeper Costa Pereira. This time the referee signalled for a goal, only for the linesman to intervene, and after a hasty consultation while surrounded by protesting Portuguese players, the man in charge reversed his decision.

We were dumbfounded but certainly not daunted and we battled on, finally gaining some reward after 35 minutes when Bobby Smith crashed the ball into the net, having been found by a superbly judged cross from John White. Our Scottish schemer, who was having another magnificent game, was at the centre of things again just after half-time when he was fouled inside the box by Coluna and Danny Blanchflower, remaining characteristically cool on the penalty spot under intense pressure, made it 2–1 to us on the night, 4–3 to Benfica on aggregate.

Now, with more than 40 minutes left to play, we were sure we could do it and we poured forward in wave after wave, completely dominating the European champions. But once more we missed our scoring opportunities. I was guilty of blazing one over the bar when maybe I should have done better, and we hit the woodwork three times, most frustratingly of all right at the death when Dave Mackay beat Pereira from 20 yards, only to see the ball clip the crossbar and fly to safety. If that had gone in we'd have secured a play-off, which I felt was the least we deserved, though in the final analysis we had to reflect that we couldn't allow opponents of such fabulous quality to score four times and expect to progress. Some critics thought we had been too frenetic in our second-half assault, so keen to get forward that too often we bypassed our creative midfield, but that might be a tad harsh on such a night of tempestuous action. We had been beaten, by the narrowest of margins, by one of the truly great teams and we had been a trifle unfortunate. The ball hadn't run for us, decisions went against us, it just wasn't to be. Now it was pointless to waste time wringing our hands when we had the clear potential to achieve so much more.

There was some consolation, too, in the reaction of Bill Nicholson. He was disappointed, of course he was, but he told us how well we had played and that he was proud of us. There were none of the misgivings he had felt following the Wembley victory over Leicester nearly a year before, which says everything about a true sportsman with wholesome values, and his reaction meant the world to us.

Later Bela Guttmann paid us an enormous compliment by declaring it had been the hardest game of his life and predicted that, very soon, we could be lifting the European crown which his mighty team was soon to retain by beating Real in the Amsterdam final. We, too, thought we were poised on the brink of the premier prize, but as it turned out that was the closest we were ever to come.

Looking back down all the long years, the thought of another missed Tottenham opportunity springs irresistibly to mind. When Alex Ferguson's Manchester United won the unique treble of European Cup, League championship and FA Cup in 1998/99, they were hailed as the team of the century, and they were, indeed, a wonderful side. But Fergie's feat caused me to ponder anew how agonisingly close we had come to scaling that same pinnacle a full 37 years earlier. But then, we have to be positive in football as in all aspects of life. We have to reflect that if we had won the European Cup in 1962, then we would never have experienced that euphoric night in Rotterdam a year later. You win some, you lose some, but most important of all, you must enjoy the journey.

CHAPTER SIXTEEN

Rapture in Rotterdam

Come the spring of 1962, I was feeling excited, confident and contented in equal measure. On the threshold of my footballing prime at 27, I was happily married with four lovely children, I was playing for what I considered to be the best side in Britain by a considerable margin, I was in demand from one or two of the continent's leading clubs, and I was looking forward to a season with Spurs which I was convinced could end with unprecedented glory. Our experience against Benfica, while it ended in defeat by an excruciatingly narrow margin, had left me in no doubt that we were comprehensively equipped to become the first team from these islands to bring home a European trophy.

The only downside to all this positivity was on the international front. We had lost to Spain, 3–2 on aggregate, in our qualifying group for that summer's World Cup finals in Chile, hindered beyond belief by the absence of John Charles. I'm well aware that no team should be totally reliant on their star player, but it's hard to recall any other individual having the same effect on a side as John on Wales. Our manager Jimmy Murphy, who was blessed with an entertainingly colourful turn of phrase, once declared: "Whenever I look at John Charles, it feels as though the Messiah has returned", and I knew exactly what he meant. Amazingly for such an influential player, the big fella collected only 38 full caps, partly due to injury, sometimes because of his commitments with Juventus, and while we could function effectively enough without him, it would be ridiculous to claim that he didn't lift us to an entirely more rarefied level of performance.

But for all our disappointment at not joining Walter Winterbottom's England in Chile, we did have our own enjoyable and prestigious South American assignment in May 1962, and it was the hard-earned product of our sterling display in 1958. The holders, Brazil, our quarter-final conquerors in Sweden, had asked us to provide the opposition for two warm-up matches in the lead-in to the latest tournament because they knew we would offer fiercely competitive opposition, just the preparation they needed ahead of the defence of their crown.

Big John was with us on this trip, deployed in both games as a mammoth presence in central defence, freeing his brother Mel to line up at centre-forward

Family time at Butlin's, Minehead in the summer of 1963. That's Joan next to me, while my sister, Val, and my mother are also at the back with our niece, Janet. The kids at the front are my nephew, Peter, on the left, next to three of our four, Steve, Debbie and Kim.

in the first encounter in Rio de Janeiro, with the promising young Graham Moore wearing the number-nine shirt four days later in Sao Paulo. We lost both encounters 3–1, with Ivor Allchurch registering in Rio and Ken Leek supplying our goal in the second game, but we gave a more than decent account of ourselves, fulfilling our hosts' requirements to the letter.

Trotting out at the Maracana, Rio's football 'cathedral', was a staggering experience. The stands towered above us in tier after tier, with the faces seeming to go on and on, and even though these meetings were friendlies, such was the level of expectation in Brazil after their triumph four years earlier that the atmosphere was electric. Once again it was a privilege to share a field with Pele, who was even better than I remembered from Gothenburg. Now he was 21, physically more developed, and there seemed to be nothing on a football pitch that he couldn't do. It was such a shame that he was injured during the Chile finals and wasn't part of the team that retained the Jules Rimet Trophy, being replaced by another youngster, Amarildo. He was a fine player, too, if not a patch on the master, who remained enduringly peerless.

Sadly, there was one appalling consequence of our South American sojourn. In Sao Paulo our fantastic goalkeeper, Jack Kelsey, injured his back so badly while diving at the feet of the Brazilian centre-forward, Vava, that he never played again. It was a cruel blow to a performer still very much in his pomp at 32, no age for a keeper, and it was bitter news, too, for his club, Arsenal, who didn't manage to replace him anything like satisfactorily until the emergence of Bob Wilson towards the end of the decade. Happily Jack, one of the nicest men in football, went on to serve the Gunners in various commercial capacities down the years, but it was for his daring exploits between the posts that he will be remembered most vividly.

Before we returned to the UK we had one more engagement to fulfil, a 'friendly' – the use of the inverted commas will become clear in due course – against Mexico, and our stay in that country proved eventful from start to finish. We checked in to a comfortable hotel in Mexico City, and I was sharing a room several storeys up with Mel Charles, with whom I'd always got on extremely well and shared plenty of laughs. But early one morning it became apparent to both of us, while we were still in our beds, half asleep, that something was seriously amiss. I can't put it any plainer than to say the room started moving! Mel shouted out to me something along the lines of "Stop messing around, Jonesy" because I had been known to enjoy the occasional practical joke and now he thought I was tipping him out of his bed.

But I was still flat on my back so I put him straight on that, and it became alarmingly clear that something extraordinary was happening. Slowly the truth dawned on us that we must be experiencing an earth tremor or, even worse, the early stages of a full-blown earthquake. We leapt up, ran to the window and saw that lots of people were running out of the hotel, which seemed like an eminently wise move, especially as we could feel the floor moving under our feet. So we threw on some clothes and dashed out of the room. Of course, we couldn't use the lift, which wouldn't have been working, so we started charging down the stairs with the walls still shaking. Then, just as suddenly as it started, it stopped. I don't know how long it lasted, maybe a minute, two at the most, but the overall feeling was of confusion rather than terror or panic. Nobody was telling us what to do, we just thought it would be common sense to get out on to the street in case the building collapsed, and as we darted out of the door we could see a gap had opened up where the wall by the entrance had parted company with the ground.

Afterwards we could only thank our lucky stars that nobody had been hurt and that the tremor did not develop into anything more serious. There have been some horrific disasters in Mexico and we could count ourselves fortunate that our incident was merely a minor one, but it certainly made life interesting while it lasted.

And for me, at least, the drama didn't end there. First I fell victim to a street conman, who did me up like a kipper. I was naïve enough to buy what looked like a lovely ring for Joan, but my delight at picking up what I thought was a bargain was short-lived. Even as I was showing it to the lads, the stone fell out, revealing itself to be a rotten fake. I can't remember how much I handed over, but it was too much, whatever it was, and the fellow who had pulled the wool over my eyes had disappeared from the scene before I could go in search of retribution. How we all laughed!

And as if that wasn't bad enough, my stay in Mexico City plumbed new depths during the second half of the match, which we lost 2–1. There was a very talented inside-forward called Antonio Jasso who had put our hosts two up with a goal either side of the interval, but not content with that, for some unknown reason he kept having a go at me, kicking me several times. Normally my response to that sort of treatment was to get on with the game, trying to get my own back in the best way possible by playing some decent football. But this time, I don't know why, I took offence. He had pushed me too far, and after one particularly horrendous tackle I swung a right hook at him, catching him squarely on the chin. Down he went, all hell broke loose and the referee had no hesitation, or alternative when I considered it in the cold light of day, but to send the pair of us off.

It wasn't an incident I was proud of because I was a stickler for discipline – the cool approach was always dinned into us at Tottenham by Bill Nicholson – and this was the first and only time in my career that I was dismissed. I was really fed up as I reached the dressing room in the bowels of the stadium, but then I thought my situation might get even worse as I heard thundering footsteps on the stairs behind me. There was a crowd of some 75,000 people making a lot of very menacing noise and the Mexicans did have a reputation for being hot-headed. Now I thought some of them might be coming to get me, so I was enormously relieved to discover that the steps were those of a few of the Welsh party, who were there to offer me support and protection if it were needed. I'm happy to report there was no further unpleasantness, but I was not sorry to be heading for home soon after that little lot.

Back in England three months later, Tottenham embarked on a bid to regain the League title which we all believed was eminently achievable. Though our captain was now in his 37th year, his sharp intelligence enabled him to spare his legs by application of that formidable Blanchflower brain, and nobody else had reached the veteran stage. Our predator in chief, Jimmy Greaves, was at his zenith, as he proved with 44 strikes, the best tally of his White Hart Lane tenure, and for all their excellent qualities, we believed we had the measure of our main challengers in recent years, Burnley, Wolves, Sheffield Wednesday and a rapidly declining Ipswich. However, there was a rising power in the land and that was big-spending Everton, now managed by Harry Catterick, who had guided Wednesday to the runners-up spot in 1960/61. They boasted top-quality performers such as the central attacking pair Alex Young and my Welsh teammate Roy

Vernon, a commanding defensive linchpin in Brian Labone, a combative midfield featuring Jimmy Gabriel and ex-Owl Tony Kay, and abrasive left winger Johnny Morrissey, who was famous for taking no prisoners.

Not that Bill Nick and the lads were daunted in the least, and we started brightly, with five wins in the first six League games, with me sneaking on to the scoresheet in four of them. In fact, we were hitting the net for fun, with one autumn sequence reading nine (against Nottingham Forest), four, two, six, five and four, a six-match tally of 30 goals with only ten against. Unfortunately four of them were whacked in by Arsenal at White Hart Lane in a 4–4 draw, which offered pulsating entertainment but did little for the peace of mind of a team chasing the championship. We led 3–0 early in the game and spurned countless other scoring opportunities, so when we ran off at half-time with a 4–2 lead – to which I had contributed a couple of goals – our fans were contemplating a massacre of the order that had overtaken Forest a week earlier. But Billy Wright's boys refused to give in and, inspired by the wily George Eastham, went away with a heroically-earned point.

But although we suffered a few hiccups from mid-November onwards, when we beat Ipswich 5–0 at the Lane on Boxing Day – Jimmy grabbed a hat-trick, just for a change – we were in second place behind Everton and confident that we could overhaul them in the New Year. But then the season went into limbo because of the Big Freeze, the whole country disappearing under an extensive layer of snow in one of the worst winters ever recorded – we played only twice in the next couple of months, including a 3–0 FA Cup exit at home to Burnley – and somehow our domestic impetus drained away. Eventually we finished as runners-up, six points adrift of the rampant Toffees, leaving us to seek solace in a competition we had entered for the first time, the European Cup Winners' Cup.

When the draw for our first tie was made, the newspapers went into overdrive. We were paired with Glasgow Rangers, and the fact that the game was part of a continent-wide tournament seemed to be forgotten as all we read about was the forthcoming 'Battle of Britain'. Though neither club were reigning champions of their own country, I think it's fair to say that we were widely recognised as the best respective teams and certainly both sides were dripping with quality. Rangers' biggest star was Jim Baxter, a supremely

*The Big Freeze didn't stop us beating Arsenal 3–2 at Highbury in February
1963. Here I've managed to skate over the snow to slip the ball past keeper
Jack McClelland for our second goal. That's Jimmy Greaves behind me, while
the Arsenal players, left to right, are John Snedden, Laurie Brown, a very
young Geordie Armstrong and Johnny Barnwell.*

gifted wing-half whose languid style sometimes gave a misleading impression that he was coasting through a game, but then, out of a clear blue sky,
he could destroy any opposition by spearing a pass through the heart of their
defence. His mastery on the pitch was apparently matched by his capacity to
enjoy himself off it, which might have had something to do with the fact that
he didn't remain at the top of the game as long as his extravagant ability
warranted, which was a shame.

But the Ibrox Blues were not a one-man team, far from it. They were nearly
all full internationals, including the brilliant wing pair Willie Henderson and
Davie Wilson, predatory marksman Ralph Brand, cool and commanding full-
back Eric Caldow and the clever midfield playmaker Ian McMillan, known

You put your left leg in ... training with Terry Dyson, a terrific little player and a grand teammate.

north of the border as 'The Wee Prime Minister.'

Sorry for the cliché, but White Hart Lane was white hot to welcome them, thanks in no small measure to the visiting Scottish fans, who practically took over the place and raised the roof, having already made their presence felt in all the pubs within walking distance – or should I say staggering distance? – of the ground. They did like their tipple, those Rangers boys, and the whole area was a heaving sea of blue.

But for all the furore, as a balanced contest the game did not live up to the heightened level of anticipation. We won 5–2, with the emphatic scoreline not exaggerating the gulf between the two sides. Ironically, the man who set us on the way to victory was one of Rangers' fellow Scots, John White, who nodded our first two goals, the others coming from Les Allen and Maurice Norman, with a wicked deflection off the visiting skipper Bobby Shearer thrown in for good measure.

But even though the tie was now tilted heavily in our direction, that did nothing to reduce the mass hysteria ahead of the second leg at Ibrox six weeks later. I've experienced some astonishing atmospheres in my time at famous grounds around the world, but rarely did I encounter such feverish intensity as was engendered that night in Glasgow. The Scottish press had whipped up a frenzy bordering on mania, declaring that Rangers could defy the odds to overturn our three-goal advantage, and the fans lapped it up. They were wild for it.

As we walked on to the pitch, the noise from the 80,000 crowd was almost unbearable. I could feel it bearing down on my head, imagined it flattening my ears. It was so loud it hurt, and it didn't lessen when we kicked off. But then suddenly, after eight minutes, there was the blissful sound of silence. Jimmy Greaves, utterly unfazed by the fury raging around him, had raced beyond three toiling Rangers to beat keeper Billy Ritchie with a fierce drive, and when that ball hit the net the din ceased abruptly. You could have heard a pin drop. It was a truly spooky moment, so totally surreal that all the Spurs players were looking round for the referee and linesman to make sure that the goal had been given.

It was, and now we were four to the good, an impregnable position. The opportunist Brand equalised soon after the break, but although the action remained passionate – Baxter was booked for a nasty foul on Greaves – two emphatic hits from Bobby Smith ensured that we prevailed 3–2 on the night, 8–4 on aggregate.

It must have been crushing for the home supporters who had arrived with such lofty expectations, and in some ways I saw it as a microcosm of the Scottish game at that time. National manager Ian McColl had such a wealth of world-class players to choose from, some of the best I've ever seen, the likes of Denis Law, Jim Baxter, Ian St John, Davie Wilson and our own Mackay and White. They should have been good enough to win the World Cup, and yet they never made the most of all that incredible quality. Somehow there was always a self-destructive element in the team's make-up which always got in their way.

Part of the reason that the fans were so rabid is the downright fearsome allegiance to their clubs. I can remember playing at Hampden Park against two of the finest wingers of modern times in Jimmy Johnstone and Willie Henderson. But when Celtic's Johnstone picked up the ball, all you could hear were Rangers chants, and the opposite applied when Henderson of Rangers took possession. The truth is that Celtic v Rangers was always more important to the supporters than the fate of the national side, an attitude which goes a long way towards explaining why Scotland have never achieved what it should have done as a country. Sadly, the question does not even arise today when the Scots don't possess one world-class footballer, let alone five or six.

Our win over Rangers took us into the quarter-finals of what was quite a limited-in-numbers competition in those early days, and our next opponents,

Slovan Bratislava, were renowned as a fine, flowing, footballing side. Sad to report, in the opening away leg we gave our worst performance of the Cup Winners' Cup campaign, and it was no excuse that the game was played on a sludgy quagmire of mud mixed liberally with snow. None of us could get going – time after time I ran into a brick wall of a full-back named Anton Urban – while they made light of the sticky conditions, and if it hadn't been for Bill Brown, putting in one of the finest displays of his life, then we would have been thrashed. Our Scottish keeper, playing on with a big plaster across his nose after taking a heavy knock, made save after save to keep us in the competition.

Naturally, the Czech crowd revelled in their team's supremacy, though towards the end I could sense a feeling of apprehension permeating the ground because the hosts had not made the most of their domination, and some bad feeling crept in, which was carried over into the after-match reception. Bobby Smith had a run-in with their goalkeeper, Willy Schroif, which threatened to get nasty, with one or two other players looking ready to get involved. It ended without physical violence but with Bobby staring at Schroif and snarling: "Londres! You've had it!" His meaning was amply clear.

Schroif did get it in Londres, too. In the first minute, he made a decent save from Jimmy Greaves, only for Bobby to follow up with a hefty whack which sent him flying into the back of the net and left him rolling in pain on the ground. He was one of the best goalkeepers in Europe at the time, known as 'The Black Cat', but after Bobby's tender attentions so early in the match, he just never turned up again and we slaughtered them. In front of him the Slovan defence, despite being marshalled by the splendid centre-half Jan Popluhar, just fell apart to the tune of 6–0. Jimmy scored two, while Dave Mackay, John White, Smith and myself got one each, but there was never any doubt that Bobby was the main man, repeatedly tearing into the opposition in a manner which they just couldn't cope with. This represented a not-uncommon scenario of continentals not being able to handle the physical side of the British game. To put it in Corporal Jones' immortal words, they didn't like it up 'em, although I do have to stress that most of the football played was impeccably fair. But it was a man's game and it would be idle to deny that there was often a hard edge.

Up for the challenge against Atletico Madrid at the Feyenoord Stadium in Rotterdam ahead of the biggest European night of our lives in May 1963. Back row, left to right: Tony Marchi, Danny Blanchflower, Maurice Norman, Ron Henry, Bobby Smith and Bill Brown. Front: Terry Dyson, myself, John White, Jimmy Greaves and Peter Baker.

The rest of us knew what was coming from Bob from the moment he declared his intentions at that Bratislava reception. We knew there was no way he was going to back off. He wouldn't have discussed his plans baldly in front of Bill Nicholson because our manager wouldn't have approved of a vendetta. But Bill realised the undercurrents, understood perfectly what was going on, and was content that it would work out in our favour. That was a fact of football life in those days, when forwards could get away with targeting a keeper to see what he was made of. Schroif wilted under fire, but by no means all of them were intimidated by tough treatment. Just imagine trying to put the fear of God into Harry Gregg – no chance!

Our 6–2 aggregate triumph over Slovan represented a cracking comeback reminiscent of our drubbing of Gornik 18 months earlier, and it set us up beautifully for our semi-final against OFK Belgrade. The first leg, taking us back behind the Iron Curtain, was to be yet another tumultuous physical contest with the sparks flying and Bobby Smith invariably in the heat of the action. It was after he had been involved in a furious tussle, which as far as I could see involved flailing elbows, that we were awarded a free-kick midway through the first period, and following that John White put us in front with a terrific 20-yard volley. Soon they equalised from the penalty spot after a harsh handball call against Dave Mackay, then early in the second period came the incident for which the game is always remembered. After retaliating to a missed punch thrown by one of their defenders, Jimmy Greaves waved a fist of his own and was sent off, making him the first Spurs man to be dismissed since 1928. Later in the dressing room, Jimmy was berated by our trainer, Cecil Poynton, for besmirching the reputation of the club and happened to ask who received matching orders some 35 years earlier. Cecil, a sturdy full-back in his day, responded in deadpan fashion: "Me" he said.

Though Jim never denied raising his hand, the lads all felt he had been hard done by, and that fuelled a deep sense of injustice which had our ten men – I was only a spectator, being out through injury – working like demons for the rest of the game. This paid off ten minutes from time when Terry Dyson came up with a smart finish to grab a deserved winner, the culmination of an uplifting team performance.

That made us overwhelming favourites to become the first British club to reach a European final, but there was no way the accomplished Yugoslavs were going to lie down for us in the second leg, and they did put up a creditably spirited fight. In the event, though, with Danny Blanchflower at his imperious best and with Bill Brown shining again, we won 3–1 with hits from Mackay, myself and Smith.

Now we had a golden chance for our second ground-breaking achievement in two years, but there was one dismal cloud hanging over White Hart Lane as we prepared for the final against the holders, Atletico Madrid, in Rotterdam. Dave Mackay, who had charged through brick walls to get us through to our showdown with the Spaniards, sometimes lifting us up by our bootstraps when we were at a low ebb, wasn't fit enough to play, having failed a fitness test on a groin strain that morning. It's no reflection on Tony

Marchi, who did a stupendous job as his deputy, putting up a tremendous show against Atletico, but there was only one Mackay.

During the pre-match team talk, Bill Nick had seemed slightly anxious, emphasising to us that the Madrid side was packed with talent, but Danny Blanchflower butted in, pointing out that we were more than a match for anyone on our day – and he was convinced that this would be our day! As we were on the point of leaving the dressing room, Bill took Terry Dyson and myself to one side and urged us to run at their full-backs at every opportunity. That advice was still ringing in my ears after 16 minutes when Bobby Smith, typically showing his intelligence and dropping deep to forage for the ball, arrowed a beautiful pass inside the left-back, Ramiro. I got up a head of steam, did the Brazilian for pace and crossed nicely into the path of Jimmy Greaves, who side-footed into the net with a characteristic minimum of fuss without even breaking his stride. That was brilliant, not least because it settled any nerves, and just after the half-hour things looked even better when Terry Dyson clipped a neat pull-back to John White, who rapped it home under the crossbar.

However, if there was any hint of complacency – not that Bill would have countenanced such a thing – it was wiped away within two minutes of the re-start when Ron Henry punched the ball clear to prevent a certain goal – he would be red-carded for such behaviour in the modern game – and their captain, Enrique Collar, beat Bill Brown from the spot. That signalled the start of a nervous 20 minutes during which they surged forward and we lost our iron grip on proceedings. Suddenly Atletico looked more than capable of retaining their trophy.

A souvenir postcard from our glorious night in Rotterdam.

Make no bones about it, we were struggling and there had to be a fear that the European Cup Winners' Cup was slipping away, which would have been terrible after such a marvellous start.

Cue Terry Dyson and a trio of interventions by the gutsy little Yorkshireman which transformed the night. First came the least spectacular but possibly the most crucial of his contributions, when he blocked a savage goal-bound shot from the right-back, Rivilla. Had the score gone to 2–2 then the classy Spaniards might have had the momentum to complete a stirring comeback. But now Dame Fortune chose to favour us and her smile was ravishing. Terry took possession on the left flank and rushed his cross, slightly mishitting it so that it curved towards the near post. It seemed like a routine take for the keeper, Edgardo Madinabeytia, but he flapped loosely at it and somehow it deceived him and he could only help it into the net. Terry might have claimed that he had delivered the centre with a deliberately devilish swerve but, to his credit, later he admitted it was a complete fluke. What's clear is that the poor keeper, who was in tears afterwards, should have done better, but that made no odds to us. This was the turning point – we were 3–1 up with one hand on the trophy.

Now all the Spanish pressure evaporated and we regained control. About a dozen minutes from time Terry crossed for Jimmy to grab his second of the night, then almost at the death the wee left winger exchanged passes with Tony Marchi, then darted through the middle to take a pass from John White before unleashing a 20-yard screamer which bulged a top corner of Madinabeytia's net. That goal was as genuinely great as his first had been fortunate, and it confirmed that the night belonged to Terry Dyson. At the final whistle, Mackay belied his lack of fitness by racing across the pitch to hug Smith, who then turned to Terry with a piece of tongue-in-cheek advice: "You should retire now," beamed Bobby, "because you'll never play so well again!"

While collectively ecstatic over our history-making 5–1 win, we were all especially delighted for Terry, who was, and remains, a smashing character. Although he was always a cracking footballer, he did tend to be characterised as something of an also-ran, and it's brilliant when a lad like that reaches such a glorious peak. It was a bit like John Aston Jnr of Manchester United, also a left winger, who enjoyed his night of nights when Matt Busby's men beat

I always loved a bus ride, especially this one, with the European Cup Winners' Cup on board. Revelling in the triumph over Atletico are, left to right, John White, Bill Brown, me, Ron Henry and man-of-the-match Terry Dyson.

Benfica at Wembley to lift the European Cup in 1968. George Best and Bobby Charlton were on the pitch on that magical evening, but it was the oft-unsung Aston who claimed the man-of-the-match accolade, and rightly so.

Back at our hotel just outside Rotterdam, we whooped it up with our supporters into the early hours, and I was delighted that, just for once, the normally reticent Bill Nick celebrated with us. He wouldn't have said as much to us, but it must have crossed his mind that we had redressed a balance that had existed ever since Hungary had humiliated England at Wembley ten years earlier. Now, at long last, the Brits were serial losers no more. I hope he also reflected, albeit in his modest, intensely private way, that only one team could ever go down in history as the first to lift a European trophy – and that team was his.

He never passed!

Terry Dyson remembers . . .

Cliff Jones was an unbelievably good footballer and he's a lovely lad, still one of my best friends after all these years.

He was a fantastic dribbler – though he used to upset Danny Blanchflower because he never passed the ball! – and he scored loads of goals, plenty of them headers. Cliff was completely fearless, always ready to throw his body in where it hurt, and he took some terrible facial knocks, especially to his nose.

We had three front-line wingers – Terry Medwin, myself and Cliff – and it was always the other Terry or me who was left out because Bill Nicholson thought so much of Cliff. I could understand why, because he scored so many goals, although I ran him close in the year we won the double. Cliff got 19 to my 17, but I always remind him that I made quite . a few of his as well, whereas he never passed to me or anyone else!

The beauty of life in our time at White Hart Lane was that everybody got on so well together. We were all close friends off the pitch as well as teammates on it. Although Cliff was essentially a quiet family man, he was always a big part of our togetherness, loving a laugh and a practical joke.

We were close to the fans, often having a drink with them after a game, and that was important to all of us. As Danny said to me when we last met, the modern players might make huge sums of money, but we have priceless memories of a glorious time, and nobody can ever take that away from us.

CHAPTER SEVENTEEN

It's lovely to be wanted

In the early 1960s I had the chance to transform my life forever. It was the era of top British footballers seeking, and sometimes finding, their fortunes in Italy. My Welsh teammate John Charles had made a massive success of his transfer to Juventus, while the Aston Villa and England centre-forward Gerry Hitchens did extremely well with Internazionale of Milan. On the other side of the coin, the star strikers Denis Law and Joe Baker, despite performing splendidly for Torino following their moves from Manchester City and Hibernian respectively, could not settle in the Piedmont sunshine, while Chelsea's Jimmy Greaves, to whom I would grow so close when eventually we became teammates at Tottenham, was not enamoured of life with AC Milan. So John and Gerry stayed and prospered and basked in the admiration of the Italian fans, while Denis, Joe and Jimmy all returned rapidly to England where, I'm delighted to say, they all thrived anew.

I also had several opportunities to join the British exodus, none more tempting than the one which came my way in the spring of 1963, shortly after scoring a hat-trick for Wales in a 4–1 victory over Northern Ireland at Windsor Park, Belfast. I was really buzzing at the time, still somewhere near my peak having scored 20 or so goals for Spurs in each of the last four seasons, and I got word from Gigi Peronace, who goes down as the first and arguably most influential football agent, that Juventus were interested in signing me. Rumours of possible approaches by a number of continental clubs had been circulating for a while, and I think the hat-trick, my only

Looking confident before kick-off against England at Ninian Park in October 1963. Alas, we lost 4-0. Back row, left to right: Mike England, Terry Hennessey, Dave Hollins, Graham Williams, Ollie Burton and Wyn Davies: Front: Len Allchurch, Roy Vernon, Stuart Williams, Ivor Allchurch and me.

triple in the red shirt of Wales, convinced them to launch negotiations before someone else stepped in.

I was ruling nothing out, keen to hear whatever might be on offer, so a rather high-powered delegation came to my house in Palmers Green, north London, consisting of Gigi himself, Gianni Agnelli, one of the biggest wheels at both the Fiat company and Juventus, and Giampiero Boniperti, who had not long retired as one of the greatest players the club had known and who had recently joined the management at the Stadio Comunale. Gigi had recruited my White Hart Lane teammate, Tony Marchi – who was of Italian extraction and had played successfully in the land of his forefathers – as interpreter, and he outlined to me what would have been a fabulous financial deal.

They were willing to pay me a signing-on fee of £10,000, which was an astronomical and life-changing amount at the time, while my weekly wage would have been £125. As a package it completely dwarfed what I was getting at Tottenham, and it was extremely tempting. They were holding out the twin carrots of long-term security for myself, my wife Joan and our four children, as well as a comparatively luxurious way of life. We talked it over and Joan would have been happy to move. She's always been a strong and capable character who would have adapted to the inevitably colossal changes in all our lives. There was also the added dimension of my friendship with John Charles, who was back in England by this time but was still able to give an invaluable insight into life in Turin. He didn't try to persuade us to go, merely gave us all the relevant information, also making the point that Juventus were spending enormous sums of money to attract some of the world's top players, so from a football point of view the switch would have been mouth-watering.

With all this whirling around in my head, I agreed that they should put the plan to Bill Nicholson, whose reaction was, I guess, utterly predictable. In that deadpan, matter-of-fact manner of his, he told Peronace and company that, yes, they could sign Cliff Jones, but they'd have to come back in four years when his current contract ran out. Of course, that amounted to an outright rejection because there was no way Juventus were going to strike a deal to sign a 28-year-old four years down the line, so that was the end of the story.

I suppose I felt a hint of regret, partly because of the new challenge, partly because of the cash on offer, and partly because I was never going to get a comparable offer, given my age. But deep down it didn't really bother me because, quite simply, I had grown to love Tottenham Hotspur. I identified with the fans, I got on brilliantly with my teammates, and I both admired and respected the way Bill Nick ran the club. The fee mentioned was a staggering £125,000, which would have been a world record, outstripping both the Law and Greaves transactions, so suddenly this little Swansea Jack would have been the costliest footballer on the planet. That aspect wouldn't have bothered me though. I've always been pretty grounded, taking most things in my stride.

In the modern era I might have been offered an improved contract to stay at the Lane, but not in those days, not by Bill Nick. In his book, just to be able to pull the white shirt over your head and wear the cockerel on your chest

I'm a pheasant plucker ... actually, this was a turkey I was getting ready for Christmas in 1962. We owned two butcher's shops at the time, one at White Hart Lane and the other at Arnos Grove.

should be enough for anyone. It was always enough for Bill, who viewed it as the ultimate sporting privilege, and he thought it should be enough for me. And in the final analysis, so it was. I guess I might have taken a different stance if the New Deal for players, inspired by Jimmy Hill, had not gone through in 1961. The old maximum wage had been consigned to history, enabling clubs to pay a greater share of the money they made to the people who, after all, facilitated what was a highly lucrative mass entertainment industry. It didn't make us rich on anything approaching the Italian scale, but it did improve our standard of living and made us feel more valued. The Juventus approach also had the fringe benefit for me of doing wonders for my confidence. Without being conceited, I knew I was one of the top wingers on the scene, and this confirmed it. As anyone in any walk of life will tell you, it's always lovely to be wanted!

In fact, it was neither the first nor the last time that a transfer overseas was mooted for me. The same Juventus had first expressed an interest in me back in the summer of 1960, when Spurs had been on a short friendly tour. I happened to have a decent game, running at defenders and going past them, and they told me I was the best left winger they'd faced, hinting at a possible move. Nothing came of that, but in the following spring I was tapped up first by Real Madrid and then by Barcelona. It was all a bit cloak-and-dagger, but then their enthusiasm appeared to cool after I had a disappointing game for Wales against Spain in a World Cup qualifier at the

Bernabeu. Three months later another, unnamed, Spanish club made discreet enquiries as to my availability, and there were frequent stories that Roma were sniffing around.

. Then in the summer of 1963 I was linked heavily with Atletico Madrid, who evidently had been impressed by my efforts against them in the European Cup Winners' Cup Final. I didn't bite, though, I just sat back and awaited any developments, which never materialised. Very little of this became public knowledge. These days the newspapers and broadcasters go wild at the slightest suggestion of a possible transfer, with constant gossip all over the pages and airwaves, and I'm absolutely convinced that a high percentage of it has absolutely no basis in fact. What it does, of course, is stimulate interest among the fans, and it can be undeniably entertaining, so who am I to knock it?

There were no major transfers involving Spurs ahead of the 1963/64 season, even though our veteran skipper Danny Blanchflower was now in his 38th year and often toiling painfully with injury. At that point, though, our captain still had the capacity to be a towering influence on most games, and clearly Bill Nick was going to keep him going as long as he was effective. It was to be a troubling season for Tottenham, however, with two members of our majestic midfield axis of Blanchflower, Mackay and White suffering grievous fitness issues, though in fairness it should be stressed that Danny and Dave's absences were mitigated, substantially

Joan was wearing scarlet for Wales in this shot outside our home at Palmers Green in the early 1960s.

though certainly not completely, by the excellence of Tony Marchi, who would have walked into any other first team in the country.

The Blanchflower knee finally gave up the ghost in the autumn, his farewell match being a 4–1 defeat at Old Trafford, an inappropriate manner for the great footballing intellectual to bow out. Manchester United were also the opponents when Mackay played his last game of the season, though in even more traumatic circumstances. Having drawn Matt Busby's men in the first round of the European Cup Winners' Cup, into which we had re-entered as holders, we monopolised possession in the first leg at White Hart Lane, but didn't break the deadlock until midway through the second period. We were becoming so frustrated by an efficient United defence that I thought I'd try something different and back-heeled into the path of a typical rampaging charge by Dave Mackay. When he received the ball he was at a narrow angle to keeper David Gaskell's goal and I didn't expect much to come of it, but Dave leathered the ball into the net with all his considerable might and was so delighted that he turned a double somersault in celebration. When Terry Dyson capitalised on a defensive error to make it 2–0 near the end, we were pretty satisfied with our night's work as we contemplated heading north for the return a week later.

Alas, despair was lurking just around the corner, and I'm not referring to David Herd's opener after six minutes which reduced the arrears. It was two minutes after the Scot's goal that our world darkened when Dave Mackay's leg was snapped in the act of shooting by a bad tackle from United's Noel Cantwell. It was not typical of Cantwell, who had a reputation as a gent within the game, but this was not a pretty challenge. I've no idea what came over him, but as Dave and he were about to collide, Cantwell turned his shoulder a split second before the impact. When you see that then you know something bad is coming, and so it proved.

Our talisman was stretchered off, and we were down to ten men for more than 80 minutes but, as if in tribute to the fallen warrior, we continued to take the game to United, even after Herd added an aggregate equaliser early in the second half. Soon Jimmy Greaves put us back in front with a neat header from a White delivery, but weight of numbers told in the end, with Bobby Charlton grabbing two late goals to settle the tie. The winner, only two minutes from time, was a typical Charlton thunderbolt, the sort that crowds

There was never a dull moment with Jimmy Greaves, who was not averse to employing whatever props came to hand in the cause of a daft picture. This time we were in Egypt.

loved him for down the years. He just took the ball in his stride and it ripped into the net past Bill Brown, who can barely have seen it.

Afterwards our concern was more for Dave than for the defeat. It was a terrible break which might have ended his career, and Cantwell was very solicitous. Mackay didn't condemn him publicly, but I don't think anyone was happy with what they had seen. In later years Dave wrote that because he eventually recovered, he could have a laugh about the incident with Noel when they met at functions, but he left his readers in no doubt that a different outcome might have produced a far less savoury response.

The Scot's enforced absence for the rest of the season enabled young Phil Beal, who would go on to a lengthy and admirably accomplished White Hart Lane sojourn, mostly as a central defender, to make his debut, though in March Bill Nicholson finally made an expert re-entry into the top end of the transfer market by paying Fulham £72,500 for their brash, devilishly steely and underratedly skilful wing-half Alan Mullery.

The big problem for Alan was in replacing such a favourite as Danny. Some fans made unfair comparisons and the newcomer took some unnecessary stick, but such was his strength of character that eventually his resilience, stamina and never-say-die motivational powers came to be widely admired, even if some supporters never quite appreciated what a technically accomplished operator he was.

That term also saw the entrance of the Scottish flankman Jimmy Robertson, a snip at £25,000 from St Mirren and so fast he could catch pigeons. Effectively I suppose Jim was a natural replacement for Terry Medwin, who had been forced to retire following a broken leg suffered when we toured South Africa during the previous summer.

We finished 1963/64 in a creditable fourth place in the First Division, only six points behind the new champions, Bill Shankly's rising power, Liverpool. They beat us 3–1 in both League meetings, twice in four days over Easter, and if only we could have reversed those results then we'd have stood a tremendous chance of winning the title again. Certainly we had championship aspirations back in October when a 4–4 draw at Highbury took us briefly to the top of the table, though I have happier personal memories of the White Hart Lane return four months later, by which time we had returned to the summit. I contributed a couple of goals, a tap-in and a header, to a 3–1 victory which revived our hopes of the top domestic prize.

In the end we fell away disappointingly, though a glance at the springtime results reveal two games worthy of comment. I managed a hat-trick, my only one of the campaign, in a 6–3 home win over Ipswich, who were about to be relegated as bottom club only two years after lifting the title; and there was a shocking 7–2 defeat at Burnley. But even thoughts of that grisly reverse would soon be rendered irrelevant, as would musings on all mere sporting matters, by the most grotesque tragedy ever to overtake Tottenham Hotspur.

CHAPTER EIGHTEEN

Calamity – but life goes on

What happened to John White, one of the best pals I ever had, was downright unthinkable. He was struck by lightning, an event which in itself is a byword for the staggeringly unlikely, while sheltering from a thunderstorm at Crews Hill golf course at Enfield, Middlesex, on 21 July 1964. I might easily have been with him when the rain starting pounding down and he dropped his clubs on the fairway to reach the supposed haven of an oak tree in the nearby rough.

That morning the players had been at White Hart Lane for the pre-season photocall and a bit of training. John asked me if I wanted a round of golf with him a bit later, but I said I didn't fancy it and would be heading home when we'd finished. Terry Medwin was there, sweating away as he attempted to fight his way back to fitness following a broken leg, and Bill Nicholson, well aware that John often liked to continue training at the end of the normal session, suggested that he have a tennis knockaround with Terry. John didn't have shorts to hand, so he took off his trousers and joined Terry on the ball court in his underpants.

For me, this was just too tempting an opportunity to pass up so, just for a laugh, I picked up John's trousers, put them in my car and drove home, chuckling at what my Scottish mate would be saying when he discovered they had gone. After that I forgot all about it, safe in the knowledge that John loved a practical joke better than most. I knew he'd be out to get his own back as soon as possible, but that was all part of the fun we used to have.

It came out later that after his tennis, he had found his football training kit and driven home. His wife, Sandra, then drove him to the golf club, where he

The best friend a man could have. Having a high old time with John White at the Tottenham Christmas party, while trainer Cecil Poynton is more interested in his grub.

bumped into Tony Marchi, who was just leaving. Apparently there had been a possibility that Jimmy Robertson might be on for a game, but in the end he didn't turn up because the weather looked uncertain.

So John strolled out on to the course on his own, heading for the tree when the rain arrived, followed swiftly by the thunder and lightning. When the investigators later tried to piece together what had happened, they surmised that he was either sat under the tree, or leaning on it, when the lightning struck, and the force of the bolt had thrown him into a nearby ditch.

Of course, the last thing you should ever do in a thunderstorm is shelter under a tree. We all know that. John knew it. But that's what he did in the haste of the moment with the sudden rain pouring down from a sky that, as people in the area were to say, had turned black. Had I been there, would I have stepped under the branches with him? That's an unanswerable question. The brutal truth is that he was alive one second and dead the next. Right to this day, the thought of what happened to John on that terrible morning fills me with horror.

I was at home when I heard the news via a Spurs supporter whom I knew well. He asked me if I knew what had happened and I didn't know what he was talking about. Then he told me: "John White's been struck by lightning. He's dead." I just couldn't take it in. It seemed completely unreal. I'd seen him only a few hours ago and I'd stolen his trousers! The first thing I did was to phone Bill Nicholson, who confirmed the worst and was obviously totally shattered. Everybody at the club, his wider circle of friends and people throughout the world of football were absolutely devastated and in a state of shock. I was distraught, knocked flat out. I had been so close to John, we were the best of mates. There was so much fun in him, he was just so good to be around, a delightfully modest lad with a tremendous sense of humour and without an ounce of malice in him.

There could be no consolation. In the days that followed, I kept thinking about all the laughs we had shared, knowing that there would never be any more. I recalled the mock swordfight on the stairs of the hotel in Portugal; the day John stuck his head out of the window of another hotel, this time in Manchester, calling for help that was not really needed and then having to make shamefaced explanations to the police; the times we had pretended to be waiters; the crazy fake phone calls; even the nicking of his trousers on that last fateful morning.

Aside from the unspeakable human tragedy, the unexpected death of a fit and healthy 27-year-old with a lovely wife and two smashing children, there were also the professional consequences to consider. Not that they amounted to a hill of beans in comparison, but Bill Nicholson and Tottenham Hotspur were not going to shut up shop, so the manager had to contemplate a future without the Scottish international.

The fact was that with Danny Blanchflower gone, John had matured into the team's main creative force and he was improving all the time. Without a shadow of a doubt, but for the horrendously freakish circumstances that snatched him away from us, he would have gone on to attain true footballing greatness. Everything was in place. As far as I could see, there wasn't a single attribute that John lacked.

He was supremely skilful and intelligent, and for a midfielder he got more than his share of goals, returning double figures in three of his five seasons at the club. He had a great engine with energy and stamina to burn, having been a cross-country champ in the Army, and his range of passing, long and short, was phenomenal – he could reach everybody. Most importantly of all, he made others play, or allowed them to. John was the ultimate playmaker, always available to help you out when you picked up the ball – not that I used to pass to him very often, I can hear him saying! He was a wonderful team member, too, so popular with everyone, a fantastic character to have around any club.

John's demise was a crippling blow to the side. He was still getting better all the time, I'm convinced that we had never seen the best of him and it took a long time to sink in that we never should. It was like the Duncan Edwards situation all over again.

With Danny gone, Dave seriously injured and now John dead, it was never the same again at White Hart Lane, the place was shaken to its very foundations. Some excellent new players arrived, but there was a devastating sense of loss which pervaded the whole place, a pall of gloom that just wouldn't disperse.

And yet, always, life goes on. You just have to get on with it. Matt Busby showed that when he fought back from much larger-scale desolation in the aftermath of the Munich tragedy, which cost the lives of eight of his players, maimed two more so that they could never take the field again and left others with lifelong psychological scars from which, in some cases, their game never recovered.

Bill Nicholson was just the man to pick up the pieces at Tottenham. Even aside from the permanent loss of John White, the retirement of Danny Blanchflower and the mercifully temporary if horribly prolonged absence of Dave Mackay – who was to suffer an excruciating second fracture to his same leg in his comeback match against Shrewsbury reserves in September – the team was faced with wholesale change. As we approached 1964/65, Bill Brown was out with injury, Peter Baker's career was coming to an end, Bobby Smith and Terry Medwin had both gone, and Les Allen barely played. It was a difficult situation, but one which Bill faced head on.

One of his initial thoughts affected me directly. Deprived of John, he needed someone to take on the midfield scheming role and he asked me if I fancied it. He had Terry Dyson and Jimmy Robertson to play on the wings, and clearly he had enough faith in me as an all-rounder to give me an extended run as a central creator. I said I'd have a go at it and he handed me the number ten shirt, but I soon discovered that being the fulcrum of the attack, the general, just wasn't my natural game. I was now required to make myself available all the time, support the man on the ball, receive his pass and then move it on quickly. But while John had been the perfect team man, fulfilling all Bill's requirements, my style was diametrically opposed to the White method. I was an individual who just wanted to keep the ball and run with it.

That was the style that had made me effective. I desperately wanted to help but although I persevered for most of that season, I just couldn't fit in with what Bill wanted, and by springtime he realised it was hopeless, coming to understand that I couldn't transform my style and still be at my best.

Oh, I had my moments as an inside-forward, but I think my first return as the regular outside-left said it all. We beat Wolves 7–4 at White Hart Lane in late March and I scored a hat-trick. It was like the hugest sigh of relief imaginable. As if any further proof were needed, I recorded another triple on the last day of the campaign when we drubbed visiting Leicester 6–2. From my own viewpoint, that had all the force of a definitive statement. I had done my best in the new position, but now I was back where I was happiest, and where I could do the most good for Spurs.

That season, in which we had finished sixth in the table – the lowest since 1958/59, understandably enough in the circumstances – we had welcomed to the club several players who would inscribe their names indelibly into Tottenham folklore.

Foremost among them was that remarkable man and, ultimately, peerless goalkeeper Pat Jennings. I first came into contact with him when he was making his Northern Ireland debut against Wales at The Vetch as a giant 18-year-old in April 1964. Few people had heard of him then and I barely registered him as we lined up before the game, but it wasn't long into the match before he made his presence felt. We were on the attack, a cross came in from the right and I ran in to meet it. Suddenly, right across my face comes this massive

In Lisbon with John White during the trip when the pair of us got up Bill Nicholson's nose with our schoolboy antics. I wish I could remember what was in the parcel.

All toffed up and ready for a move into politics? I can just imagine Jimmy Greaves as PM and me as the Chancellor of the Exchequer!

hand, which grabs the football out of the air as though it were a tennis ball. The next thing I know this big boy, because that's all he was, has volleyed the ball some 50 yards to a wisp of a lad, who was also making his entrance on the international stage and who was now lurking unobtrusively on their right wing. George Best – for that's who it was – pulled it down effortlessly, went past two players and set up a scoring chance for one of his teammates, all in one flowing sequence of action.

I was dumbfounded. I thought: "Who are these players?" With Pat being at Third Division Watford and George having played only a relative handful of games for Manchester United, I knew nothing of either of them. As it turned out I was there to witness the emergence of two of the greatest footballers ever to play the game, and now I see it as a treasured privilege to have been in their company on the pitch. It was a very special moment for me, even if I was on the wrong end of it, with the Irish beating us 3–2 that day.

With that experience in mind, I was so delighted a couple of months later when Spurs paid £27,000 to sign Pat from the Hornets. I knew in my bones that he was something special and I can't say I was the tiniest bit surprised when he went on to become the finest goalkeeper of them all. He was a natural at every aspect of his art, and I suspect that he picked up and honed a lot of his skills in earlier days as a successful Gaelic footballer, particularly the kicking, at which he was superb. I'm certain that if Pat had not been so exceptional between the posts, he could have excelled as a centre-half.

Like Jack Kelsey, he always loved being an outfielder in training games, but in sharp contrast to my dear old Welsh international mate, he was brilliant with the ball at his feet. Pat was a natural defender, reading the action often before it unfolded and stepping in to do the right thing. He was quick, the power of his physique was matched by the sharpness of his brain, his ball control was as assured as an inside-forward's and his kicking was invariably crisp. Keepers have to be good on the ball now – Spurs' Hugo Lloris is a fine example – and I know Pat would have been a sensation in the modern game. As it was he proved a magnificent long-term successor to Bill Brown, and Tottenham were so lucky to have him.

Bill Nicholson pulled off another recruitment coup midway through that 1964/65 season when he paid Dundee £72,500 for the services of their subtly sensational centre-forward Alan Gilzean, who had been such a major force as the Dens Park club had been crowned champions of Scotland and reached the semi-finals of the European Cup in the year after Spurs made it to the same stage. Gilly had made a huge impression on our manager when he had shone for a Scotland XI that had put six past Spurs at the Lane in a memorial match for John White. That night it was clear that Alan was a special talent, and Bill was positively watering at the mouth. He didn't cut a dominant rumbustious figure like Bobby Smith, always ready to bash opponents out of the way, far from it. Rather Gilly specialised in delicate little nudges and touches with his head and both feet, the intelligent kind of centre-forward who puzzled many big defenders, who preferred going up against the more traditional tough-nut type of spearhead so common in the British game. Almost immediately Alan forged a seemingly telepathic link with Jimmy Greaves, the pair of them knowing instinctively what his partner was going to do and what he required. They became known as the 'G-Men' and they did Spurs proud for half a decade, with the Scot remaining several years after Jimmy had left to join West Ham.

If you met Gilly on the street, and didn't know what he did for a living, you would never have thought he was a professional footballer. Pale and balding and not obviously athletic in appearance, he looked more like a businessman or an accountant. But there was never the slightest doubt about his fitness for his job, even after one of the lengthy drinking sessions that he relished so much. No matter how much he took on board – and he could take a bit! – he was always up to the mark in training, so it was never an issue for Bill Nick.

Having said that, there was one extraordinary occasion when Gilly imbibed a wee bit more than he could comfortably handle. We had been playing in a post-season tournament in Amsterdam in May 1965, and after one game we were relaxing outside a local bar, as was our custom. There had been a military tattoo taking place in the city and, as we sat there shooting the breeze and watching the world go by, a Scottish regiment marched past on its way back to base. The colour sergeant happened to glance across at us, he spotted Gilly and he was transfixed. The last time Scotland had met England at Hampden Park, Alan had scored the winning goal, and recently there had been a ceremony north of the border to mark his achievement, so he had been in the news.

It was a tremendous honour to take part in Stanley Matthews' testimonial match at Stoke in April 1965. Alan Gilzean is on the bench between Jimmy Greaves and myself, with the maestro making meticulous preparations, as ever, before the action gets under way.

Clearly, the patriotic sergeant was not going to let such an opportunity pass him by. He marched over to Gilly, saluted smartly and said something along the lines of: "Aye Laddie, come with the boys, we'll take you to see the captain." At first Alan said he couldn't accept this kind invitation because he was with the Tottenham party, but the fellow wouldn't give up. Now Gilly had already had a few drinks anyway and the next thing we knew, he was on his feet, and the sergeant had fitted him out with the regimental sash. Of course, Alan had done his National Service so he knew how to march and he played along with the situation. Before we knew it he was marching off into the distance and we didn't see him again for 12 hours. When he did finally rejoin the Spurs party he was, uniquely for him, in a hell of a state. Safe to say those Scottish boys know how to drink and, clearly, Alan had joined in enthusiastically. Bill Nick wasn't impressed, making it clear that he wouldn't last long at the club if he went on like that, but our wise manager, having made his point, had the nous to realise that fit young athletes were prone to let off steam, and providing there was no malice involved, there was no harm done.

Gilly, who from that incident onwards was known to his irreverent teammates as 'The Scottish Soldier', was always fun to be around, loving to perform tricks, much like his countryman Dave Mackay. We might be standing at a bar when, out of the blue, he'd toss a coin into the air, catch it on his forehead, then walk around with it balanced below that receding hairline. Next, all of a sudden, there'd be a plop and he would have dropped it into somebody's drink. The unsuspecting teammate would glance down and there, staring back at him from the bottom of his beer glass, would be a two-bob piece.

Another major Tottenham character in the second half of the 1960s was the full-back Cyril Knowles, who was to earn national cult status through the pop record *Nice One, Cyril*. Few people at White Hart Lane had heard of the 19-year-old Yorkshireman when he joined Spurs from Middlesbrough for £45,000 in the spring of 1964, but we weren't long in finding out about him. As a player Cyril was so many things – exceedingly powerful, pacy, adventurous, composed and very skilful – and had his career not coincided with those of Ray Wilson and Terry Cooper then I'm certain he would have collected far more than his four England caps. But there was so much more to Cyril than his football. He bubbled with sheer zest for life, he loved a practical joke, he was great company, and it was the cruellest of tragedies when he lost his life to a brain tumour at the hideously premature age of 47. But back in the summer of 1965, when he switched from right flank to left to replace the retiring Ron Henry, Cyril was ready to entrench himself as one of Spurs' key performers over the next ten seasons.

Change had engulfed White Hart Lane, as it does every football institution, no matter how successful it might be, but throughout my time at Tottenham it remained a friendly place, an enjoyable environment where there was always fun to be had alongside the business of winning football matches. I had lost my chief partner in humour, John White, but there were still laughs to be had as I demonstrated – in a rather crazy fashion, some thought – on a mid-decade visit to Nottingham Forest's City Ground. As the players were having a wander across the pitch before the game, some police dog-handlers were staging a show for those fans who had turned up early, putting their hounds through a succession of party tricks on an obstacle course, which included leaping through some hoops. Instinctively I turned to Alan Mullery and said: "I could do that." Alan reckoned I couldn't and told me to put my money where my mouth was, adding that he'd get together a few quid from the lads which would be mine if I accepted the challenge. Well, there was no way I could resist that and so, heedless of the consequences, I duly dived through the hoops at top speed, causing much hilarity and cheering from the terraces and stands in the process, as well as drawing a few puzzled looks from the dogs.

Bill Nicholson, of course, was aghast, especially when one of our directors demanded of him: "What on earth is Jones up to? Is he mad?" But, thinking on his feet, our manager flashed back with: "He's having a fitness test, obviously." Then, after covering for me until the director had shuffled away, Bill grabbed me and asked me what the hell I thought I was doing. Rather shamefacedly I told him how the daft escapade had come about, and somehow he kept a straight face as he bollocked me, telling me I was old enough to know better. It was a joy to work for such a wise, fair and resourceful man alongside a bunch of players who were as much mates as colleagues.

If I had any regret around this time it was that rumours of Bill signing former England captain Johnny Haynes from Fulham to replace John White

I shared some of the happiest moments of my life with John White, and this was one of them.

as our midfield general proved to be misleading. Johnny was a sumptuously gifted player, arguably the finest passer of his generation, and he had been born not too far from the Lane, in Kentish Town, so he would have been the ideal local hero. I believe he would have been the perfect fit for us, creating endless scoring chances for Jimmy and Gilly, but it wasn't to be.

Still, although most of the double-winners were now out of the picture, Spurs had new bulwarks in Jennings, Gilzean and Knowles, there was always the incomparable Greaves, Mackay would soon be swashing his buckle once more and Mullery was in his influential pomp. I had celebrated my 30th birthday but still felt like a spring chicken – well, more or less! – so as we looked ahead to 1965/66 Tottenham supporters had plenty of blessings to count.

CHAPTER NINETEEN

The times they are a-changing

There was no problem with my form in 1965/66. In fact, I averaged almost a goal a game in my League appearances. The difficulty was getting on the pitch in the first place. I had a severe hamstring injury and didn't play until December, then put together a little mid-season run of appearances before relapsing in February and being out for the rest of the campaign. It seemed that no matter how much treatment and rehabilitation I underwent, I just couldn't get it right. At one point a doctor removed what seemed to me an enormous amount of blood with a big syringe, and the blood was almost black. At that point I was told the problem would never have cleared up without that procedure, but that wasn't the end of it. There was lots of cortisone, the leg was immobilised in plaster for four weeks, then the movement had to be regained and the muscle built up, and finally I had to find some proper all-round fitness. It was an incredibly frustrating episode, not only on my own behalf but because I felt the team needed me. True, my absence enabled Derek Possee and Keith Weller, a couple of hugely promising youngsters, to pick up some invaluable experience, but at a time when Bill Nick was still rebuilding the team while results were extremely variable, I felt I still had plenty to offer.

One big plus for the manager was a return to full fitness at last of the indomitable Dave Mackay, who had defied the medical odds to bounce back from two fractures of the same leg. He was now the club captain and he led by buccaneering example, underlining the fact that he was one of the most outstanding footballers the British game has known.

That was all very well for the regeneration process, but any feel-good factor was offset in the autumn when Jimmy Greaves went down with a bout of hepatitis which was to sideline him for three months. Not even a team purring along in top gear could afford to lose the most lethal finisher in the land, and Spurs were going through an inconsistent patch when Jimmy fell victim to the debilitating illness. It was particularly infuriating because he had been in such fine fettle, scoring ten goals in 14 games, and his partnership with Alan Gilzean was improving all the time. The growing understanding between the pair was a joy to witness, and the last thing they needed was to have their impetus interrupted for such a lengthy period.

The up-down nature of Tottenham's progress was illustrated perfectly by our two meetings with the reigning champions, Manchester United. At White Hart Lane in October, when my devastated hamstring had me confined to the role of spectator, Dave and company absolutely murdered the Red Devils. We won 5–1 and one of the goals, by Jimmy Greaves, was fit to grace any stage. Jim picked the ball up around the centre circle and dribbled past half their team before pushing the ball into the vacant net. It was poetry in motion, definitely one of the most amazing sequences of action I've ever witnessed. The whole team was buzzing that day – young Eddie Clayton, who was playing at inside-right, had a terrific game and also contributed a goal – while all United could muster in return was a Bobby

The cast had changed as the 1960s wore on, but there was still fabulous fun to be had as a Spurs player. Joining me in the wardrobe are, left to right, the amiable Scot Jimmy Robertson, Terry Venables with a characteristic twinkle in his eye and the irrepressible Cyril Knowles.

Charlton special after Dave had goaded him, mistakenly as it turned out, about shooting from distance!

But in the return fixture on an Old Trafford mud patch shortly before Christmas, by which time I was back in the side, it was like a game between two different teams. This time they won 5–1, starting with another snorter from my old Army chum Bobby, a 25-yard half-volley which rose all the way into the net with such fearsome power that Pat Jennings was probably a lucky lad that he didn't get a hand to it. Quite how our form could be so variable was a taxing conundrum which Bill Nick somehow had to address.

Another stand-out memory from that term was a 4–3 home victory over Burnley in the fourth round of the FA Cup which evoked shades of the epic battles between the two clubs earlier in the decade. We were two down, and then 3–2 adrift, before turning it around thanks principally to a Gilzean hat-trick. Then there was my own White Hart Lane afternoon when everything went right as I managed three goals in a 4–3 win against Fulham in February. Alas, that was to be my last game of the campaign as my hamstring twanged again, leaving me an extremely unhappy man. I had thought I was back in form with my injury troubles behind me, but I was left to reflect on what might have been, with eight strikes from nine League appearances suggesting I might have been able to make a significant contribution if only I could have maintained my fitness.

Towards the end of the season two debutants afforded grounds for optimism over Bill Nick's continued restoration project. In early April a chirpy young Irish full-back called Joe Kinnear enjoyed an impressive run of outings in the number-two shirt. He was quick and energetic on the overlap, a polished passer and a solid defender, as well as being a cheerful soul to have around the place. I expected him to carve out a decent Spurs career, and so he did.

The other newcomer, who arrived just in time to help achieve a 1–0 victory at Blackburn on the last day of the season, was Terry Venables, another bright and breezy individual and, more importantly, a sharply clever creative inside-forward whom Bill hoped might go some way towards filling the void left by the death of John White. I thought Terry, who cost £80,000 from Chelsea, was a tremendous footballer, although not quite on John's level. That should not be

The changing face of Tottenham Hotspur. This is 1966/67, the season in which we won the FA Cup, by which time only Dave Mackay and myself were left as regulars from the side that won the double. Back row, left to right: Pat Jennings, Mike England, Cyril Knowles, Eddie Clayton, Alan Mullery and Joe Kinnear. Front: Jimmy Robertson, Jimmy Greaves, Alan Gilzean, Dave Mackay, Terry Venables, Frank Saul and me.

taken as criticism, however, because the world is still waiting for the new John White, and I'm sure it will continue to do so. Terry, who survived an early training ground dust-up with Dave Mackay of all people – strictly not recommended! – did pretty well for us, but without fitting into the quick-fire Tottenham style quite as seamlessly as had been hoped. For all that, when he moved on to Queen's Park Rangers in 1969 he was greatly missed at White Hart Lane because he was such a fun guy, a joker liked by everyone and who was also talented enough to be a singer and a writer.

But despite those positives, there was no disguising the fact that Spurs finished in eighth position in the First Division, our lowest since 1958/59 and with no fewer than 14 defeats, a third of the programme. That's proper mid-table standard, not what we'd come to expect, and it was clear that drastic improvement was needed quickly.

For several seasons now we had been conceding far too many goals, and Bill addressed that in August 1966, at a time when the majority of football-lovers were still toasting the fantastic achievement of Alf Ramsey's team in winning the World Cup on home soil, by signing a man widely acknowledged within the game as the best centre-half in the land. Our manager paid Blackburn Rovers a whopping £95,000, a British record for a defender, to clinch the much sought-after signature of Mike England – but not before he had asked me to chat up my fellow Welshman. Though Bill was a great one for doing everything by the book, he didn't want to miss out on a player whom Manchester United were known to be chasing hard, and he wanted to leave no stone unturned. I thought it was never going to be easy, what with United being right on Blackburn's doorstep and with Mike having a close Old Trafford connection in Matt Busby's assistant manager, the former Welsh national boss Jimmy Murphy.

But when I rang Mike, he told me he would be interested in joining Tottenham, and he came down to talk to Bill Nick. He ended up living with us for about two months, while looking for a suitable house for himself and his family. I was so pleased when the deal was done because Mike was exactly the dominant stopper that we needed. He was a colossal lad, commanding in the air, with a fierce competitive spirit, but he was also composed and skilful with the ball at his feet. He was a top character, too, a tremendous addition to our dressing room, so you could say he was the whole package. The only centre-half I have played with or against who I would put above Mike England would be John Charles, and it would be impossible for me to praise anyone more highly than that.

Soon, too, Mike and I had something more in common than our country and our club – we both hated playing against the flamboyant and provocative Northern Irish centre-forward Derek Dougan. For Mike's part, he loathed the bloke. He had been a youngster at Blackburn when Dougan had been an established player at the club, and he told me the Ulsterman did not treat the young boys at Ewood Park very well. He always said that if he ever had the opportunity to pay Dougan back then he'd take it, and so he did on plenty of occasions. Whenever they faced each other Dougan had to look out for himself or he'd be in trouble. He was a fine player, nobody's arguing with that, but he did have an unpleasant edge to him.

I recall a painful incident when he was playing for Leicester and we both went for a ball in midfield. He came right over the top, smashed into me, dislocated my shoulder and did my leg in. I was out of action for a lot of games. As I was struggling off the pitch I said to Mike: "Get that bastard!" I'm delighted to say that Mike didn't let me down. He sorted out Dougan that day, made sure he felt the pain for what he had done to me. I finished up in the Prince of Wales hospital and stayed there for quite a while. After that I had quite a bit of trouble with my shoulder, which kept slipping out. I'd expected I'd have to get it pinned in place, but instead the medics had me build up the muscles with weight training which supported the joint and solved the problem.

I also remember that day at White Hart Lane in December 1966, when we beat the Foxes 2–0, for being replaced by an up-and-coming lad named Roy Low, best remembered now, perhaps, for being Spurs' first ever substitute in League football during the previous season. He was a specialist half-back but was versatile enough to fill any attacking role at need, and he did have a lot of ability. His problem was that he had just too much of a swagger about him. It's all right talking the talk but you have to walk the walk, too, and Roy never quite managed it at Tottenham.

That 1966/67 season started on a highly positive note for Spurs with a 3–1 home win over Don Revie's ultra-competitive Leeds United in a game which gave to the world one of the most iconic of all football images. The Leeds skipper, Dave Mackay's countryman Billy Bremner, was a fantastic footballer but he could also be a fiery, confrontational little so-and-so and in the heat of battle he made the mistake of kicking our Mr Mackay on his newly healed leg. The two men were friends but for a couple of seconds the red mist descended on Dave, not surprisingly given all he'd been through, and he later admitted that, albeit fleetingly, he felt capable of wreaking immediate violent revenge. So he grabbed Billy by the scruff of his neck, lifting him from the ground, and it just so happened that the photographer Monty Fresco was right on the ball, capturing the moment for all eternity.

In all the years that followed, whenever a snap has been needed to depict Mackay the Warrior, this is the one that's been trotted out and Dave came to detest it. He felt that it characterised him wrongly and unfairly as a bully, picking on an obviously terrified smaller man, and as such it was totally misleading. Dave was never a bully. This was retaliation, and retaliation in the light of his two horrific recent breaks. No wonder he took offence, and that Bremner bore the brunt of his anger. Of course, it would be ridiculous to contend that Dave wasn't a fearsomely hard man or that he didn't deploy his awesome power on the pitch. But first and foremost he was a wonderful all-round footballer, one of the most skilful I have ever seen, certainly a passer as much as a tackler, and he was inherently fair. It's just a shame that such a brilliant photograph – and it is certainly that – should cause so much anguish over so many years.

For me, I was looking forward to 1966/67 as the season in which I could put injury worries behind me and get back on track, but in that I was only partially successful. Thanks in large measure to the assault by Dougan, I spent far too much time on the treatment table again, though I did manage 25 appearances in all competitions and in a team playing arguably its best football since we lifted our European trophy. We finished third in the title race, on the same number of points as second-placed Nottingham Forest and only four behind the champions, Manchester United. I was sidelined for both our meetings with Matt Busby's men, but was cheering the lads on as we beat them 2–1 at White Hart Lane in September thanks to goals in the last four minutes from Gilly and Jim, who were now a truly magical pairing. That was a wonderful day, with the sun beating down on a shirt-sleeved crowd, a good-natured pitch invasion at the final whistle and the distinct feeling in the air that we were in with a genuine opportunity of winning the League.

Unfortunately we went down 1–0 in a tight encounter in the Old Trafford return in January – what a difference it would have made if we had shaded that – but then didn't lose again all season, taking 19 points out of a possible 20. But for our early stumbles we would have been in with a great chance, but at least there was consolation in the FA Cup, which we won by beating Chelsea 2–1 at Wembley. I played in the first four games of our knockout run, but after that my only appearance was as a substitute for Mackay in our 2–1 semi-final victory over Forest at Hillsborough.

I did make history at the final, though not in the way I would have chosen. This was the first season in which subs were permitted, a change in the rules which was long overdue because so many showpieces had been ruined by injuries in the past. I was really disappointed when I wasn't picked to start, but I couldn't complain because I'd had lots of fitness difficulties, and the team was playing so well with Jimmy Robertson and Frank Saul in the wide positions. It was hugely frustrating for me, but Bill Nick was always honest, he had to make a call and I could only accept it, knowing he would always be doing what he thought was right for the team. He didn't make a big thing of explaining his decision, and I wouldn't have expected him to. In the end I wasn't called into action, so became the first man to get a winner's medal without kicking a ball.

Tottenham trainer Cecil Poynton sends me on as a substitute in 1967, when I could no longer quite count on starting every game.

The scene was changing, as it always has to, but still it was amazing to reflect that Dave and I were the only two players left from our great team. Was I granted any extra status because I'd been a part of the Glory Glory Days? Perhaps, to a limited extent. I was part of the history of the club and that might have come into the thinking when I got the shout over the excellent and unlucky Eddie Clayton to sit on the bench – remember there was only one substitute allowed in those days. But Bill would never have picked me out of sentimentality and it would have been wrong if he had. Frank Saul had come in, done well, scored goals and deserved the number-11 shirt. That's the nature of the game, and fairness has to be preserved at all times.

After all, I was now 32, carrying the legacies of various injuries and was unlikely to have too long left at the top end of professional football. That said, I proved I had something in common with a rubber ball by bouncing back in 1967/68, making 37 appearances in all competitions and contributing 14 goals. My pace had decreased somewhat but I had changed my style to accommodate that. Finally I was making the ball do more of the work instead of running with it at every opportunity, as was my natural inclination. Danny Blanchflower would have appreciated the irony of that.

Bill Nicholson was still preaching his gospel in his own inimitable way and the ethos of the old Spurs was still intact, dripping quality with the likes of Greaves, Gilzean, Jennings, England, Mullery and Venables all in their pomp. The colossally promising young centre-forward Martin Chivers was signed from Southampton in January in a deal which involved Tottenham forking out £125,000 and allowing Frank Saul to make the opposite journey to The Dell. Still, we slipped to seventh in the First Division table, and went out of the FA Cup to Liverpool after beating Manchester United, which was an underwhelming return for our efforts.

The feeling of ongoing transition accelerated at season's end when it was announced that Dave Mackay, now in his 34th year but still our touchstone, would be leaving to join Derby County of the Second Division. The boss at the Baseball Ground, a forthright young man called Brian Clough, must have thought all his birthdays had come at once when he signed Mackay, and he wasn't wrong. In his first campaign with the Rams Dave played masterfully alongside future England centre-half Roy McFarland, proving inspirational

A fine way to say goodbye, signing off as a Spur with a goal against Manchester United in a 2–2 draw at White Hart Lane in October 1968. United keeper Alex Stepney doesn't seem too overjoyed on my behalf.

as they rose to the top flight as Second Division champions, while Dave shared the Footballer of the Year award with another thirtysomething, Tony Book of Manchester City. Of course, it begged the question: couldn't Dave Mackay have gone on doing a superlative job for Spurs? Pretty certainly he could, but he felt he had run his course at White Hart Lane and was up for a fresh challenge, a stance which could only be respected.

Now I was the last double-winner still standing at Tottenham and at the outset of 1968/69, Bill called me into his office and told me, plainly but with a degree of compassion, that I had given marvellous service to the club, but soon he was going to let me go. But first he had one last job for me. The games come thick and fast at the start of a season and he asked me to hang around to help him through that rush, then I would be free to leave with his blessing. So I hung in there, made eight starts – and scored six goals!

For this battle-scarred 35-year-old, however, there was to be no eleventh-hour reprieve. On the morning after I had whacked in a goal against the new holders and first English winners of the European Cup, Manchester United, in a 2–2 draw at White Hart Lane, Bill called me again with a list of clubs who wanted to sign me, and this really was the end.

Since arriving in north London in February 1968, I had played 380 competitive games and scored 159 goals as a Spur. In three seasons I had exceeded 20 strikes, with a best of 25 in 1959/60, and attained double figures on seven occasions. I had been a member of one of the finest sides ever to play our lovely game, I had helped to make British football history, there had been no shortage of silverware, I had served under the best boss imaginable, I had made friends to last a lifetime and I had brought up my family in what I came to see as a delightful part of the world. As I reflected on my plans for the next stage of my life, the thought occurred to me – that move to Tottenham Hotspur all those years ago, it didn't work out too badly, did it?

CHAPTER TWENTY

The Cottage and beyond

Still possessed of a childlike wonder at being able to play football for a living after a decade and a half in the professional game, I was delighted that five or six clubs were keen to take me on following my departure from White Hart Lane. The list Bill Nicholson gave me of potential future employers included Fulham, Wolves, Leicester and a couple of others, but the one which I fancied from the off was Fulham. I had grown to love life in London, which had become home to me, and the family was well settled, so I lost no time in getting in touch with their new young manager, Bobby Robson, and he agreed to take me to Craven Cottage.

But the Fulham I was joining in October 1968 was not what you might call a buoyant outfit. They were already virtually certain to be demoted from the First Division when Bobby accepted his first British managerial job with the club in the previous January, and he had not been able to save them. Their greatest ever player, the superlative midfield general Johnny Haynes, was fast approaching the end of his career and their England World Cup winner, the excellent right-back George Cohen, was shortly to be invalided out of the game with a chronic knee injury. Allan Clarke, an outstanding striker, had been sold to Leicester in the summer following demotion – it's fair to say that cash was not abundant – and the atmosphere around the place left a lot to be desired.

Still, I had genuine hopes of making a worthwhile impact at a good club, but sad to say it never worked out for me at the Cottage. There were a number of better-than-decent players – Les Barrett, Jim Conway, Stan Brown

A fresh start beside the Thames, but it never quite worked out for me at Fulham.

and the young Malcolm Macdonald were among them – but there were also a few who behaved like Jack-the-Lads and at that early stage of his career, perhaps, Bobby didn't have the authority to handle them. He had been playing at Fulham himself as recently as 1966/67, and maybe there were one or two who knew him then but wouldn't take orders from him now. This led to problems and he was sacked in November, only a few weeks after my arrival. Of course, he went on to become a hugely successful boss with Ipswich, then later he took the helm of England, Barcelona, Newcastle and others, so obviously the Fulham experience stood him in good stead.

Bobby was replaced by Bill Dodgin Jnr but it was a thankless task and the team was all over the shop. I played 18 League games that season – mostly on the left wing, a few on the right and a handful in midfield – and scored a couple of goals, but I didn't enjoy it. I kept myself fit, although like any professional my age I was playing with the legacy of various injuries and the years were catching up with me. I always put in a shift, but whereas I should have been laying the ball off even more to make up for the reduction in pace, I was still trying to carry it and got caught in possession too often.

Results were appalling, we won only six of 42 League games and for the second season in succession, Fulham were relegated as bottom club, once again five points adrift of the next team up the table, Bury. The situation didn't improve for me in the Third Division. I was injured in only the second game of the campaign, never playing regularly again and making my last League appearance as a substitute for Steve Earle shortly before Christmas 1969. Soon after that I left the club.

I'd be lying if I said my memories of Fulham were happy ones, and my sojourn at the Cottage made me realise how lucky I'd been to spend so many years at White Hart Lane. Not that I want to criticise Fulham as a club. They were going through an extremely rough period when I was there, but since then they have known many better days, including a dozen or so seasons in the top division, and I wish them nothing but well.

Meanwhile my international days had drawn to a close with my 59th cap, against The Rest of the United Kingdom at Ninian Park in July 1969, in a match to mark the Prince of Wales' investiture. A strong Welsh side including my old Spurs mate Mike England, the workaholic wing-half Terry Hennessey and the big strikers John Toshack and Ron Davies, lost 1–0 to exceptionally strong opposition featuring the likes of George Best, Jack Charlton and two more from the White Hart Lane brigade, Pat Jennings and Alan Mullery.

Our goalkeeper was the Leeds man Gary Sprake, who was an excellent all-round performer, brave and athletic, his only trouble being that whenever the television cameras were on him he seemed to make a serious mistake. As a result he picked up a reputation as a blunder waiting to happen, which hurt him a lot because it was so unfair – fundamentally, Gary was such a safe keeper. He did tend to be hot-headed, though, and had to be careful with his behaviour because if anybody upset him he was likely as not to try and knock them out.

At the other end of the pitch we were well equipped with strikers, with lots of people outside the Principality assuming that Ron and Wyn Davies were brothers, which was not the case. Ron was incredibly classy, brilliant in the air and on the floor and an extremely heavy scorer. As for Wyn, if anything he was even better in the air than Ron and although he was not as comfortable on the ball, I actually preferred him of the two because he was such an unselfish battler. The fans of Newcastle, where he played during the peak of his career, used to idolise him for his courage and his effort. They called him 'Wyn the Leap' and sang "You'll not see nothing like the mighty Wyn" to the tune of the Bob Dylan song, *The Mighty Quinn*. He was ferocious all right, but only in a competitive way, there was nothing remotely dirty about the way he played the game. He would hand out stick and take it in return without a murmur of complaint, which I believe is the way it should be. I did think a lot of Wyn.

At the time of our clash with The Rest of the UK, I was 34 and could say I'd had a good innings, though it was a lasting disappointment that we never qualified for the finals of another major tournament after our exploits in Sweden way back in 1958. But I always loved playing for my country, it was the ultimate honour and I was privileged to share my time in the red shirt with so many colleagues whom I would class as all-time greats.

After all that, although it might sound corny, the fact was that I was still in love with football and wanted to continue playing at as high a level as possible for as long as I could. To achieve that I dipped into the Southern League, where the standard was really rather demanding. I'm happy to say that I never got found out like some old professionals did, and that was because I committed myself to it wholeheartedly and respected it.

Anyone who dropped from the Football League into the Southern expecting to have an easy billet had another think coming. You had to work really hard because there were lots of keen young lads on the rise and out to make a name for themselves, as well as loads of battle-hardened veterans at the other end of their career, so it was a truly competitive environment. Some of my opponents knew about my previous days and tried to take the rise out of me. Basically it was along the lines of: who do you think you are, coming in here as an international and lording it over us? But in all honesty, I never swaggered about my past and took a lot of satisfaction in applying myself properly. One hundred per cent is the only way I know how to do something, that's the way I am. If I embark on anything then I give it my absolute all.

Despite that, I soon discovered that all was not sweetness and light at non-League level. Almost straight after leaving Fulham I signed for King's Lynn, where my old Wales international teammate Reg Davies was the boss. Unfortunately the team was toiling terribly and I had only been there for a few months when Reg was sacked. That was a blow to me, but it seemed I might be lucky when Laurie Brown, who played with me at Tottenham, was appointed as the new manager. But he took what I thought was an unreasonably hard line, insisting that anyone who played for the club had to train at the club, too, and that just wasn't a practical option for me. I explained to him that I lived 120 miles away, and couldn't be expected to make such a journey twice a week for training sessions as well as travelling for matches. So that was the end of that.

Next I had a brief spell with Wealdstone, before fetching up at Cambridge City, where I did quite well under a Scottish coach, Tommy Bickerstaff, then later I enjoyed myself at Bedford Town with Barry Fry, the one-time Busby Babe who went on to a colourful career in management.

Of course, while all this was going on, I had to be making a living outside football. I had never considered coaching because I knew it wasn't for me. I was an instinctive sort of footballer rather than a deep thinker like Bill Nicholson, and it's the thoughtful types who make successful bosses. So I decided initially to return to my old trade as a sheet-metal worker, enrolling on a six-month course at a government training centre to get me back into the ways of the industry. Naturally there had been sweeping changes in the time I had been away, mainly with tasks which I used to perform by hand now being done by machines. The course gave me confidence and I got a job at a firm not far away from White Hart Lane, which might seem incongruous to fans of the current team, who might have trouble imagining Harry Kane or Christian Eriksen rocking up at a local factory when their playing days are over. You might say times have changed!

I have to admit I found it difficult going back to metalwork after such a long time as a professional footballer, and I was lucky to be able to make a fundamental change of direction. I was talking one day to my old friend Micky Dulin, who had been a young winger with Spurs before his prospects were sabotaged by injury, and he had become a games instructor at

Highbury Grove, an enormous state school catering for 2,000-plus pupils in Islington, north London. Now he was about to leave the job and asked me if I would fancy it. The post sounded right up my alley, so he put my name forward and I had an interview with the headmaster, Rhodes Boyson, who later became an MP, government minister and knight of the realm. Our chat went well, I was offered the work and set about getting the necessary qualifications. I already had a provisional certificate for football coaching, but now I moved into cricket, tennis, badminton and basketball. It turned out to be one of the best moves I made in my life. I stayed at Highbury Grove for nigh on 30 years, concentrating wholly on sport with no secondary subject, my job description being games instructor with specialised skills.

I have a great deal of respect for teachers. They do one of the most difficult and at times most rewarding jobs there are. I remember so many of them with pleasure from my Highbury Grove days, particularly my best mate Pete Whitecross, Head of PE Danny Goulden, swimming instructor Dave Fraser, Head of Sixth Form Ernie Mudd, and Pete Hepburn, who adored his football so much and who I used to call the poor man's Len Shackleton! I loved all aspects of life at Highbury Grove – working at the school, being with young people who kept me on my toes, it all made a huge difference to me in later life. My way of getting through to them was showing them how to do things and you've got to be in good shape to achieve that.

The badminton turned out to be particularly fantastic fun. I don't mean this to be boastful – I know I'm one of the lucky ones with my naturally lean physique and my good health – but the fact was that nobody could beat me. Not once in 15 years. I suppose I was quick about the court and had decent coordination, which made it difficult for them. I put the challenge out to all the boys aged 12 to 17 – do you fancy your chances this year, lads? There were a lot of them who thought they could beat an old man, but none of them ever did. When I'd won I'd tell them to go home and let their parents know they'd been beaten by an ancient fella. I just loved the winding up, it was like the banter in the football dressing rooms of days gone by.

I think the whole process helped to increase respect for what I did, and I made some great friends along the way. Years later someone might come up to me on the street and say something like: "Hello Sir, remember me? Johnson from Bedford House." I might come back with: "Oh yes. Still a pain in the ass?" It was smashing, a really rewarding job and I enjoyed it enormously, all the way to retirement.

During the 1990s, I also enjoyed organising and hosting soccer schools for youngsters in the little town of Cuffley in Hertfordshire, not far from where I have lived for the last 30 years. I ran it in conjunction with my son, Steve, who was a more than useful footballer as a boy and who might have

PE won't be the same without football legend

LAST Wednesday marked the end of an era when former Spurs legend Cliff Jones took his last PE Lesson at Highbury Grove School.

By **PAUL CHRONNELL**

It brought to an end to 27 years at the Highbury New Park school for Jones who joined at the end of his professional playing days in 1973.

"I had no idea I'd stay here this long when I took the job at the time," admitted Cliff, who joined after finishing his professional career.

"But I'm glad I did as it's been a great place for me and I've got some wonderful memories from over the years.

Generations of Highbury Grove boys have benefited from his coaching over the years – and have also given him plenty of stick for his Spurs connections!

Now 65, Cliff still works at White Hart Lane on match days and admitted he has been involved in more than a little banter in the school which is less than a quarter of a mile from the Gunners Highbury home.

"I've been surrounded by Gunners fans for nearly 30 years – but I've loved every minute of it," said the former Spurs winger last week.

"All the kids know about my Spurs

background so I did get a few insults thrown at me but it was all good-natured stuff," he added.

"But I always ask them was the first team to win the double and that usually gets them going," added Cliff, who was a member of that fabled Spurs 1960-61 double-winning side.

"That was 40 years ago now though and Arsenal have been so good lately so I've had a hard time of it," laughed Jones.

He was also capped 59 times by Wales and was recently included in a specially-compiled list of the top 100 footballers of all time – not a bad man to have as a PE teacher!

"I think the kids always had a bit of respect for me because they knew what I had achieved and that I had played at the highest level," he added.

"The school has had some hard times over the years but it has always had a good heart. I always told them there was more to life than exams," added Cliff who has also seen a few famous faces pass through the Highbury Grove gates.

"Of course we had Chris Whyte who went on to play for Arsenal and

Leeds and there's been plenty of other good footballers produced by this school over the years.

"I remember Peter Ebdon the snooker player as well – he was more of a cricketer back then and played for the county a few times.

"We had Eddie Kidd here as well and Sid Owen from EastEnders – so I've seen a few characters in my time here."

Although it was a long time since Cliff used to fly down the wing for Spurs, he is still in good shape.

"That's one thing this job has been brilliant for and I'm still fighting fit – I've had to be to keep challenging all this lot," he laughed.

Colleague Danny Golding will certainly miss Cliff's presence and added: "He still runs around like he's 30 years younger than he is and has been brilliant for this school.

"He's done so much in his time here and has been the reason behind so much of the success the school has had on the football field."

As a parting gift, Cliff has left the school with a new competition, the Hartlington Cup, which will see them take on the champions Hertfordshire every year.

In the inaugural match earlier this month, Highbury Grove ensured a final win for their long-serving teacher, winning 5-2.

■ CLIFF Jones admits he is sad to leave Highbury Grove School

I spent nearly three decades at Highbury Grove, and they represented some of the happiest years of my life.

made it at League level but for a knee injury. He's terrific at coaching and we both got a lot of fulfilment and fun from the experience, and if the feedback from parents and kids is anything to go by, we didn't do a bad job.

Throughout my football career I very rarely played golf; somehow in those days it never grabbed me. That said, a number of the Spurs players were very talented and immensely enthusiastic golfers, particularly the Scots, to whom it was their second game, with one-handicap man Bill Brown being the prime example. When I played for Swansea back in the 1950s the usual second string was snooker, and some of those boys at The Vetch earned more money with their side bets on the green baize than they did at football.

My own second sport in my twenties and thirties was cricket. I was a useful wicketkeeper and could get a few quick runs as a middle-order batsman. Over the years, during our pre-season training weeks as a member of the Spurs cricket team, I spent many an enjoyable afternoon in action against local clubs.

But since those far-off days my horizons have changed, and now I derive a huge amount of pleasure from golf, which remains a big part of my sporting and social life at the time of writing. I became a member of West Essex Golf Club some 40-odd years ago and now I'm in my early eighties, part of the senior section. I'm playing off a handicap of 17, maybe struggling a bit at that level, and can only look back wistfully to the middle 1970s, when I got down as far as ten. But I think I don't do badly for my age, while it still keeps me in good physical shape and, whatever else, I'm as keen as ever. Some of the best friends I have ever made are at the West Essex, for example Martin Tyler (he looks after me), Peter Dawson (what would we do without him?), Robin Hunt (come on you Hammers!) and Ronnie Forecast (the same age as me and he lives next door to Harry Kane). For an 80th birthday present, my Saturday morning group took me down to Celtic Manor, where the sun shone and Gareth Edwards, the rugby union great, was there to greet us. Some 50 years ago my White Hart Lane teammate Bobby Smith and his family were our neighbours and now his son, Stephen, is the senior captain at the West Essex – what an amazing coincidence. Fingers crossed, I shall continue to enjoy that lovely course with my mates for the foreseeable future.

But I am far from done with football. There are a large number of ex-players employed by Tottenham as matchday hosts in their corporate hospitality lounges, and round about 2004 Spurs asked me to join their ranks. I jumped at the chance to work at the club I will always love and respect, and I relish my duties at White Hart Lane, sometimes also travelling away for European games. When Spurs played Benfica in a pre-season friendly, I went with the team on a private jet to Lisbon, and then we had a motorcycle escort from the airport to our hotel. You might say that was a slightly different experience from my first game for Tottenham against the Arsenal, when Joan and I stayed at a bed-and-breakfast in Finsbury Park and made our way to the marbled halls of Highbury on the top of a double-decker bus.

Over the last dozen years I have mainly acted as host in the Legends Lounge. Before every game I give a rundown of the opposition and a prediction, seeking to enhance the fans' matchday experience. Unfortunately I have not always been too successful with my forecasting, and lounge members have been known to tell me: "Cliff, you are the worst judge in the world!" Well, you can't have everything can you?

I relish what I'm doing, engaging with the fans, and watching my beloved Spurs, especially during the 2015/16 campaign when Mauricio Pochettino and his hugely promising young team achieved Tottenham's highest placing for years. I have been thrilled by the exploits of Harry Kane, Dele Alli, Christian Eriksen and the rest, and there is no limit to what they might achieve over the next few seasons. In my opinion, they are the best Tottenham side since we won the double, and I hope so much that they will emulate us one day. I do believe their time will come.

As for talking to our supporters, sharing stories and jokes with them, I couldn't wish for anything more fulfilling. As Bill Nick would always say, they are the most important people at the football club.

Cliff's to blame!

Gareth Edwards remembers . . .

When my sister got married, no picture of myself or my brother was to be found in the family album. In fact, we were conspicuous by our absence – and for that Cliff Jones must shoulder a major share of the blame.

It just so happened that her wedding coincided with the 1961 FA Cup final, in which Spurs were facing Leicester City, so the pair of us slipped out of the reception early to find a television set on which we could watch that historic game.

Having been raised in the Upper Swansea Valley, I always followed Cliff's career closely, albeit from afar when he moved to north London, but he was always a hero to me and there was no way I was going to miss him in action on his biggest day – even if I was AWOL for part of my sister's!

People often say you should never meet the heroes of your youth because you'll be disappointed, but Cliff shoots that theory down in flames. Though I never saw him in the flesh during his playing pomp, I have been lucky enough to get to know him at golf days and other events in recent years, and you could never wish to meet a nicer person. In no time at all it felt like I had been his friend all my life.

I've been fortunate enough to travel the world as a sportsman, but still one of my most cherished memories is playing alongside Cliff and the equally brilliant Ivor Allchurch in a charity football match at Hungerford. Both of them still retained a magical touch with the ball at their feet, which made me realise just how special they must have been in their prime.

As a boy, like many of my pals, I couldn't get enough sport and I used to play rugby for my school on a Saturday morning, then football for my village in the afternoon. Like Cliff I was a winger and his success was an inspiration to me. I loved the round-ball game so much that for a brief spell in my mid-teens I was on the books of Swansea Town, but then my rugby took me off in a different direction.

Although the Swansea, Spurs and Wales teams that Cliff served so magnificently will be thankful that he never gravitated to rugby, I'm absolutely sure he could have made the grade with the oval ball. He was deft and fast, he had balance and control, he could drop a shoulder and execute a magnificent sidestep, he was brave, he had the lot. I'm certain that such a marvellous natural athlete could have adapted to either code – what an outside-half he might have been!

The word 'great' is bandied about much too freely when it comes to modern sportspeople, but occasionally it fits perfectly and Cliff Jones is a case in point, both as a fabulous footballer and a lovely man.

CHAPTER TWENTY-ONE

There *is* a road back from alcoholic hell

This might shock a lot of people who have followed my football career down the decades, but I want to make the frankest of admissions – I'm a recovering alcoholic and have been for more than 30 years.

I have visited the darkest pits of human misery, I have put my loyal and beloved wife and family through hell on earth, but I've emerged to tell the tale, and am living proof that there is always hope, there is always a way back from the most horrific depths of despair. But first, as I shall explain in soul-searing, humiliating detail, there must be unconditional acceptance of the problem and an iron will to reclaim all that is dearest to you.

Throughout all the glory years with Tottenham Hotspur, some of the lads had a motto, and in the light of my subsequent experiences it doesn't seem very clever. We used to delight in telling each other: "Win or lose, on the booze." And yet, believe it or not, the drinking I did with my mates during my playing days had absolutely nothing to do with the alcoholism which over-whelmed me later in life. Admittedly, there were times when I might have put away too much of the amber fluid, but I was a fit young athlete and I coped with it easily. It had no effect on my personal life or my ability to give my best as a professional footballer. Certainly it never controlled me, it was the game that did that and which gave me the buzz which I needed to get the most out of life.

My problems cut in only when the game had gone, when I no longer had the regular exhilaration of running out on to the pitch, beating defenders, scoring goals, relishing the camaraderie of the dressing room. I found I desperately needed something to replace those feelings and sensations, a substitute for the rarefied buzz of football, and that's when I turned to alcohol. I found that it gave me confidence, made me easier among people and it was all so simple. But gradually it got worse and turned into a nightmare beyond my wildest imagining.

The excess drinking started at home. I'd wait until Joan had gone to bed, then I'd just sit in a darkened room, stick a record on – probably Frank Sinatra – and get quietly inebriated. Up to a point, maybe, it was merely relaxing and, I guess, not necessarily harmful, but I took it too far. Before too long I'd be hiding drinks all around the house – under the sink, at the back of cupboards, on top of wardrobes, in the loft – hoping that Joan didn't find them. Then I could wander casually into different rooms and have a drink whenever I fancied one. The loft was a great place for me to hide booze because Joan couldn't get up there and I knew it. She'd shout up and ask me what I was doing – though knowing all along what I was up to, I'm sure, and hating it – and I'd call back to say I was looking for something and that I wouldn't be long. It's clear to me now that my behaviour was that of an out-and-out alcoholic, but for a long time I was in denial and just didn't realise the seriousness and implications of what was going on.

As to what I was drinking, I would have a go at practically anything – beers, wines or spirits – but Special Brew was my favourite, I got through an ocean of that stuff in my time. It was so strong, it would hit the mark straight away, and that was exactly what I wanted.

Sometimes I would go out to drink, and things came to a head, probably in the early 1980s, when I got involved in a fracas in a pub in Islington, close to where I worked as a school games instructor. Police were called and I finished up in Highbury Vale nick for the night. For Joan and my four adult children – who now knew what was going on and were more than worried by it – that was the lowest point to date. For myself, too. I felt terrible, desperate, utterly consumed with guilt.

I experienced the deep shame of appearing at Highbury Magistrates' Court on a charge of being drunk and disorderly and I was fined £30. I felt even worse because my son Steve, then in his twenties, was in the courtroom to witness me at my lowest ebb. Afterwards, as he was driving me home, he was so full of anguish and told me: "Dad, you've got to do something about your drinking. You're tearing the family apart, you must know that." Of course, I did know that only too well and I promised to address the situation, but even while I was saying that, issuing those calming words to my son, I didn't even want to be with him. Not deep down inside me. When I was in the court there were three other fellows on a similar type of charge and they were real bad cases, complete alcoholics. They had been planning their next drink after being dealt with by the magistrates and I knew they were headed for a pub in Highbury Fields, a tough place where people used to go for drugs, a really disreputable joint.

Now I know it beggars belief, and I shudder to recall it, but even while I was talking to Steve, who was doing such a wonderful job of looking after me, I didn't truly want to be in his caring company, I wanted to be with those three blokes. The reason? I was an alcoholic, pure and simple and unadorned. That's the stark, honest truth of the predicament I was in, even though I was not admitting it. I had crossed that line between being a heavy drinker into being a problem drinker – an alcoholic in anyone's language. At that point, without using the dreaded A-word, I understood that I had a compulsion which had me in an unholy grip, but I didn't know what to do about it.

I was a games instructor at the time and, looking back, I wonder how I managed to do my job. The fact was, although I had become very good at hiding the state I was in, the situation was coming to a head. I had got into the regrettable habit of going into a local pub during the school dinner hour, and there was this particular occasion when I returned to work with quite a few drinks inside me. I knew I had to take a challenging class that afternoon, with one or two difficult characters, and I had hoped to get them outside on the football pitch. However, it was hammering down with rain so I decided we'd do circuit training in Highbury Grove's grand hall instead. But when I announced this to the boys, one of them swore at me and said he wasn't doing that. I was incensed and I reacted stupidly, grabbing him by the scruff of his neck and starting to shake him. But he was very savvy, he smelt the alcohol on my breath and he exclaimed loudly: "You've been drinking!" I just pushed him away roughly, as if in contempt, but I knew that he had realised my condition. Still, I thought that was the last I would hear of it. After all, I reasoned to myself, it was a very minor incident and the whole thing was out of character, nothing like me at all.

But this lad went to the headmaster, Lorrie Norcross, and at the end of the day there was a message on the Tannoy for me to report to the head's office. Now I sensed trouble and Lorrie came straight out with it. "Cliff, I've had a complaint from this boy that you got hold of him and you'd been drinking." I couldn't deny it, and didn't even try to. He went on: "Your drinking has been noticed before and there have been one or two incidents which have been overlooked until now. But it can't go on. Now, we respect you very much, both for who you are and what you do for the school, and I hope you understand that. But I have to tell you that if anything like this happens again, there can be only one outcome, which will be the sack. For now, all I'm going to do is record it in the incident book.'

I was appalled at myself, dismayed at the depths to which I was sinking. The consequences of grabbing the boy brought it home to me that I was facing an extremely serious, potentially disastrous life-changing situation. I kept telling myself that it was all so out of character, but the evidence before me was very plain. Nobody else was doing this, it was me!

Domestically, too, I was approaching a crisis. Joan was worried sick and I couldn't blame her. She had tried for several years to control my drinking, but now she realised she couldn't. It was enough to drive her off her head, and the fact that she maintained her sanity, while keeping the family on a relatively even keel, speaks volumes for her incredible strength of character.

But even for Joan, breaking point was at hand, and it arrived with the premature end of Christmas Day 1984 at our house when I upset my family, that's my extended family, big time. My brother Bryn, for whom I'd always felt the utmost love and respect, and whom I played alongside at Swansea, was a long-term renal patient who had suffered abominably with his kidneys. I had been boozing freely for some hours and, after watching me pour myself yet another drink, Bryn walked over to me and told me I'd had enough. I can recall his exact words: "Just give it a rest, Cliff." But I was very drunk and I saw red. "Who do you think you're talking to, you f****** w*****." Then I lost all control and, with a mighty bump, I kicked the tray he was carrying out of his hands. Glasses and drink went everywhere, all over the furniture and the carpet. The music stopped, everybody stared at me in horror and then, very rapidly, they started to leave. I had allowed things to get badly out of hand in my own house, completely ruining what should have been a happy Christmas. Any momentary anger I had felt towards poor Bryn evaporated immediately and I experienced utter despair. I couldn't believe that I had allowed such a thing to take place. I knew I wasn't that sort of person, that it was totally against my nature and everything I had ever been to abuse anyone, let alone someone so close to me, but I couldn't escape the bald fact that it had happened. I had let myself down and betrayed everybody that I loved.

Before and after this horrendous meltdown, Joan was magnificent, but now, for the moment, she had to take a step to one side. I think she had the impression that I'd had enough of anyone interfering with my drinking, she thought all I wanted was to be left alone, and so she left me and went to stay with one of our daughters. Of course, she came back after a few days and she continued to stand by me, every distressing step of the way, but the time had come when she had to do something for herself and our children.

Joan also did something else, something which, a little way down the road, was to prove decisively inspirational in my fight to come back from alcoholism. Not knowing which way to turn, or what else to do, she got in touch with Jimmy Greaves, my former teammate, who a few years previously had battled with the same debilitating illness that was now bringing me so low. He had hit rock-bottom through his addiction to booze. He had lost everything that he valued in his life.

He came to our house in the New Year, when the raw shame of my Christmas outburst was still seared on the memories of my family, and he was deeply compassionate but, crucially, he pulled no punches. He said to me: "Cliff, you've got a smashing wife, a beautiful family, a lovely home, a good job, everything you could possibly want. Do you really want to lose all that?"

I just goggled at him. "Of course I don't want to lose it. What in the hell are you f****** talking about?" He was firm and clear in his response: "Let me tell you something, Cliff, if you keep on drinking then you will lose the whole lot. I know because it happened to me." I was shocked, but still aware how much I needed to drink, so I asked him: "What can I do?" His immediate answer was: "Try Alcoholics Anonymous. Go there with an open mind and

A friend, indeed – Jimmy Greaves stood by me when the going was at its toughest.

see how you get on." I just exploded: "You must be f****** joking Jim, I'm not an alcoholic." I think he had expected this reaction from me but he repeated his message once again. He was compassionate, and understood me completely because he had been through exactly the same experience. Since that day, we have kept in touch and he has willingly offered support when needed. But it was that eventual admission that I was an alcoholic, and was powerless over alcohol, that was the first step on my road to recovery.

When I had overcome my initial resistance that I should give AA a try, I screwed up my courage and went along to a meeting. It might seem hard to believe but the moment I walked into the room I picked up a sense of hope. I felt that at least I was in the right place because there were people there who had clearly made progress from the low places they had been. It was explained to me that there was a programme that I needed to follow one day at a time if I wanted what the people in that room had. That was fundamental to all human beings - the simple thing called hope.

At first, if I'm honest, I didn't make the kind of progress I had hoped for. I just didn't get it. The problem was that I had gone to AA for the wrong reasons. I had gone for my wife, I had gone for my family, but I hadn't gone for Cliff. If you want AA to help then you have to want to give up alcohol for yourself. For me the admission and acceptance that I was an alcoholic took an excruciatingly painful amount of time. It took at least another six months for the penny to properly drop. Then one day something just clicked in my head and I still don't know why. But at last I saw the way forward, the way to save my life as something worthwhile.

AA meetings gave me the opportunity to share my own experiences and listen to other people's stories. It's very hard to do this but it's extremely uplifting and it means so much to know, at last, that you're not on your own after all. I gradually learned that the more involved I got in the meeting rooms – doing service such as making the tea, being secretary for a term, acting as literature secretary, helping with administration, sometimes taking the chair at a gathering – the more my confidence increased and the more my self-esteem improved. In time, when I achieved the all-important state of acceptance, I realised the truth of the enduring adage, that half measures avail us of nothing. Now more than 30 years later, I still go to meetings on a regular basis, I try to practice the twelve steps of AA myself, and welcome, encourage and understand other alcoholics. I have grown from someone who was desperately in need of urgent help, with low self-esteem and a complete lack of confidence, to someone who now feels he's giving something back and helping other alcoholics.

The last time I took an alcoholic drink was 29 June 1985, that date is seared into my very consciousness. I think of it as Acceptance Day, and I remember it vividly. I was praying for God to help me. Our daughter, Mandy, had a baby boy that morning and very much wanted Joan and I at her bedside, but we couldn't go for hours and hours because I was in such a dreadful state with the alcohol and Joan was looking after me. It drove it home to me that day that we simply couldn't go on living like that, I had to do something about myself. It was acceptance of my condition at long, long last.

That was a red-letter day in the history of the Jones family for another reason – our grandson, Tony, was born. He's 31 now, a smashing young man, very grounded, working in local government in London. I look at him now and he's a symbol of my sobriety. He has never seen me the worse for drink and, God willing, he never will.

Now it seems like I've come a very long way from the day I behaved so disgracefully, upsetting everybody at that Christmas party. But despite all the progress I've made, I'll never say I've beaten the booze. All I can say is that, just for today, I'm a winner because I haven't had a drink. I've engaged with it every day for 31 years, and during that time so much has happened in my life to underline the obvious truth that, finally, I took the right direction.

I have made lots of very close friends through AA over the years, individuals I'd trust with my life. Happily it doesn't bother me in the slightest if the people I'm with want to have an alcoholic drink. I'm just happy to be with them, relaxing, having fun, quaffing a glass of lemonade or fruit juice, though I would stress over and over again I can never become complacent. Although I'm no longer consumed with a longing for alcohol, I know it's just one day at a time.

In the early years of my sobriety I didn't want people to know that I was an alcoholic, albeit a recovering one, because I felt self-conscious I suppose. Today I don't think like that. Some of my friends know and others don't, although they will all find out if they read this book and I'm more than happy with that. I've reached the stage where I'm willing to tell my story. A great scenario for me would be if someone struggling with a drinking problem picks up this book and finds it helps them. I tend to be a very negative person by definition, but I continually try to be more positive at all times. My motto is and always will be 'Just for today I will be happy.' I've come to believe that a person, any person, is as happy as they make up their mind to be. That doesn't work all the time, of course, but it certainly works for me most days.

When we lost our daughter, Debbie, to cancer in 2006, at least I was able to be of use to my family at a time of crisis and grief. I was able to spend precious time at her side, and to help the rest of the family. She knew we were there, we were able to bring her some comfort and that meant everything in the world to all of us. Crucially for me, I had lost the feeling of uselessness that had engulfed me for so many years, and the self-pity which every alcoholic wallows in had also gone. Then, and now, I can be supportive instead of supported.

So much has flowed from the death of my daughter. I'm now a patron of St Francis' Hospice in Romford, which is where Debbie died with all our family around her. The hospice was fantastic throughout her time there and I wanted to show some sort of gratitude for that, so with the help and support of family and friends I put on a fund-raising golf day at the West Essex club where I play. It was supported by a wonderful charity, the Willow Foundation, which was launched by the old Arsenal goalkeeper, Bob Wilson, after he lost his daughter to cancer and which put its arms around us when we needed it. Bob's a marvellous man, so very compassionate and strong, and he gave me magnificent help on the day, which raised more than £26,000.

Returning to a positive slant, as well as preserving my family life, the AA programme also saved my working life. I simply couldn't have gone on the way I was going. Unquestionably I did my job far better as an optimistic recovering alcoholic than when I was a miserably active one. I was much more clear-headed, I could deal with difficult situations when they presented themselves, and I saved so much mental energy which had previously been squandered in subterfuge – hiding drinks, sliding off to the pub, telling lies to cover my tracks.

All that negativity was gone, the time freed up for overdue positive use. If you're at the bottom and you want to stop drinking, then Alcoholics Anonymous is one way to do it. It's not easy but it can work for you. Becoming aware of other people's success will give you hope and encourage you to seek help for yourself. Truly there is a road back from alcoholic hell if you wish to find it.

CHAPTER TWENTY-TWO

Through Joan's eyes

In 1958 we left Swansea for north London, "up to the Smoke" as they said back home, to begin a completely different lifestyle. Very few footballers could afford to buy houses then and we rented a club house in Palmers Green and Tottenham teammates Bobby Smith, Mel Hopkins and Terry Medwin were our neighbours. When the maximum wage of £20 per week was abolished we bought our house from Spurs and lived there for 22 years. London was such a whole new world to us. For the first time in our lives we had our own telephone, so we had no further need to find a callbox or ask a neighbour for help. We bought a second-hand fridge and for a while we switched it off when we went to bed as we thought we were saving electricity! Nevertheless we were so much better off than the average person and Cliff often said how wonderful it was to get paid so handsomely for doing something he would have done for nothing – playing football. Life was sweet, and it became even sweeter in 1959 when our second daughter, Kim, was born at home. She arrived unexpectedly and Cliff added the role of midwife to his CV before calmly heading off to training.

The early 1960s were the start of the Spurs Glory Days, our social life became hectic and exciting, and there were countless invitations to functions, special events, posh London restaurants and even breaks at Caister Holiday Camp. After home games players would spend an hour or so at The Bell and Hare pub on the Tottenham High Road and although the back room was specifically allocated to the footballers, there was easy access for the fans to mingle with their idols. Drinking was the main social recreation for everybody at that time and it certainly didn't seem a problem for Cliff in his playing days.

His second career, as a games instructor at Highbury Grove Boys School in Islington, lasted nearly 30 years. From the age of 12 until he was in his late thirties he had played football and had been surrounded by people who willingly dealt with everything on his behalf. When football finished he had to take on new responsibilities, but he seemed able enough to cope with these changes, and I thought how well he had adapted to life after his playing days were over. But I was wrong.

***

By the early 1980s everything was changing. We had moved house, our four children had all left home to get married and we had become grandparents. Cliff was still at Highbury Grove School and I had a successful career in the Civil Service. This should have been the start of the best years of our lives with opportunities to do whatever we wished together. Something was going wrong, however, and I couldn't pinpoint what it was. It was something that had crept up on me insidiously over the years, masked to a large extent by his essentially benign nature.

Drinking had never been an issue when our four children were growing up because football had always given him the buzz he needed and he was the perfect family man. But slowly Cliff's social drinking evolved into hard drinking and even now I can't identify when it nudged over the line into addictive drinking.

I had always willingly taken responsibility for running the home, organising, taking decisions and paying all the bills. In fact, I had taken total control over everything, the main reasons being that I thought I could do it better myself and Cliff wasn't really interested in anything not connected with football. But I started to feel resentful that he left everything to me to sort out. I'd always thought I knew him better than I knew myself – I was wrong on both accounts.

Gradually Cliff's behaviour changed. Sometimes when we went out socially he would be drunk by the end of the evening and eventually we never went out anywhere together because his behaviour had become an embarrassment.

He became resentful over petty things, verbally aggressive, unreliable, uninterested in family life – all traits never before associated with my husband. On more than one occasion he would go out and get drunk, forget where he'd left his car, then ring me late at night to go and pick him up. I often tried to talk to him about his excessive drinking, sometimes I blamed it on his colleagues, and often I felt if he loved me he would stop drinking to please me.

I thought as he was getting older his tolerance for alcohol was decreasing as he didn't appear to drink any more than anyone else – all that denial! He mostly convinced me there was no problem, it was all in my mind. I called him an alcoholic but I didn't really believe he was one. I think there is a stigma attached to that word. I had always imagined an alcoholic as someone living on a park bench, a desperate outsider with nobody to care for him or her, and Cliff was nothing like that.

I never told anyone how bad his drinking had become because I felt ashamed. The person I had grown up with had become a stranger to me. Although I was surrounded by a large, loving, caring family, at times I felt completely isolated. I tried everything I could think of to stop him drinking, hiding his money, throwing the booze down the drain, shouting at him and nagging him, threatening to leave, and even bribery – when I was left some money, I spent most of it buying Cliff a new car. I suppose I was trying to buy myself back into favour but that didn't work either.

I lost my own identity, I was attached to my husband by an invisible bit of

Joan and I at Buckingham Palace and, for once, it was not all about me. My wife had just retired after 30 years in the Civil Service and was invited to a garden party to mark the occasion. Afterwards she told me that I had ate so many little cakes it was embarrassing!

Full house: our grandchildren around 1990. On the sofa, left to right, are Danny, Lisa, Scott, Holly, Matthew, Tony and Katy. That's Emma and Sarah at the front.

string. If he was happy (which wasn't often) I felt good, but when he was feeling depressed so did I. My life became more and more unmanageable and the thought that I could somehow control his drinking made me more determined to sort him out. I don't know why I thought that because I had been trying for a long time and the clear evidence was that I wasn't succeeding.

The disastrous Christmas when Cliff's drinking spiralled out of control proved to be the turning point in my continuous battle to stop him. Looking back I can identify the traumatic events of that day as the spur to starting the long climb back to normal living. Suffice to say that Christmas Day 1984 ended early for the Joneses and for the only time in 29 years of marriage I left home. In truth, Cliff wanted me gone as I had become an irritant and was constantly interfering with his drinking. I returned home after a few days, however, and his drinking continued to get progressively worse.

We were in serious trouble and I knew it. Our daughter Kim, appalled like the rest of us at what was happening to her father, who had always been the most loving, gentle, considerate and caring person imaginable, had listened to a programme on the radio a few days earlier about Al-Anon, a fellowship to help families of alcoholics. I suppose I was desperate enough to try anything and so, nursing the hope that someone was going to hand me a magic formula to put things right, I rang the number and told them I needed help for my husband. They explained to me that Al-Anon was not there for the alcoholic, it was there for the family, friends and colleagues of people whose drinking was causing problems.

But I clearly needed help, and so, along with our four adult children, I went along to a meeting. Immediately I walked through the door I felt an enormous sense of empathy, I knew I was in the right place, everybody there was facing similar problems to me and had been affected by someone's drinking. It was suggested I attend six meetings to decide if Al-Anon was for me and I readily agreed. In time I realised just how little I knew about the subject. I had never for an instant characterised alcoholism as an illness, or known that it was progressive. I certainly didn't know it was an incurable disease.

The Al-Anon programme gradually clarified my thinking – mercifully I now had the opportunity to tell my story and listen to other people who had been affected by someone's drinking. I could share their experiences, their strength and their hope. I've often said that Cliff found sobriety despite me, not because of me. I came to understand that every person is responsible for their own actions. It became clear that so much of what I'd been doing for the right reasons were actually the wrong things to do. I stopped covering up for him, stopped trying to sort out his problems, I stopped doing everything which enabled him to carry on drinking. It's true that only a person who has lived with an alcoholic, and has experienced the mental anguish that goes with it, can understand the problems of the alcoholic's family and friends.

A couple of months after Cliff stopped drinking, on the spur of the moment we decided to go on holiday to tour northern France. For a long time holidays had been spoiled because of his behaviour, but now I felt safe to ride in our car and although at times it seemed I was treading on eggshells, being

*Cliff and I in Las Vegas with our four children in 2004 when Steve's eldest
daughter, Emma, got married. The kids are, left to right, Debbie, Kim, Steve
and Mandy.*

afraid I might do or say something that would upset him, we had a lovely
holiday, just like the old days.

That was my new beginning. Over many years, by showing me how to
detach with love, and concentrate on myself, Al-Anon has enabled me to cope
with my difficulties and find a more serene approach to life. For me it has
been the salvation of my home and my marriage.

On 29 June 1985 Cliff had his last drink, by coincidence just a few hours
after the birth of our second grandson, Tony, and I firmly believe there
should have been two births recorded that day because it proved to be a
brand new beginning for my husband and myself. Since then, 31 years have
passed and the Cliff I've always known and loved has returned to us to play
a full part in our family life. In particular, when our beloved daughter
Debbie was diagnosed with breast cancer in 2001, he was my rock, a deeply

caring, dependable, loving man. He was such a massive and influential presence in our family right through to her death in March 2006.

The year 2015 was a landmark for us because it marked our diamond wedding anniversary and Cliff's 80th birthday. And, as our son, Steve, remarked at the celebration party, 2015 also signified 30 years of unbroken sobriety for his dad. I am so, so proud of Cliff. It has, indeed, been a wonderful life!

CHAPTER TWENTY-THREE

A glorious postscript: Euro 2016

For anyone with Wales in their heart, Euro 2016 was a gloriously uplifting experience. Now, after Chris Coleman's boys made us all so proud by reaching the semi-finals in such a glorious and entertaining manner, it gives me overwhelming pleasure to declare that the Spirit of '58, of which I was a part as we made it to the last eight of the World Cup more than half a century ago, can be laid to rest.

Of course, it won't ever be forgotten, and nor should it be, but it's time to move over for the new generation and hail the Spirit of 2016. The modern team is magnificent, a fantastic bunch of men full of passion, commitment and talent, and they are matched by our wonderful fans. They sang their hearts out in France and truly graced the tournament, creating such an unforgettable atmosphere. Particularly after all the adverse publicity about rampaging supporters from other countries, the Welsh set the best possible example, having a great time but conducting themselves sensibly and with honour. They were a credit to themselves and to their nation.

For me, there was a huge element of serendipity involved in the whole scenario. When I decided to write this book, I could never have known it would coincide with Wales getting to the finals of a major tournament for the first time in 58 years. With each failed qualification attempt down the decades, the team which included the likes of John and Mel Charles, Ivor Allchurch, Jack Kelsey and myself became more revered and embedded in Welsh sporting folklore. World-class players such as Ian Rush and Ryan Giggs were unable to show their quality on the grandest stage, while fans and pundits alike wondered if we would ever make it to the latter stages of another big competition.

Then in 2010 Gary Speed was appointed manager and he brought a different approach, implementing new training methods, introducing sports scientists and embracing state-of-the-art technology. Following Gary's tragic and untimely death, his good friend Chris Coleman accepted the reins, continued to build on the foundations laid by his predecessor and took the Euro 2016 qualifiers by storm.

Wales started the tournament on a high note by beating Slovakia in Bordeaux, then I was absolutely delighted to be invited by the Welsh FA to attend their next game, which just happened to be against England. On the way through customs with my son, Steve, at Cardiff airport I was recognised by a customs officer, who asked me: "Off to the Euros, Cliff?" That made me smile because it offered such a vivid contrast to our homecoming from Sweden more than half a century earlier, when the chap on the gate didn't even know where we'd been! This time there was no doubt about our destination, with the Wales team's 'Together Stronger' banners much in evidence wherever we looked.

We travelled along with the families of many of our players, including Gareth Bale's mum and dad, who are really great people. It's no wonder Gareth is who he is, a modest, unassuming, approachable lad who is always ready with a smile and a handshake, having been brought up in such a happy, loving environment.

We flew to Ostend before transferring by coach to our hotel in the seaside resort of Le Touquet, an elegant town favoured mainly by wealthy Parisians, although the local history reveals close ties to Britain. Land there was purchased in 1903 by an enterprising Englishman who developed luxury properties to sell to the rich and famous, for instance the Duchess of Westminster and literary greats H.G Wells and P.G Wodehouse. The architecture of the houses is beautiful, a sight to behold, and we enjoyed a leisurely stroll in the sunshine, fantasising how fine it would be to own one. In our dreams!

Back at the hotel there was a welcome meal organised by the Welsh FA and hosted by the TV presenter Frances Donovan, a lovely lady who made me feel very relaxed and comfortable as she interviewed me – and also got me out of a slightly embarrassing situation with consummate skill.

Along with me as a guest speaker was the Wales international Steve Morison, who understands the modern game exceedingly well and gave an excellent insight into Chris Coleman's squad. I think we worked well together, apart from when I suffered what I can only describe as a senior moment.

Question from the floor: "Who do you think would make the best defensive pairings for the game against England?"

Me: "I don't think I'm qualified to answer that so I'll pass it to Steve, who is a centre-half."

Steve: "No Cliff, I'm a centre-forward!"

Me (looking puzzled): "Are you?"

That's when Frances stepped in so nimbly, declaring: "Perhaps he's like John Charles, Cliff, a centre-forward and a centre-half."

The audience roared with laughter and I was so glad Frances had come to my rescue.

There followed lots of warm memories from 1958 before Frances decided we should finish with a song. My Steve, sitting beside me, asked what I would choose and I decided on 'It's A Grand Old Team To Play For.' He said: "You can't sing that, Dad, it's a Spurs song" but I assured him: "Don't worry, I'll change the words!" As it turned out there weren't many Tottenham fans in the room, but I did some nifty improvisation and I think it went down pretty well. Frances posted a clip on YouTube so if it's still there you can judge for yourself.

The day of the big game meant another long coach trip, this time to Lens, and it reminded me of all the times as a player when I had endured hours of being cramped on a bus with my teammates ahead of being expected to perform at the highest level. It's so different now, with most journeys made well in advance, often by plane, which means the footballers can more easily be at their peak come kick-off.

When we arrived in Lens the atmosphere was amazing, with both sets of fans mingling outside bars and cafes. We were taken to a VIP venue for the Welsh, a nightclub opposite the ground, and I found it very strange going from the bright daylight into a very dark room with loud disco music blaring from the speakers. I had not been in a crowded nightclub for many a year and was not enjoying the experience, but my son steered me to a quieter area, where I was interviewed again by Frances.

She asked about Sweden all those years ago, but I wanted to make the point: "That was then, Frances, now the time has come for this team to make its own history. Let's not talk about the Spirit of '58, we have had our time, now it's the Spirit of 2016." I found myself adding: "I want all you supporters to listen. What you have to do is go out there today, out-cheer and out-sing the English, get behind our boys 100 per cent and I'm sure we'll win."

A huge cheer went up, which I found very moving, and then Frances asked me to finish with another song. Steve reminded me to choose a different one and I came up with 'We'll Keep A Welcome In The Hillside.' I must admit I did it justice and by the end the whole nightclub was joining in. It was an emotional moment shared by many Welsh hearts. After we had finished I was engulfed by fans requesting autographs and photographs, selfies I think they are called, and it took quite a while for Steve and I to reach the stadium.

Though the Welsh fans were outnumbered by a ratio of around three to one, they were in fabulous voice as always and our rendition of the national anthem gave me goosebumps. Unfortunately our team was not at its best and we lost 2-1. Some might say we were unlucky to concede a goal in added time, and yes, that was hard, but we had to admit it was a fair result and there could be no complaints. England had the best of the game, with the two Spurs full-backs, Kyle Walker and Danny Rose, showing up to great advantage, especially on their attacking overlaps. But after that events turned dramatically, with England unfortunately falling by the wayside and Wales kicking on superbly.

For me it was time to go home to enjoy the rest of the tournament from the comfort of my sofa, and the first instalment was a tremendous 3-0 victory over Russia in Toulouse. I thought it was going to be a tight contest, but we got on top early in the match and never relaxed our grip. All the players contributed terrifically, but one who especially caught my eye that night was Joe Allen. What a fabulous few weeks he had. I always liked the lad, and now he really blossomed. He reminds me of Luka Modric, having the ability to change a game by keeping it flowing, constantly probing the opposition with his lovely, accurate passing, and the Russians never remotely came to terms with him.

Beating them put us through to the last 16, where we faced what was always going to be a really tense affair with Northern Ireland. The sides knew each other very well, they play a similar sort of game, there was never going to be much between us. The Irish were totally committed and made it very difficult for us, though I must admit that my heart went out to their defender, Gareth McAuley, who deflected the only goal of the game past his own keeper. That was harsh on the young man, who had played very well, but football can be cruel sometimes. Mind you, sitting at home, wearing my Wales shirt as I watched every kick, I have to admit that I was celebrating excitedly when the final whistle went.

Still in store was Wales' finest performance of the tournament, arguably our country's best display in living memory, when we came from behind to beat Belgium in the Toulouse quarter-final. It was a superb all-round display against opponents whom many people fancied to lift the trophy. They had so many top Premier League players such as Eden Hazard, Romelu Lukaku and Spurs' magnificent centre-half Toby Alderweireld, and could beat anybody on their day.

But this was not their day. This was Wales' day and I think it's fair to say we outplayed them, fully meriting our 3-1 triumph. Our midfield was exceptional, with Aaron Ramsey and Joe Allen particularly outstanding. What astounded me was that Belgium left Moussa Dembele, one of my favourite players at Tottenham, on their bench. That made no sense at all to me. I was pleased from a Welsh point of view, but staggered because he is one of the top midfielders in the world by my reckoning.

The Belgians started as if they were going to walk away with the game, and scored an early goal, but that proved merely to be the cue for our centre-half and captain, Ashley Williams of Swansea City, to show what an inspirational figure he can be. Just when we needed it, he popped up with a sensational headed equaliser, and wasn't his celebration a tonic? After the ball hit the net, the delight on his face as he tore towards his teammates was just like an enthusiastic schoolboy, so refreshing and so genuine.

That was a special moment, but Ashley was always lifting the lads, dictating to them, setting a stirring example, demanding and receiving utter commitment from everybody.

Astonishingly, there was an even more sensational sequence of action to come, one which lit up the night for Wales and which will live forever in our collective sporting memory. To say that our second goal, dispatched by Hal Robson-Kanu, was a bit special is a chronic understatement – truly it took the breath away. I always knew Hal was an excellent player, both strong and smart, but I hadn't appreciated he was capable of the sheer magic he served up after being fed so expertly by the splendid Ramsey. Our centre-forward controlled the ball sumptuously, executed the Cruyff turn to perfection, sent three defenders lunging in different directions and then placed the ball past the keeper in the manner of Jimmy Greaves – and I can't offer higher praise than that. They won't be calling it the Cruyff turn in future – it'll be the Kanu twist!

Then, as Belgium threatened to bounce back near the end, we struck again with a towering header from Sam Vokes. For those who remember, it was just like watching Trevor Ford, a remarkable effort which had me bouncing off my sofa and nearly bumping my head on the ceiling.

Now, suddenly, the hitherto impossible dream of reaching the final became a realistic possibility. We were only one game away and nothing seemed to be beyond us. Alas, we couldn't quite produce the same creative spark against Portugal, our semi-final opponents, for whom Cristiano Ronaldo almost burst our net with a header which conjured up memories of John Charles. Yes, it really was that impressive. In the end we went down 2-0 without reaching the heights of which we had proved ourselves capable, but still turning in a display of which the Welsh people could be proud.

Throughout the tournament, nobody let Wales down. Perhaps Gareth Bale was not at his very best – although he did contribute three goals, including two trademark free-kicks – but he worked his socks off constantly and was marked so tightly that I'm certain he created extra space for his mates.

Arguably the star of the show was Aaron Ramsey, who found the net against Russia and set up so many of Wales' other goals. He made the whole team tick with the imagination and accuracy of his passing and the non-stop industry which always made him available to receive the ball. He had the legs and he had the head, and to me he was reminiscent of John White in his heyday, which puts him in the very highest bracket. It seemed ridiculously harsh that he was ruled out of the semi-final for only his second booking in five games, and that for an innocuous handball. Of course, we have to have rules, but it seemed rough justice that he missed the biggest game in Welsh history for such a marginal misdemeanour. And if he had played, what a difference he might have made but, oh dear, it's no use going there now!

Although I've singled out a few individuals, in fact every player shone and all deserve the highest praise. For instance the Spurs full-back Ben Davies, who also missed the semi through suspension, was exemplary and I expect big things from him in the future.

Finally, I come to the boss, Chris Coleman, for whom no tribute can be too extravagant. He created a fantastic spirit, organised the team brilliantly and tended to make inspired decisions, such as the bringing on of Vokes as a substitute against Belgium.

I always place immense importance on establishing a spine to any side, and Chris has done just that with the exceptional Wayne Hennessey in goal, Ashley Williams at the core of the defence, Aaron Ramsey and Joe Allen in central midfield and Hal Robson-Kanu up front, with Gareth Bale floating dangerously to all attacking areas. Chris found his best team and, whenever possible, he stuck to it, reaping the benefits accordingly.

Another Swansea Jack – how I love to hail that 'Made in Swansea' tag – he is a friendly, down-to-earth character brimming with enthusiasm and knowledge, an inspirational speaker who ensures that his players are never in awe of the opposition. In so many ways he reminds me of Jimmy Murphy, even if he's not quite so talkative – mind you, nobody is! I can't speak too highly of Chris and the job that he's done for Welsh football.

I'm so pleased and proud for all the boys, and they deserved the tumultuous homecoming that contrasted so vividly with ours in 1958. They went to Cardiff and were greeted by a cheering multitude, while we were met by Mel Charles' chum, who wondered where we'd been for the summer. Of course, the success of 2016 has created great expectations for the future, but I'm absolutely convinced that Chris and company are capable of meeting them. I can hardly wait!

Two Spurs with plenty in common – both Ossie Ardiles and I helped to bring the FA Cup back to White Hart Lane.

A happy moment with Tottenham's main man, the late, great Bill Nicholson.

Still part of the Tottenham team. It's always a pleasure to meet up with my fellow matchday hosts at White Hart lane, lovely lads such as Pat Jennings (right) and Alan Mullery.

Two peas in a pod, same dress sense, same football club. I'm so proud of my grandson, Matt Wells, who is the assistant coach of Tottenham's under-21 side. Matt was a very promising young player who joined the Spurs academy at the age of ten, only to suffer injury a few years later and adjust his ambitions in the direction of coaching. He's got a lot of ability and he's ambitious. You never know, he might be the next Bill Nick ...

Memories, memories... standing, left to right: Dave Mackay, Terry Medwin, Ron Henry, Maurice Norman, Les Allen, Tony Marchi, Peter Baker, Mel Hopkins and Bobby Smith. Bill Nicholson is seated, flanked by Terry Dyson and myself.

Club statistics

SWANSEA TOWN 1952/53 to 1957/58

Managers: Billy McCandless to July 1955, then Ron Burgess

1952/53 – 11th in Div 2; FA Cup 3rd rd
League: 3 games, 1 goal
Total: 3 games, 1 goal

1953/54 – 20th in Div 2; FA Cup 4th rd
League: 25 games, 4 goals
FA Cup: 3 games, 0 goals
Total: 28 games, 4 goals

1954/55 – 10th in Div 2; FA Cup 5th rd
League: 40 games, 10 goals
FA Cup: 4 games, 1 goal
Total: 44 games, 11 goals

1955/56 – 10th in Div 2; FA Cup 3rd rd
League: 40 games, 12 goals
Total: 40 games, 12 goals

1956/57 – 10th in Div 2; FA Cup 3rd rd
League: 31 games, 9 goals
FA Cup: 1 game, 0 goals
Total: 32 games, 9 goals

1957/58 – 19th in Div 2; FA Cup 3rd rd
League: 28 games, 12 goals
FA Cup: 1 game, 0 goals
Total: 29 games, 12 goals

SWANSEA GRAND TOTALS: 176 games, 49 goals

TOTTENHAM HOTSPUR 1957/58 to 1968/69

Manager: Bill Nicholson

1957/58 – 3rd in Div 1; FA Cup 4th rd
League: 10 games, 1 goal
Total: 10 games, 1 goal

1958/59 – 18th in Div 1; FA Cup 5th rd
League: 22 games, 5 goals
FA Cup: 4 games, 2 goals
Total: 26 games, 7 goals

1959/60 – 3rd in Div 1; FA Cup 5th rd
League: 38 games, 20 goals
FA Cup: 4 games, 5 goals
Total: 42 games, 25 goals

1960/61 – 1st in Div 1; FA Cup winners
League: 29 games, 15 goals
FA Cup: 6 games, 4 goals
Total: 35 games, 19 goals

1961/62 – 3rd in Div 1; FA Cup winners; European Cup semi-finalists; Charity Shield winners
League: 38 games, 16 goals
FA Cup: 7 games, 4 goals
Europe: 8 games, 4 goals
Charity Shield: 1 game, 0 goals
Total: 54 games, 24 goals

1962/63 – 2nd in Div 1; FA Cup 3rd rd; European Cup Winners' Cup winners; Charity Shield winners
League: 37 games, 20 goals
FA Cup: 1 game, 0 goals
Europe: 6 games, 2 goals
Charity Shield: 1 game, 0 goals
Total: 45 games, 22 goals

1963/64 – 4th in Div 1; FA Cup 3rd rd
League: 39 games, 14 goals
FA Cup: 2 games, 0 goals
Europe: 2 games, 0 goals
Total: 43 games, 14 goals

1964/65 – 6th in Div 1; FA Cup 5th rd
League: 39 games, 13 goals
FA Cup: 4 games, 0 goals
Total: 43 games, 13 goals

1965/66 – 8th in Div 1; FA Cup 5th rd
League: 9 games, 8 goals
FA Cup: 2 games, 0 goals
Total: 11 games, 8 goals

1966/67 – 3rd in Div 1; FA Cup winners; League Cup 2nd rd
League: 20 games, 6 goals

FA Cup: 4 (1) games, 0 goals
Total: 24 (1) games, 6 goals

1967/68 – 7th in Div 1; FA Cup 5th rd; Charity Shield shared
League: 27 (3) games, 12 goals
FA Cup: 1 (3) games, 1 goal
Europe: 3 games, 1 goal
Total: 31 (6) games, 14 goals

1968/69 – 6th in Div 1; FA Cup quarter-finalists, League Cup semi-finalists
League: 6 (1) games, 5 goals
League Cup: 2 games, 1 goal
Total: 8 (1) games, 6 goals

SPURS GRAND TOTALS: 372 (8) games, 159 goals

FULHAM 1968/69 to 1969/70

Managers: Bobby Robson to November 1968, then Bill Dodgin Jnr

1968/69 – 22nd in Div 2; FA Cup 4th rd; League Cup 2nd rd
League: 18 games, 2 goals
Total: 18 games, 2 goals

1969/70 – 4th in Div 3; FA Ciup 1st rd; League Cup 2nd rd
League: 5 (2) games, 0 goals
League Cup: 1 game, 0 goals
Total: 6 (2) games, 0 goals

FULHAM GRAND TOTALS: 24 (2) games, 2 goals

OVERALL CLUB TOTALS: 572 (10) games, 210 goals

International statistics

WALES 1954–69 (59 caps), 15 goals

Managers: Jimmy Murphy 1956 to 1964, then Trevor Morris for one match, then Dave Bowen

Cap 1: Austria in Vienna, 9 May 1954, lost 2–0
Friendly
Team: Jack Kelsey; Stuart Williams, Alf Sherwood; Bill Harris, John Charles, Ron Burgess; Harry Griffiths, Derek Tapscott, Trevor Ford, Ivor Allchurch, Cliff Jones

Cap 2: England in Cardiff, 22 October 1955, won 2–1, one goal
Home International
Team: Jack Kelsey; Stuart Williams, Alf Sherwood; Mel Charles, John Charles, Roy Paul; Derek Tapscott, Noel Kinsey, Trevor Ford, Ivor Allchurch, Cliff Jones
Other scorer: Tapscott

Cap 3: Scotland in Glasgow, 9 November 1955, lost 2–0
Home International
Team: Jack Kelsey; Stuart Williams, Alf Sherwood; Mel Charles, John Charles, Roy Paul; Derek Tapscott, Noel Kinsey, Trevor Ford, Ivor Allchurch, Cliff Jones

Cap 4: Austria in Wrexham, 23 November 1955, lost 2–1
Friendly
Team: Jack Kelsey; Stuart Williams, Alf Sherwood; Mel Charles, John Charles, Roy Paul; Len Allchurch, Derek Tapscott, Trevor Ford, Ivor Allchurch, Cliff Jones
Scorer: Tapscott

Cap 5: Northern Ireland in Cardiff, 11 April 1956, drew 1–1
Home International
Team: Jack Kelsey; Alf Sherwood, Mel Hopkins; Alan Harrington, John Charles, Roy Paul; Cliff Jones, Derek Tapscott, Trevor Ford, Ivor Allchurch, Roy Clarke
Scorer: Clarke

Cap 6: Scotland in Cardiff, 20 October 1956, drew 2–2
Home International
Team: Jack Kelsey; Alf Sherwood, Mel Hopkins; Alan Harrington, Ray Daniel, Derrick Sullivan; Terry Medwin, John Charles, Trevor Ford, Ivor Allchurch, Cliff Jones
Scorers: Medwin, Ford

Cap 7: England at Wembley, 14 November 1956, lost 3–1
Home International
Team: Jack Kelsey; Alf Sherwood, Mel Hopkins; Alan Harrington, Ray Daniel, Derrick Sullivan; Terry Medwin, Mel Charles, John Charles, Ivor Allchurch, Cliff Jones
Scorer: J Charles

Cap 8: Northern Ireland in Belfast, 10 April 1957, drew 0–0
Home International
Team: Jack Kelsey; Trevor Edwards, Mel Hopkins; Mel Charles, Ray Daniel, Dave Bowen; Terry Medwin, Derek Tapscott, John Charles, Roy Vernon, Cliff Jones

Cap 9: Czechoslovakia in Cardiff, 1 May 1957, won 1–0
World Cup Qualifier
Team: Jack Kelsey; Ron Stitfall, Mel Hopkins; Mel Charles, John Charles, Dave Bowen; Terry Medwin, Derek Tapscott, Colin Webster, Roy Vernon, Cliff Jones
Scorer: Vernon

Cap 10: East Germany in Leipzig, 19 May 1957, lost 2–1
World Cup Qualifier
Team: Jack Kelsey; Trevor Edwards, Mel Hopkins; Bill Harris, John Charles, Dave Bowen; Terry Medwin, Derek Tapscott, Mel Charles, Roy Vernon, Cliff Jones
Scorer: M Charles

Cap 11: Czechoslovakia in Prague, 26 May 1957, lost 2–0
World Cup Qualifier
Team: Jack Kelsey; Dai Thomas, Mel Hopkins; Mel Charles, Ray Daniel, Bill Harris; Terry Medwin, Des Palmer, John Charles, Roy Vernon, Cliff Jones

Cap 12: East Germany in Cardiff, 25 September 1957, won 4–1, one goal
World Cup Qualifier
Team: Graham Vearncombe; Dai Thomas, Mel Hopkins; Bill Harris, Mel Charles, Dave Bowen; Len Allchurch, Reg Davies, Des Palmer, Roy Vernon, Cliff Jones
Other scorer: Palmer 3

Cap 13: England in Cardiff, 19 October 1957, lost 4–0
Home International
Team: Jack Kelsey; Stuart Williams, Mel Hopkins; Bill Harris, Mel Charles, Dave Bowen; Terry Medwin, Reg Davies, Des Palmer, Roy Vernon, Cliff Jones

Cap 14: Scotland in Glasgow, 13 November 1957, drew 1–1
Home International
Team: Jack Kelsey; Stuart Williams, Mel Hopkins; Alan Harrington, Mel

Charles, Dave Bowen; Len Allchurch, Bill Harris, Terry Medwin, Roy Vernon, Cliff Jones
Scorer: Medwin

Cap 15: Israel in Tel Aviv, 15 January 1958, won 2–0
World Cup Qualifier
Team: Jack Kelsey; Stuart Williams, Mel Hopkins; Alan Harrington, Mel Charles, Dave Bowen; Len Allchurch, John Charles, Terry Medwin, Ivor Allchurch, Cliff Jones
Scorers: Bowen, I Allchurch

Cap 16: Israel in Cardiff, 5 February 1958, won 2–0, one goal
World Cup Qualifier
Team: Jack Kelsey; Stuart Williams, Mel Hopkins; Alan Harrington, Mel Charles, Dave Bowen; Terry Medwin, Ron Hewitt, John Charles, Ivor Allchurch, Cliff Jones
Other scorer: Allchurch

Cap 17: Northern Ireland in Cardiff, 16 April 1958, drew 1–1
Home International
Team: Jack Kelsey; Stuart Williams, Mel Hopkins; Alan Harrington, Derrick Sullivan, Dave Bowen; Len Allchurch, Ron Hewitt, Terry Medwin, Ivor Allchurch, Cliff Jones
Scorer: Hewitt

Cap 18: Hungary in Sandviken, Sweden, 8 June 1958, drew 1–1
World Cup
Team: Jack Kelsey; Stuart Williams, Mel Hopkins; Derrick Sullivan, Mel Charles, Dave Bowen; Colin Webster, Terry Medwin, John Charles, Ivor Allchurch, Cliff Jones
Scorer: J Charles

Cap 19: Mexico in Stockholm, Sweden, 11 June 1958 , drew 1–1
World Cup

Team: Jack Kelsey; Stuart Williams, Mel Hopkins; Colin Baker, Mel Charles, Dave Bowen; Colin Webster, Terry Medwin, John Charles, Ivor Allchurch, Cliff Jones
Scorer: Allchurch

Cap 20: Sweden in Stockholm, Sweden, 15 June 1958, drew 0–0
World Cup
Team: Jack Kelsey; Stuart Williams, Mel Hopkins; Derrick Sullivan, Mel Charles, Dave Bowen; Roy Vernon, Ron Hewitt, John Charles, Ivor Allchurch, Cliff Jones

Cap 21: Hungary in Stockholm, Sweden, 17 June 1958, won 2–1
World Cup
Team: Jack Kelsey; Stuart Williams, Mel Hopkins; Derrick Sullivan, Mel Charles, Dave Bowen; Terry Medwin, Ron Hewitt, John Charles, Ivor Allchurch, Cliff Jones
Scorers: Allchurch, Medwin

Cap 22: Brazil in Gothenburg, Sweden, 19 June 1958, lost 1–0
World Cup
Team: Jack Kelsey; Stuart Williams, Mel Hopkins; Derrick Sullivan, Mel Charles, Dave Bowen; Terry Medwin, Ron Hewitt, Colin Webster, Ivor Allchurch, Cliff Jones

Cap 23: Northern Ireland in Belfast, 22 April 1959, lost 4–1
Home International
Team: Vic Rouse; Stuart Williams, Mel Hopkins; Vic Crowe, Derrick Sullivan, Dave Bowen; Terry Medwin, Derek Tapscott, Tony Rowley, Ivor Allchurch, Cliff Jones
Scorer: Tapscott

Cap 24: England in Cardiff, 17 October 1959, drew 1–1
Home International
Team: Jack Kelsey; Stuart Williams, Mel Hopkins; Vic Crowe, Mel Nurse,

Derrick Sullivan; Terry Medwin, Phil Woosnam, Graham Moore, Ivor All-church, Cliff Jones
Scorer: Moore

Cap 25: Scotland in Glasgow, 4 November 1959, drew 1–1
Home International
Team: Jack Kelsey; Stuart Williams, Mel Hopkins; Derrick Sullivan, John Charles, Colin Baker; Terry Medwin, Phil Woosnam, Graham Moore, Ivor Allchurch, Cliff Jones
Scorer: Charles

Cap 26: Northern Ireland in Wrexham, 6 April 1960, won 3–2
Home International
Team: Jack Kelsey; Stuart Williams, Graham E Williams; Vic Crowe, Mel Nurse, Colin Baker; Terry Medwin, Phil Woosnam, Graham Moore, Roy Vernon, Cliff Jones
Scorers: Medwin 2, Woosnam

Cap 27: Republic of Ireland in Dublin, 28 September 1960, won 3–2, two goals
Friendly
Team: Graham Vearncombe; Stuart Williams, Graham E Williams; Vic Crowe, Mel Nurse Colin Baker; Terry Medwin, Phil Woosnam, Graham Moore, Roy Vernon, Cliff Jones
Other scorer: Woosnam

Cap 28: Scotland in Cardiff, 22 October 1960, won 2–0, one goal
Home International
Team: Jack Kelsey; Alan Harrington, Graham E Williams; Vic Crowe, Mel Nurse, Colin Baker; Terry Medwin, Phil Woosnam, Ken Leek, Roy Vernon, Cliff Jones
Other scorer: Vernon

Cap 29: England at Wembley, 23 November 1960, lost 5–1
Home International

Team: Jack Kelsey; Alan Harrington, Graham E Williams; Vic Crowe, Mel Nurse, Colin Baker; Terry Medwin, Phil Woosnam, Ken Leek, Roy Vernon, Cliff Jones
Scorer: Leek

Cap 30: Northern Ireland in Belfast, 12 April 1961, won 5–1, two goals
Home International
Team: Jack Kelsey; Stuart Williams, Mel Hopkins; Mel Charles, Mel Nurse, Vic Crowe; Cliff Jones, Phil Woosnam, Ken Leek, Ivor Allchurch, Graham G Williams
Other scorers: Allchurch, Charles, Leek

Cap 31: Spain in Madrid, 18 May 1961, drew 1–1
World Cup Qualifier
Team: Jack Kelsey; Stuart Williams, Mel Hopkins; Mel Charles, Mel Nurse, Vic Crowe; Cliff Jones, Graham Moore, Ken Leek, Ivor Allchurch, Graham G Williams
Scorer: Allchurch

Cap 32: Hungary in Budapest, 28 May 1961, lost 3–2, one goal
Friendly
Team: Jack Kelsey; Stuart Williams, Mel Hopkins; Mel Charles, Mel Nurse, Vic Crowe; Cliff Jones, Phil Woosnam, Ken Leek, Ivor Allchurch, Graham G Williams
Other scorer: Allchurch

Cap 33: England in Cardiff, 14 October 1961, drew 1–1
Home International
Team: Jack Kelsey; Alan Harrington, Stuart Williams; Mel Charles, John Charles, Vic Crowe; Cliff Jones, Phil Woosnam, Dai Ward, Ivor Allchurch, Graham G Williams
Scorer: G G Williams

Cap 34: Scotland in Glasgow, 8 November 1961, lost 2–0
Home International

Team: Jack Kelsey; Alan Harrington, Stuart Williams; Vic Crowe, Mel Charles, Colin Baker; Len Allchurch, Phil Woosnam, Ken Leek, Ivor Allchurch, Cliff Jones

Cap 35: Northern Ireland in Cardiff, 11 April 1962, won 4–0
Home International
Team: Jack Kelsey; Stuart Williams, Mel Hopkins; Mal Lucas, Mike England, Terry Hennessey; Len Allchurch, Phil Woosnam, Mel Charles, Roy Vernon, Cliff Jones
Scorer: Charles 4

Cap 36: Brazil in Rio de Janeiro, 12 May 1962, lost 3–1
Friendly
Team: Jack Kelsey; Stuart Williams, Mel Hopkins; Terry Hennessey, John Charles, Vic Crowe; Len Allchurch, Roy Vernon, Mel Charles, Ivor Allchurch, Cliff Jones
Scorer: I Allchurch

Cap 37: Brazil in Sao Paulo, 16 May 1962, lost 3–1
Friendly
Team: Jack Kelsey (sub Dave Hollins); Stuart Williams, Mel Hopkins; Mike England, John Charles, Terry Hennessey; Phil Woosnam, Roy Vernon, Graham Moore (sub Ken Leek), Ivor Allchurch, Cliff Jones
Scorer: Leek

Cap 38: Mexico in Mexico City, 22 May 1962, lost 2–1
Friendly
Team: Dave Hollins; Stuart Williams, Mel Hopkins; Mal Lucas, Mike England, Vic Crowe; Roy Vernon, Ivor Allchurch, John Charles, Ken Leek, Cliff Jones
Scorer: Charles

Cap 39: Scotland in Cardiff, 20 October 1962, lost 3–2
Home International
Team: Tony Millington; Stuart Williams, Mel Hopkins; Terry Hennessey, John

Charles, Mal Lucas; Barrie Jones, Ivor Allchurch, Mel Charles, Roy Vernon, Cliff Jones
Scorers: Allchurch, J Charles

Cap 40: Hungary in Cardiff, 20 March 1963, drew 1–1, one goal
European Championships Qualifier
Team: Dave Hollins; Stuart Williams, Graham E Williams; Terry Hennessey, Mike England, Ollie Burton; Barrie Jones, Phil Woosnam, Graham Moore, Ivor Allchurch, Cliff Jones

Cap 41: Northern Ireland in Belfast, 3 April 1963, won 4–1, three goals
Home International
Team: Dave Hollins; Mel Hopkins, Graham E Williams; Ollie Burton, Mike England, Barrie Hole; Barrie Jones, Phil Woosnam, Graham Moore, Ivor Allchurch, Cliff Jones
Other scorer: Woosnam

Cap 42: England in Cardiff, 12 October 1963, lost 4–0
Home International
Team: Dave Hollins; Stuart Williams, Graham E Williams; Terry Hennessey, Mike England, Ollie Burton; Len Allchurch, Roy Vernon, Wyn Davies, Ivor Allchurch, Cliff Jones

Cap 43: Scotland in Glasgow, 20 November 1963, lost 2–1
Home International
Team: Gary Sprake; Stuart Williams, Graham E Williams; Terry Hennessey, Mike England, Mel Nurse; Barrie Jones, Graham Moore, John Charles, Roy Vernon, Cliff Jones
Scorer: B Jones

Cap 44: Northern Ireland in Swansea, 15 April 1964, lost 3–2
Home International
Team: Gary Sprake; Roy Evans, Graham E Williams; Mike Johnson, Mike England, Barrie Hole; Barrie Jones, Graham Moore, Ron Davies, Brian

Godfrey, Cliff Jones
Scorers: Davies, Godfrey

Cap 45: Scotland in Cardiff, 3 October 1964, won 3–2
Home International
Team: Gary Sprake; Stuart Williams, Graham E Williams; Barrie Hole, John Charles, Terry Hennessey; Cliff Jones, Ken Leek, Wyn Davies, Ivor Allchurch, Ronnie Rees
Scorers: Davies, Leek 2

Cap 46: Denmark in Copenhagen, 21 October 1964, lost 1–0
World Cup Qualifier
Team: Gary Sprake; Stuart Williams, Graham E Williams; Terry Hennessey, Mike England, Barrie Hole; Barrie Jones, Brian Godfrey, Wyn Davies, Cliff Jones, Ronnie Rees

Cap 47: England at Wembley, 18 November 1964, lost 2–1, one goal
Home International
Team: Tony Millington; Stuart Williams, Graham E Williams; Terry Hennessey, Mike England, Barrie Hole; Ronnie Rees, Ron Davies, Wyn Davies, Ivor Allchurch, Cliff Jones

Cap 48: Greece in Athens, 9 December 1964, lost 2–0
World Cup Qualifier
Team: Gary Sprake; Peter Rodrigues, Graham E Williams; Terry Hennessey, Mike England, Barrie Hole; Ronnie Rees, Ken Leek, Wyn Davies, Herbie Williams, Cliff Jones

Cap 49: Greece in Cardiff, 17 March 1965, won 4–1
World Cup Qualifier
Team: Dave Hollins; Peter Rodrigues, Graham E Williams; Herbie Williams, Mike England, Barrie Hole; Cliff Jones, Ivor Allchurch, Ken Leek, Roy Vernon, Ronnie Rees
Scorers: Allchurch 2, Vernon, England

Cap 50: Northern Ireland in Belfast, 31 March 1965, won 5–0, one goal
Home International
Team: Dave Hollins; Peter Rodrigues, Graham E Williams; Cyril Lea, Mike England, Barrie Hole; Cliff Jones, Ivor Allchurch, Wyn Davies, Roy Vernon, Ronnie Rees
Other scorers: Vernon 2, Allchurch, Williams

Cap 51: Italy in Florence, 1 May 1965, lost 4–1
Friendly
Team: Dave Hollins; Colin Green, Graham E Williams; Cyril Lea, Mike England, Barrie Hole; Cliff Jones, Ivor Allchurch, Brian Godfrey, Roy Vernon, Ronnie Rees
Scorer: Godfrey

Cap 52: USSR in Moscow, 30 May 1965, lost 2–1
World Cup Qualifier
Team: Tony Millington; Colin Green, Graham E Williams; Terry Hennessey, Mike England, Barrie Hole; Cliff Jones, Ivor Allchurch, Wyn Davies, John Charles, Ronnie Rees
Scorer: Davies

Cap 53: Scotland in Cardiff, 22 October 1966, drew 1–1
European Championships Qualifier
Team: Gary Sprake; Peter Rodrigues, Graham E Williams; Terry Hennessey, Mike England, Barrie Hole; Gil Reece, Wyn Davies, Ron Davies, Cliff Jones, Alan Jarvis
Scorer: R Davies

Cap 54: England at Wembley, 16 November 1966, lost 5–1
European Championships Qualifier
Team: Tony Millington; Colin Green, Graham E Williams; Terry Hennessey, Mike England, Barrie Hole; Ronnie Rees, Wyn Davies, Ron Davies, Cliff Jones, Alan Jarvis
Scorer: W Davies

Cap 55: England in Cardiff, 21 October 1967, lost 3–0
European Championships Qualifier
Team: Gary Sprake; Peter Rodrigues, Colin Green; Terry Hennessey, Mike England, Barrie Hole; Ronnie Rees, Alan Durban, John Mahoney, Roy Vernon, Cliff Jones

Cap 56: Scotland in Glasgow, 22 November 1967, lost 3–2
European Championships Qualifier
Teams: Gary Sprake; Peter Rodrigues, Colin Green; Terry Hennessey, Glyn James, Barrie Hole; Ronnie Rees, Wyn Davies, Ron Davies, Alan Durban, Cliff Jones
Scorers: R Davies, Durban

Cap 57: West Germany in Cardiff, 8 May 1968, drew 1–1
Friendly
Team: Tony Millington; Rod Thomas, Colin Green; David Powell, Mike England, Barrie Hole; Ronnie Rees, Wyn Davies, Ron Davies, Alan Durban, Cliff Jones
Scorer: W Davies

Cap 58: Italy in Cardiff, 23 October 1968, lost 1–0
World Cup Qualifier
Team: Tony Millington; Rod Thomas, Graham E Williams; Ollie Burton, David Powell, Barrie Hole; Ronnie Rees, Wyn Davies, Ron Davies, Colin Green (sub Barrie Jones), Cliff Jones

Cap 59: Rest of the United Kingdom at Cardiff, 28 July 1969, lost 1–0
Friendly
Team: Gary Sprake; Peter Rodrigues, Rod Thomas; Terry Hennessey, Mike England, Graham Moore; Barrie Jones, Cliff Jones, Ron Davies, John Toshack, Ronnie Rees (sub Gil Reece)

Post-retirement honours

1998 Welsh Football Association Hall of Fame
2001 Welsh Football Association Special Award
2004 Tottenham Hotspur Hall of Fame
2013 Lifetime Achievement Award from Wales Sport
2013 National Football Museum, Manchester, Hall of Fame
2013 Swansea City Wall of Fame
2014 Honorary Fellow of the University of Wales, Trinity St David

Acknowledgements

CLIFF JONES

My wonderful family; all at Swansea Town (now City) and Tottenham Hotspur; Ryan Giggs and Gareth Bale for their warm words; the Bale family; Jimmy Greaves; Sir Gareth Edwards; Alcoholics Anonymous; Al-Anon Family Groups; West Essex Golf Club; St Francis Hospice, Romford.

IVAN PONTING

Pat, Rosie and Joe Ponting, as always; Steve Jones, ever resourceful; Les Gold, a firm friend and a walking Tottenham Hotspur encyclopedia; Tom Morgan, a gifted young journalist and another Spurs aficionado; all at VSP, especially Jim Drewett and Toby Trotman for their calmness and expertise, Paul Baillie-Lane for his excellent editing and endless patience, and Doug Cheeseman for his crisp design; the ever-optimistic Will Bebb.

ILLUSTRATIONS

All images supplied by Mirrorpix, Getty Images, Colorsport, the Neville Evans Collection, Les Gold, Spurs photographer Ray Pickard and the Jones family.

CLIFF JONES
(Spurs)

The perfect way to sign off this book, with a jaunty cartoon of me in my prime in a Spurs shirt. A wonderful life? Not half!